.

UN PEACE OPERATIONS

UN PEACE OPERATIONS

EVOLUTION OF DOCTRINE, PRACTICE AND INTEGRATION OF HUMAN RIGHTS ISSUES

RAVINDRAN DANIEL

Los Angeles | London | New Delhi
Singapore | Washington DC | Melbourne

First published in 2022 by

SAGE Publications India Pvt Ltd
B1/I-1 Mohan Cooperative Industrial Area
Mathura Road, New Delhi 110 044, India
www.sagepub.in

SAGE Publications Inc
2455 Teller Road
Thousand Oaks, California 91320, USA

SAGE Publications Ltd
1 Oliver's Yard, 55 City Road
London EC1Y 1SP, United Kingdom

SAGE Publications Asia-Pacific Pte Ltd
18 Cross Street #10-10/11/12
China Square Central
Singapore 048423

Published by Vivek Mehra for SAGE Publications India Pvt Ltd and typeset in 10.5/13 pt Berkeley by AG Infographics, Delhi.

Library of Congress Control Number: 2021950960

ISBN: 978-93-5479-221-2 (HB)

SAGE Team: Amrita Dutta, Satvinder Kaur and Anupama Krishnan

To my granddaughter,
Anisha.

Thank you for choosing a SAGE product!
If you have any comment, observation or feedback,
I would like to personally hear from you.

Please write to me at **contactceo@sagepub.in**

Vivek Mehra, Managing Director and CEO, SAGE India.

Bulk Sales

SAGE India offers special discounts
for purchase of books in bulk.
We also make available special imprints
and excerpts from our books on demand.

For orders and enquiries, write to us at

Marketing Department
SAGE Publications India Pvt Ltd
B1/I-1, Mohan Cooperative Industrial Area
Mathura Road, Post Bag 7
New Delhi 110044, India

E-mail us at **marketing@sagepub.in**

Subscribe to our mailing list
Write to **marketing@sagepub.in**

This book is also available as an e-book.

CONTENTS

LIST OF ABBREVIATIONS

A4P	Action for Peacekeeping
ACHR	Advisory Council for Human Rights
ADHOC	Association for Human Rights in Cambodia
AFDL	Alliance of Democratic Forces for the Liberation of Congo-Zaire
AMIS	African Mission in Sudan
AMISOM	African Mission in Somalia
APC	All People's Congress
AQIM	Al-Qaida in the Islamic Maghreb
ASEAN	Association of Southeast Asian Nations
AU	African Union
BLDP	Buddhist Liberal Democratic Party
BONUCA	UN Peacebuilding Support Office in the Central African Republic
CAVR	Commission on Reception, Truth and Reconciliation
CCTP	Cambodian Court Training Project
CDVR	Commission for Dialogue, Truth and Reconciliation
CGDK	Coalition Government of Democratic Kampuchea
CIA	Central Intelligence Agency
CICIG	International Commission against Impunity in Guatemala
CONARIV	National Committee for Reconciliation and Victim's Compensation
CPA	Comprehensive Peace Agreement
CSEI	Special Investigation and Examination Unit
DDPD	Doha Document for Peace in Darfur

DK	Democratic Kampuchea
DPA	Darfur Peace Agreement
DPKO	Department of Peacekeeping Operations
DRC	Democratic Republic of the Congo
DSRSG	Deputy Special Representative of the Secretary-General
EC	Electoral Committee
ECOWAS	Economic Community of West African States
FARDC	Military of the Democratic Republic of the Congo (Forces armées de la République démocratique du Congo)
FIB	Force Intervention Brigade
FMLN	Farabundo Marti National Liberation Front (Frente Farabundo Martí para la Liberación Nacional)
FNLA	National Liberation Front of Angola
GoNU	Government of National Unity
GoS	Government of Sudan
GOSS	Government of South Sudan
HAC	Humanitarian Aid Commission
HIPPO	High-level Independent Panel on Peace Operations
HNEC	High National Election Commission
HNP	Haitian National Police
HoR	House of Representatives
HRD	Human Rights Division
HRDAG	Human Rights Data Analysis Group
HRDDP	Human Rights Due Diligence Policy
HRFOR	Human Rights Field Operation in Rwanda
HRU	Human Rights Unit
ICC	International Criminal Court
ICISS	International Commission on Intervention and State Sovereignty
ICJ	International Court of Justice
ICTJ	International Center for Transitional Justice
ICTR	International Criminal Tribunal for Rwanda
ICTY	International Criminal Tribunal for the former Yugoslavia
IGAD	Intergovernmental Authority on Development

IMTFs	Integrated Mission Task Forces
INTERFET	International Force East Timor
IPTF	International Police Task Force
ISAF	International Security Assistance Force
ISIL	Islamic State of Iraq and the Levant
JEM	Justice and Equality Movement
JIUs	Joint Integrated Units
JSC	Joint Situation Centre
LURD	Liberians United for Reconciliation
MARA	Monitoring, analysis and reporting arrangements
MICIVIH	International Civilian Mission in Haiti
MILAD	Military Advisers
MILOB	UN Military Observers
MINJUSTH	United Nations Mission for Justice Support in Haiti
MINUCI	United Nations Mission in Cote d'Ivoire
MINUGUA	United Nations Verification Mission in Guatemala
MINURCA	UN Mission in the Central African Republic
MINURSO	UN Mission for the Referendum in Western Sahara
MINUSAL	United Nations Mission in El Salvador
MINUSCA	UN Multidimensional Integrated Stabilization Mission in the Central African Republic
MINUSMA	United Nations Multidimensional Integrated Stabilization Mission in Mali
MINUSTAH	United Nations Stabilization Mission in Haiti
MIPONUH	United Nations Civilian Police Mission in Haiti
MJP	Movement for Justice and Peace
MNLA	Mouvement national pour la libération de l'Azawad
MONUA	United Nations Observer Mission to Angola
MONUC	United Nations Organization Mission in the Democratic Republic of the Congo
MONUSCO	United Nations Organization Stabilization Mission in the Democratic Republic of the Congo
MOSS	Minimum Operation Security Standard
MoU	memorandum of understanding
MPIGO	Ivorian Popular Measure of the Great West
MPLA	Popular Movement for the Liberation of Angola
MRM	Monitoring and Reporting Mechanism

MRND	Mouvement Revolutionnaire National pour le Developpement
MSCSIV	Ministry of Solidarity, Social Cohesion and Victim's Compensation
MUJAO	Mouvement pour l'unicité et le jihad en Afrique de l'Ouest
NAP	National Action Plans
NCP	Nepali Congress Party
NEC	National Election Commission
NGOs	Non-governmental organizations
NHRI	National Human Rights Institutions
NISS	National Intelligence and Security Services
NPLF	National Patriotic Front
NTC	National Transitional Council
OAS	Organization of American States
OAU	Organization of African Unity
OHCHR	Office of the High Commissioner for Human Rights
ONUC	United Nations Operation in the Congo
ONUSAL	United Nations Observer Mission in El Salvador
PCA	Permanent Court of Arbitration
PDK	Party of Democratic Kampuchea
PMSS	Peace Missions Support Section
PMSU	Peace Mission Support Unit
PNC	National Civilian Police
POC	Protection of Civilian
PRK	People's Republic of Kampuchea
PSOs	Peace Support Operations
QUIPS	Quick Impact Projects
RPF	Rwandan Patriotic Front
RRP	Relief, Reintegration and Protection
RUF	Revolutionary United Front
SAF	Sudan Armed Force
SCU	Serious Crimes Unit
SGBV	Sexual and gender-based violence
SIU	Special Investigations Unit
SLM/A	Sudan Liberation Movement
SLPP	Sierra Leone People's Party

SOC	State of Cambodia
SOPs	Standard operating procedures
SPLM/A	Sudan People's Liberation Movement/Army
SRF	Sudan Revolutionary Front
SRSG	Special Representative of the Secretary-General
SRSG–CAC	Special Representative on Children and Armed Conflict
SRSG–SVC	Special Representative on sexual violence in conflict
SSHRC	Southern Sudan Human Rights Commission
SWAPO	South-West Africa People's Organisation
T/PCCs	Troop/Police contributing countries
TFG	Transitional Federal Government
TNG	Transitional National Government
UNAMA	United Nations Assistance Mission in Afghanistan
UNAMET	UN Mission in East Timor
UNAMI	United Nations Assistance Mission for Iraq
UNAMID	United Nations–African Union Mission in Darfur
UNAMIR	United Nations Assistance Mission for Rwanda
UNAMSIL	United Nations Mission in Sierra Leone
UNAVEM	United Nations Angola Verification Mission
UNDSS	UN Department of Safety and Security
UNEF	United Nations Emergency Force
UNFICYP	United Nations Peacekeeping Force in Cyprus
UNIFIL	UN Interim Force in Lebanon
UNIOSIL	United Nations Integrated Office in Sierra Leone
UNIPSIL	United Nations Integrated Peacebuilding Office in Sierra Leone
UNISFA	United Nations Interim Security Force for Abyei
UNITA	National Union for the Total Independence of Angola
UNITAF	US-led Unified Task Force
UNITMAS	United Nations Integrated Transition Assistance Mission in Sudan
UNMAS	UN Mines Action Service
UNMIBH	United Nations Mission in Bosnia and Herzegovina
UNMIH	United Nations Mission in Haiti
UNMIL	United Nations Mission in Libya
UNMIN	UN Mission in Nepal
UNMIS	United Nations Assistance Mission in Sudan

UNMISET	United Nations Mission of Support in East Timor
UNMISS	UN Mission in the Republic of South Sudan
UNMIT	United Nations Integrated Mission in Timor-Leste
UNMOGIP	UN Military Observer Group in India and Pakistan
UNOA	United Nations Office in Angola
UNOCI	United Nations Operations in Cote d'Ivoire
UNOGIL	UN Observer Group in Lebanon
UNOL	United Nations Peacebuilding Support Office in Liberia
UNOMIL	United Nations Observer Mission in Liberia
UNOMSIL	United Nations Observer Mission in Sierra Leone
UNOSOM	United Nations Operation in Somalia
UNOTIL	UN Office in Timor-Leste
UNPCRS	United Nations Peacekeeping Capability Readiness System
UNPOS	United Nations Political Office for Somalia
UNPROFOR	United Nations Protection Force
UNSAS	United Nations Standby Arrangement System
UNSCOB	UN Special Committee on the Balkans
UNSF	United Nations Security Force
UNSMIH	United Nations Support Mission in Haiti
UNSMIL	United Nations Support Mission in Libya
UNSOM	United Nations Assistance Mission in Somalia
UNTAC	UN Transitional Authority in Cambodia
UNTAES	United Nations Transitional Administration in Eastern Slavonia
UNTAET	United Nations Transitional Administration in East Timor
UNTAG	United Nations Transition Assistance Group
UNTEA	United Nations Temporary Executive Authority
UNTMIH	United Nations Transition Mission in Haiti
UNTSO	United Nations Truce Supervision Organization
URNG	Guatemalan Revolutionary National Unity

FOREWORD

When in 1985 I joined Amnesty International as the head of the Asia region of its Research Department, one of the first—and best— professional relationships that opened up to me was with the legal officer for Asia of the International Commission of Jurists (ICJ), Ravindran Daniel. Although Amnesty and ICJ were then the two most consequential non-governmental organizations engaging with the United Nations (UN), neither of us had the slightest inkling that we would both one day work for the UN. It would be eight years before I stumbled into my first UN role, soon after leaving Amnesty; Ravi had spent a decade contributing to the development of civil society activism for human rights in Asia before he did so. Among our various UN roles, over more than 20 years, we would find ourselves working at different times in the same country, in East Timor (later Timor-Leste) and Sudan, and eventually (but not coincidentally) would work closely together in Libya.

These and our other respective UN roles came about as the organization's work to promote and protect human rights moved beyond the committee rooms of Geneva, where we had first engaged with it, into the field. The New York departments for political affairs and peacekeeping discovered the value of including human rights components in their peace operations, and the post-Cold War Security Council became willing to mandate them. The creation of the post of High Commissioner for Human Rights and development of the High Commissioner's office saw Office of the United Nations High

Commissioner for Human Rights (OHCHR) move to the ground with its own field presences.

Although OHCHR fielded substantial stand-alone operations in Rwanda, Colombia and Nepal, and significant offices in Cambodia and elsewhere, the story of the UN's work for human rights in conflict and post-conflict countries has become mostly bound up with the development of peace operations, whether peacekeeping or special political missions. The pages that follow first set out the categories of such operations and the evolution of peacekeeping doctrine, up to and beyond the 2015 review by the High-level Independent Panel on Peace Operations (HIPPO) established by Secretary-General Ban Ki-moon, of which I was a member. They go on to tackle the most difficult issue our panel wrestled with: the appropriate use of force by UN peacekeeping operations and its limits. After the shameful failures in Rwanda and at Srebrenica, those concerned with the protection of human rights rightly insist on the responsibility of military peacekeepers to intervene where they have the possibility to prevent massacres of civilians. But no mission can protect civilians at all times in all places: At the time of the HIPPO report, a little over 100,000 uniformed UN peacekeepers were operating across 11 million sq. km, and expectations are often unrealistic. Robust peacekeeping is not to be confused with war fighting, and HIPPO drew a red line in concluding that UN missions are not suited to engage in military counter-terrorism operations.

The integration of protection mandates within peace operations has been a highly positive development, but overlapping concepts have brought managerial complexities and sometimes confusion. HIPPO noted that monitoring and reporting of human rights issues in peace operations are often dispersed and fragmented, with competing requests for resources and duplication of activities, and called for coherence in the overall monitoring and reporting on human rights and the protection of civilians. Moreover, structural integration does not always bring integration into the overall political strategy of a peace operation. Those with UN political responsibilities have sometimes been inclined to see human rights engagement and reporting as complicating the task of mediation and political compromise. However, there has been growing recognition that, as a recent study argues, the human rights components of peace missions 'also play fundamental roles in creating the political conditions essential for such missions to build sustainable peace and relaunch development progress when conflict recedes'.[1] There is a mutual obligation on the Special Representatives of the Secretary-General who are the leaders of peace operations and the heads who direct the work of the human rights components, as well as their respective headquarters in New York and Geneva, to ensure that the priorities of human rights work are those which contribute to the political strategy of peace operations. The author of the following pages has participated in the political work of a UN peace operation as well as headed human rights components and in the case studies which describe his personal experience brings to life aspects of the relationship between them.

I have sometimes been asked how someone who had worked for Amnesty International found my transition to the UN, the assumption behind the question usually being that the constraints of an intergovernmental organization must have limited principled action for human rights. A part of my answer was to compare the ability to research a country situation mostly from afar, dependent on very limited staff resources and only occasional opportunities to undertake field visits, with the immediate access of a substantial cadre of human rights officers (HROs) to places of detention, torture and killing and face-to-face engagement with local and national authorities. Working for an organization of member states, including the government giving its consent to a UN presence, requires particular skill in handling the sensitivities of human rights work, but the Charter, the Universal Declaration of Human Rights and the body of international human rights law and standards provide a framework which transcends the political interests of governments. There is thus no

---

[1] UN Office of the High Commissioner for Human Rights. (2020, 1 October). *Going further together: The contribution of human rights components to the implementation of mandates of United Nations field missions.*

contradiction between the work for non-governmental organizations in which Ravindran Daniel and I were partners in the 1980s, and our collaboration as UN colleagues, which is reflected in his constructively critical analysis.

Ian Martin

Ian Martin has headed UN human rights and peace operations in a number of countries, including as the Special Representative of the Secretary-General in East Timor (now Timor-Leste), Nepal and Libya. He is a former Secretary-General of Amnesty International.

ACKNOWLEDGEMENTS

As part of the UN peace operations, I worked in East Timor (officially Timor-Leste), Libya and Sudan. As a senior staff of the OHCHR, I worked in Cambodia and did a short stint in Uganda. My family and friends often proposed that I write about my experiences in conflict and post-conflict situations. The pandemic and the lockdown gave me an opportunity to consider sharing my ideas and experience regarding UN peace operations. Once I made the decision to write, I resolved that it should not be restricted to sharing my own personal experiences; rather, it should add to the existing literature on peace operations. The idea is to contribute to understanding the evolution of UN peace operations (doctrine and practice) and its complexities. Unlike many UN staff, I did not spend my whole career in UN missions. Mine was short but intense. At times, it was frustrating to witness people caught in conflicts with no hope. Other times I have also witnessed the resilience and commitment of people to strive for peace despite the odds.

I went to East Timor in October 1999 as secretary of the UN Enquiry Commission to investigate the atrocities committed by the Indonesians. When I reached there, the country literally had nothing: Houses were burnt, and the infrastructure was destroyed. The population that had fled to the mountains gradually returned. It was a young population. Despite the destruction, I noticed that people were happy. It would be difficult to describe the joyous mood of the people amid the destruction. In their happiness, I realized the value of freedom. They were happy because they were free from the Indonesian occupation. They had reclaimed their dignity as free people.

Nyala in Darfur, Sudan, housed the largest internally displaced peoples' (IDPs) camp in the world with thousands of people living in harsh desert conditions. The camps in Nyala and other regions of Darfur made me, at times, wonder at the futility of peacekeeping. I was doubtful of my own purpose and wondered if I was just part of a charade called peacekeeping. However, at Nyala University, I met a father and his daughter. The daughter had come to submit her application to join the university. The father was keen that his daughter should continue her higher education despite the ongoing conflict. Meeting them reassured me that people wanted peace, and they would achieve it with or without the assistance of UN or other international organizations. This book is written with the conviction that however difficult a conflict may be, caught up in the nexus of local political leaders and international powers, there is always hope that people who live through the conflict would find ways to end it.

I owe much to the patience and guidance of Amrita Dutta, Associate Commissioning Editor, Academic Books, of SAGE. I must thank Mihir Vatsa for painstakingly editing my first draft of several hundred pages. Thanks are due to Sabitha Suresh for her meticulous work with the footnotes, references and in preparing the bibliography. I thank Ashna D., who assisted with the initial compilation of different peace operations' human rights mandates.

My former colleague and friend Marieke Wierda read the first draft and encouraged me to publish the manuscript. I benefited constructively from the commitment and friendship of my colleagues who worked with me in difficult situations. I extend my gratitude to Marieke Wierda, Bela Kapur, Joanna Oyediran, Rafeef Dajani, Sanne van den Bergh, Francesca Marotta, Marlene Alejos, Alisa Tesic and numerous other national and international colleagues with whom I have shared many memorable moments.

I am grateful to Ian Martin for reading the manuscript, providing valuable comments and sharing and/or pointing to resources related to my book. I feel honoured that he very kindly agreed to write a foreword to the book. I owe much to his friendship and guidance that has spanned across nearly 40 years.

Finally, I thank Sandeep, Vandana and Sundari. Sundari, in particular, for prodding me regularly about sharing my experiences in writing and not giving up. This book is dedicated to Anisha with the hope that she would grow up in a world with greater peace and justice than the one I have experienced till now.

INTRODUCTION

UN deployed its peace operations mostly to respond to conflicts arising from global, regional and national dynamics. UN does not operate in a vacuum; Member states' concerns influence its response. For example, in 2000, US President George Bush was elected with an administration dominated by UN sceptics. The distrust about multilateral institutions became even stronger after the 9/11 terrorist attack on its soil. However, the USA sought the UN's role in Afghanistan after overthrowing the Taliban regime. The Security Council's refusal to endorse the US invasion of Iraq resurrected its animosity towards the UN, but six months later, it sought the UN's presence in post-war Iraq. The UN's deployments in Afghanistan and Iraq reaffirmed its relevance in peace and security issues.[1]

The arrival of international cable television news networks and their coverage of the UN Security Council debates, particularly during the discussion on Iraq, made a wider audience aware of the member states' role (including bullying by some) and that of the Secretary-General's balancing act. Those unfamiliar with the UN Security Council's complex political dynamics, their peacekeeping image is all about the UN's glossy publications that show young soldiers with blue helmet standing in front of gleaming UN emblem-embossed four-wheel drive vehicles. In addition, Hollywood movie images of army generals planning for war might influence their perception that

---

[1] Durch, W. J., Holt, V. K., Earle, C. R., & Shanahan, M. K. (2003). *The Brahimi report and the future of UN peace operations*. The Henry L. Stimson Center. https://www.stimson.org/wp-content/files/file-attachments/BR-CompleteVersion-Dec03_1.pdf

UN peacekeeping is based on infinite resources and strategic planning by generals.

However, the reality is very different. UN is constrained by the politics of its members while planning and resourcing its peace operations. The 2016 war film *The Siege of Jadotville*[2] depicts the real story of Irish peacekeepers sent to Congo in 1962 UN's effort to prevent the secession of the mineral-rich Katanga region. The film shows how the Irish soldiers defended the UN compound in Jadotville from Belgian-backed mercenaries. The film demonstrates the reality of peacekeeping that includes global power dynamics, Security Council members' interests and personality clashes among UN personnel on the ground.

There have been numerous success stories of UN peace operations. However, the UN's credibility was at stake by the failure of the UN Protection Force (UNPROFOR) in former Yugoslavia, the UN Assistance Mission for Rwanda (UNAMIR) and the UN Operation in Somalia (UNOSOM I & UNOSOM II). These and other missions constantly demonstrate that UN peace operations are complex and challenging. This book aims to capture the context, complexities and evolution of the doctrine, including integrating thematic issues into peace operations.

Chapter 1 examines the first phase of evolution of peacekeeping doctrine despite any reference to such processes in the xter. It also includes classification of context such as Cold War, interstate conflicts, intrastate conflicts, etc., in which the UN responded to deploy peace operations. Chapters 2–6, based on the classification, provide information and analysis of major UN peace operations deployed in the last 70 years. Chapter 7 addresses the evolution of UN peace operations doctrine in the second phase (1992–2015). Chapter 8 examines the controversial idea of the use of force, which is the latest challenge in doctrinal development and in implementing peacekeeping operations. Chapter 9 traces the evolution and integration of thematic areas such as human rights, the rule of law, women's role in peace and security, children and armed conflict and the protection of civilians in armed conflict. Chapter 10 examines the institutional and programmatic

---

[2] See https://time.com/4408017/the-siege-of-jadotville-the-true-story-netflix-film/

integration of human rights in the UN's peace operations (1990–1998). Chapter 11 examines the institutional and programmatic integration of human rights in the UN's peace operations post 2000. Chapter 12, based on the author's first-hand experience, discusses human rights components in Timor-Leste (East Timor), Sudan and Libya as case studies.

UN's peace operations may reflect UN Charter's ambition to 'save succeeding generations from the scourge of war', but it required Dag Hammarskjöld's idealism to begin its journey by responding to the conflicts that emerged in the initial years. This book attempts to capture that journey. The evolution of peace operations in the last 70 years demonstrates that Dag Hammarskjöld's idea that the UN embodied the 'edge of the development of human society' and worked on the 'brink of the unknown' remains an inspiring vision.[3]

---

[3] As quoted in Bildt, C. (2013). Dag *Hammarskjöld and United Nations peacekeeping.* UN Chronicle. https://www.un.org/en/chronicle/article/dag-hammarskjold-and-united-nations-peacekeeping

Legal Framework, Initial Doctrinal Evolution and Thematic Classification of Operations

UN CHARTER AND PEACEKEEPING OPERATIONS[1]

The UN Charter came into force on 24 October 1945, and it provides the legal framework and shapes the United Nations' (UN) vision, structure and operations. Constituted by nation states, the UN's edifice was built on the notion of sovereignty of its members. The organization, therefore, is based on the principle of respecting the sovereign equality of its members. The Charter stipulates that the members 'shall refrain in their international relations from the threat or use of force against the territorial integrity or political independence of any state'.[2]

[1] The report of HIPPO defines the term 'UN Peace Operations' as 'a broad suite of tools managed by the UN Secretariat'. These instruments range from special envoys and mediators, political missions (including peacebuilding missions), regional preventive diplomacy offices, observation missions (both ceasefire and electoral missions) to small, technical specialist missions (such as electoral support missions), multidisciplinary operations both large and small drawing on civilian, military and police personnel to support peace process implementation (including even transitional authorities with governance functions), as well as advance missions for planning. All these missions draw upon expertise mobilized by the Secretariat, including mediation and electoral specialists, and human rights, administrative law, gender, police and military experts. United Nations. (2005). *Report of the Independent High-Level Panel on Peace Operations*, para 18. https://peacekeeping.un.org/en/report-of-independent-high-level-panel-peace-operations

[2] United Nations. (1945). *Charter of the United Nations and statue of the International Court of Justice* (Article 2(4)). https://upload.wikimedia.org/wikipedia/commons/a/a4/Uncharter.pdf

The UN emerged after the Second World War with fresh memories of devastation, crimes committed against humanity and the effects of aggression by some states against others. The Charter affirmed its vision for the maintenance of international peace and security. It conferred upon the Security Council the primary responsibility for maintaining peace and security.[3] The Charter tried to strike a balance between the sovereignty of its members and collective interventions to maintain peace and security.

THE UN CHARTER: CHAPTER VII

Based on the experience of the two World Wars, the Charter, in Chapter VII, provided for collective security and cooperation against 'threats to the peace, breaches of the peace and acts of aggression'.[4] Chapter VII is about the collective use of measures, including force, to restore international peace and security. It deals with addressing instances of aggression by one or more states and the member states' response through collective measures. The UN founders were concerned about state security. In creating a collective security system, their focus was on states joining together to prevent aggression against one state by another.[5]

Since its establishment, in two instances, the Security Council authorized the collective use of force to maintain international peace and security. The first was in 1950, when the Security Council authorized collective action to prevent the North Korean aggression against South Korea. The second was in 1990, when the Security Council authorized enforcement action after Iraq invaded Kuwait. Both cases involved aggression by one state against another and impacted on the

[3] United Nations. (1945). *Charter of the United Nations and statue of the International Court of Justice* (Articles 24 and 26). https://upload.wikimedia.org/wikipedia/commons/a/a4/Uncharter.pdf

[4] United Nations. (1945). *Charter of the United Nations and statue of the International Court of Justice* (Chapter VII). https://upload.wikimedia.org/wikipedia/commons/a/a4/Uncharter.pdf

[5] United Nations. (2004). *A more secure world: Our shared responsibility* (Report of the High-Level Panel on Threats, Challenges and Change, A/59/565). https://www.un.org/en/ga/search/view_doc.asp?symbol=A/59/565

interests of some of the permanent members of the Security Council. The Security Council authorized enforcement action by one or more members in Rwanda and Somalia to create conditions for humanitarian relief and in Haiti for restoration of democracy.[6] In 2011, the Security Council authorized the North Atlantic Treaty Organization (NATO) intervention in Libya for the protection of civilians.

The UN Charter even envisaged the creation of a UN armed force through conclusion of special arrangements between the Security Council and member states. It proposed that the force operate under the strategic direction of a 'Military Staff Committee' to enable 'combined international enforcement action'.[7] This ambitious goal never materialized. However, the UN has established United Nations Peacekeeping Capability Readiness System (UNPCRS), formerly known as the United Nations Standby Arrangement System (UNSAS), through which member states pledge force contributions to missions. Consequently, there is no permanent standby peacekeeping force, only individual operations.[8]

THE UN CHARTER: CHAPTER VI

The Charter, in Chapter VI, provides for peaceful settlement of disputes between states that are 'likely to endanger the maintenance of international peace and security'.[9] When a dispute arises, the parties, with the assistance of the Security Council, should seek 'a solution

[6] United Nations Secretary General. (1995). Supplement to an *agenda* for peace: *Position paper of the Secretary-General on the occasion of the 50th anniversary of the United Nations* (United Nations Secretary-General Reports [1994–1995], A/50/60-S/1995/1). https://digitallibrary.un.org/record/168325?ln=en

[7] United Nations. (1945). *Charter of the United Nations and statue of the International Court of Justice* (Chapter VII, Articles 45 and 47). https://upload.wikimedia.org/wiki-pedia/commons/a/a4/Uncharter.pdf

[8] Labuda, P. I. (2015, 2 September). UN peace operations: Tracking the shift from peacekeeping to peace enforcement and state-building. *EJIL: Talk! Blog of the European Journal of International Law*. https://www.ejiltalk.org/un-peace-operations-tracking-the-shift-from-peacekeeping-to-peace-enforcement-and-state-building/

[9] United Nations. (1945). *Charter of the United Nations and statue of the International Court of Justice* (Chapter VI, Article 33(1)). https://upload.wikimedia.org/wikipedia/commons/a/a4/Uncharter.pdf

by negotiation, enquiry, mediation, conciliation, arbitration, judicial settlement, resort to regional agencies or arrangements, or other peaceful means of their own choice'.[10] It is clear that Chapter VI provides for peaceful settlements of disputes between states, and Chapter VII stipulates collective action, including the use of force to maintain international peace and security.

THE UN CHARTER: CHAPTER VIII

The UN Charter's Chapter VIII provides for the involvement of regional organizations in the maintenance of international peace and security. Article 52 provides for their involvement in peaceful settlement of disputes, and Article 53 provides for their enforcement action but with explicit authorization of the Security Council. Article 54 obligates regional organizations to inform the Security Council of their activities for the maintenance of international peace and security at all times.[11]

Until 1990, the Security Council did not refer to regional organizations in its resolutions. Since 1991, references to the role of regional organizations in prevention and resolution of conflicts became common.[12] Increasing collaboration between the UN and regional organizations led to collaboration in several operations. The examples include the African Union (AU)'s role in Burundi, Ethiopia and Eritrea and the Democratic Republic of the Congo, Somalia and the Sudan. Similarly, the Organization of American States (OAS) was involved in Haiti. The 2015 High-Level Independent Panel on Peace Operations (HIPPO) observed that regional entities have emerged as important

---

[10] United Nations. (1945). *Charter of the United Nations and statue of the International Court of Justice* (Chapter VI, Article 33).https://upload.wikimedia.org/wikipedia/commons/a/a4/Uncharter.pdf

[11] United Nations Security Council. (2010). *Regional arrangements* (Chapter VIII of UN Charter). https://www.un.org/securitycouncil/content/regional-arrangements-chapter-viii-un-charter

[12] United Nations. (2008). *Report of the Secretary-General on the relationship between the United Nations and regional organizations, in particular the African Union, in the maintenance of international peace and security* (Report No. S/2008/186). https://archive.globalpolicy.org/images/pdfs/0407africanunion.pdf

and significant actors, and the UN should strengthen these partnerships. It proposed that the UN should make regional entities part of an increasingly global and regional peace and security architecture. In the context of Africa, the HIPPO report pointed the experiences in Central African Republic, Mali and Somalia and stated that troops from the region bring political commitment, understanding of the context and a direct link to regional political influence.[13]

THE INTERNATIONAL COURT OF JUSTICE'S RULINGS ON PEACEKEEPING

The International Court of Justice (ICJ) affirmed the legality of establishing peacekeeping operations despite any reference to such operations in the Charter. In 1949, the Court declared that under international law, the organization must be deemed to have those powers which, though not expressly provided in the Charter, are conferred upon it by necessary implication as being essential to the performance of its duties.[14] In 1962, regarding the establishment of the United Nations Operation in the Congo (ONUC), the ICJ reasoned that it was not necessary to identify specific provision for the legal basis of the creation of ONUC by the Security Council. It further noted that 'the operations of ONUC did not include a use of armed force against a state which the Security Council, under Article 39, determined to have committed an act of aggression or to have breached the peace'.[15] According to the Court, the UN forces were not authorized to take military action against any state and were not permitted to implement enforcement measures under Chapter VII and, therefore, did not constitute 'action' as that term is used in Article 11.[16]

[13] United Nations. (2015). *Report of the High-Level Independent Panel on Peace Operations on Uniting our strengths for peace: Politics, partnership and people* (Report No. A/70/95-S/2015/446). https://www.un.org/en/ga/search/view_doc.asp?symbol=S/2015/446

[14] Henry, E. (2015). *Use of force and peacekeeping operations*.https://www.academia.edu/37018831/Use_of_Force_and_Peacekeeping_Operations

[15] Ibid.

[16] Ibid.

EVOLUTION OF THE TYPE OF
PEACEKEEPING OPERATIONS

In pursuing its mandate on maintenance of peace and security, the UN responded to conflicts as they emerged around the world. During the first two decades of its existence, the UN conducted investigations and deployed unarmed military observers and armed peacekeepers around the world to prevent escalation of conflicts between states and create conditions for political solutions.

In 1947, the UN set up the United Nations Special Committee on the Balkans (UNSCOB). It authorized military observers to assist the committee (UNSCOB) in its investigations on neighbouring states' interference in the internal affairs of Greece. The Security Council's debate on the committee witnessed the beginning of Cold War politics that continued for the next six decades.[17] The Cold War impacted the UN's functioning, and the first casualty was the collective action to maintain peace and security. In the absence of a consensus on responding to interstate and intrastate conflicts, Secretary-General Dag Hammarskjöld improvised by deploying peacekeeping forces.

In 1948, the UN set up its first peacekeeping operation called the United Nations Truce Supervision Organization (UNTSO). More than 500 military observers participated in UNTSO to supervise the truce between Israel and its neighbours—Egypt, Jordan, Lebanon and Syria.[18] In 1949, the UN set up the UN Military Observer Group in India and Pakistan (UNMOGIP) to observe the ceasefire between the two countries.[19] Both missions are still in operation.

In 1956, against the Suez Crisis, the UN deployed the United Nations Emergency Force (UNEF) to ensure the withdrawal of British, French and Israeli forces to restore peace.[20] Two years later, in 1958, the UN Observation Group in Lebanon (UNOGIL), with 600-strong contingent

---

[17] Lewis, P. (1992). *A short history of United Nations peacekeeping.* https://www. historynet.com/short-history-united-nations-peacekeeping.htm

[18] United Nations. (2000). *United Nations truce supervision organization.* https:// untso.unmissions.org

[19] Ibid.

[20] United Nations. (2003). *First United Nations emergency force: November 1956–June 1967.* https://peacekeeping.un.org/en/mission/past/unefi.htm

to investigate complaints against Egypt and Syria's interference in Lebanon, was deployed.[21] In 1960, ONUC marked its involvement in an internal civil war. It was the most complex and large-scale operation at the time.[22] In 1962, the United Nations Temporary Executive Authority (UNTEA), along with the United Nations Security Force (UNSF), was deployed to administer West New Guinea (West Irian) as an interim measure prior to its transfer to Indonesia.[23] UNTEA was the harbinger of the UN; it assumed interim administration of territories and not just monitored ceasefire or kept peace. In 1964, the United Nations Peacekeeping Force in Cyprus (UNFICYP) was established to prevent communal violence between Greek Cypriots and Turkish Cypriots.

Gradually, two types of operations emerged—peacekeeping operations and special political missions. Peacekeeping missions deploy armed forces under the UN command as peacekeepers to provide security in UN's peacebuilding efforts to help countries make the difficult and early transition from conflict to peace. Peacekeeping operations include civilian components to implement the mandate of a mission such as protection of civilians. Special political missions are defined as UN civilian missions (without the presence of peacekeeping forces) that are deployed for a limited duration to support the member states in good offices, conflict prevention, peace-making and peacebuilding.

DEVELOPMENT OF DOCTRINE[24]: INITIAL PHASE

In a report on UNEF presented to the Security Council on 9 October 1958, Dag Hammarskjöld expounded the principles of peacekeeping operations and set the doctrine for future operations. He identified

---

[21] United Nations. (2003). *United Nations observation group in Lebanon: June–December 1958.* https://peacekeeping.un.org/mission/past/unogil.htm

[22] United Nations. (2001). *United Nations operation in the Congo: July 1960–June 1964.* https://peacekeeping.un.org/en/mission/past/onuc.htm

[23] United Nations. (1962). *West New Guinea—UNSF: Background.* https://peacekeeping.un.org/en/mission/past/unsfbackgr.html

[24] The UN does not use the term 'doctrine'. Due to lack of consensus on institutionalizing peace operations, states have left it to the Security Council and the General Assembly's Special Committee on Peacekeeping to make ad hoc pronouncements on various elements of peace operations.

three principles: consent of the member state party to the conflict, impartiality and the non-use of force except in self-defence. These principles, known as the 'holy trinity', continue to be the basis for peacekeeping operations and have posed challenges in applying them in contemporary peacekeeping operations.[25]

The UN's Harry Potter Moment

In 1960, the Security Council deployed ONUC. Unlike UNEF that was deployed to separate two warring parties, ONUC was deployed to deal with an internal civil war. The Congolese government requested the UN's intervention after the separatists in the wealthy province of Katanga declared independence. The Belgian troops and European mercenaries supported the secessionists. Secretary-General Dag Hammarskjöld sought a restricted mandate limiting the use of force only for purposes of self-defence. However, the intensity of the conflict soon increased, and the Security Council, in February 1961, authorized the UN forces to 'take all appropriate measures to prevent the outbreak of civil war in the Congo including arrangements for ceasefire … if necessary, to use force as a last resort'.[26] In September 1961, Dag Hammarskjöld died in an air crash in the region while travelling to negotiate ceasefire in Congo. After his death, the Security Council authorized the use of mass force against the Katanga secessionists and foreign troops.[27] In 1964, the UN withdrew from Congo after its intervention prevented the break-up of the country and for Congo to cope with the post-Independence crisis. ONUC was a forerunner among the UN missions that dealt with complexities of intrastate conflicts. Dag Hammarskjöld, based on his experience in setting up ONUC and other missions, declared that peacekeeping operations

[25] Hatto, R. (2013). From peacekeeping to peacebuilding: The evolution of the role of the United Nations in peace operations. *International Review of the Red Cross, 95*(891/892), 495–515. https://www.icrc.org/en/doc/assets/files/review/2013/irrc-891-892-hatto.pdf

[26] Shagalov, V. A., Letyaev, V. A., Grishin, Y., & Vladimirova, M. M. (2018). Dag Hammarskjold's role in the development of peacekeeping. *Revista Publicando 5, 16*(1), 606–616. https://pdfs.semanticscholar.org/41df/60a0c1372dfdbe07e3cec07885a0eb1f3f76.pdf

[27] See note 25.

belonged to 'Chapter six and half' of the Charter.[28] He situated the peacekeeping missions between the traditional methods of resolving conflicts peacefully under Chapter VI and more forceful action as authorized by UNSC under Chapter VII of the Charter. Long before J. K. Rowling created the fictional train platform 9¾ in Harry Potter series, Dag Hammarskjöld had created the non-existent 'Chapter six and half' in the UN Charter. Peacekeeping, as it came to be known as, is the 'epitome of Hammarskjold's pragmatism and creativity'.[29]

PEACEKEEPING OPERATIONS RESPONDING TO GLOBAL PEACE AND SECURITY CHALLENGES

The UN expanded its first two decades of experience to respond to situations that threatened peace and security around the world.[30] To understand the context that led to the deployment of peacekeeping operations in various regions/countries, we are proposing a thematic classification of the context in which the conflict occurred that led to the deployment of peacekeeping operations.

Thematic Classification of UN Peacekeeping Operations[31]

1. Contributing to decolonization
2. Responding to post-Independence crisis

---

[28] Emmanuel, O. O. (2018, August). *Peacekeeping operations and the United Nations Security Council* (Essay submitted to the Faculty of Law, Osun State University, Ifetedo Campus, Nigeria in Partial Fulfilment of the Requirements for the Award of Bachelor of Law [LLB Hons] Degree. https://www.academia.edu/40397927/PEACEKEEPING_OPERATIONS_AND_THE_UNITED_NATIONS_SECURITY_COUNCIL20190919_46081_1 lcnoun?auto=download&email_work_card=download-paper

[29] Bildt, C. (2013). *Dag Hammarskjöld and United Nations peacekeeping*.https://www.un.org/en/chronicle/article/dag-hammarskjold-and-united-nations-peacekeeping

[30] United Nations. (2020). *United Nations peacekeeping: Where we operate.* https://peacekeeping.un.org/en/where-we-operate

[31] Some peace operations would fall under more than one thematic area; for example, UNMISS could come under 'post-Independence crisis' as well as 'internal ethnic and other conflicts'. Similarly, the United Nations Organization Mission in the Democratic Republic of the Congo (MONUC) and the United Nations Organization Stabilization Mission in the Democratic Republic of the Congo (MONUSCO) could come under the thematic areas of 'conflicts arising from the Cold War and its aftermath', 'internal ethnic and other conflicts' as well as 'transition from authoritarian rule to democracy'.

3. Cold War, the aftermath and peacekeeping operations
4. Intrastate conflicts
5. Conflicts arising from transition to democracy from authoritarian rule
6. Peacekeeping operations deployed post US-led interventions

In Chapters 2–6, we discuss major UN peacekeeping operations under each of these categories to demonstrate the complexities and challenges involved in implementing the mandate of the respective missions.[32]

---

[32] The narration includes author's observations as a staff member of peace operations in Timor-Leste (East Timor), Sudan and Libya.

Operations Contributing to Decolonization and Responding to Post-Independence Crisis

CONTRIBUTING TO DECOLONIZATION

When the UN was established in 1945, a vast number of countries were still under colonial rule. The UN, as mandated under the Charter, assisted in decolonization of such states.[1] In addition to its role in facilitating decolonization, it also deployed missions to expedite the process.

Operation	Year	Purpose
UN Security Force in West New Guinea (West Irian)— UNTEA and UNSF	1962–1963	Monitor ceasefire during the transition of West Irian from Dutch to Indonesian rule
UN Transition Assistance Group (UNTAG)	1989–1990	Supervise Namibia's elections and its transition to independence
UN Mission for the Referendum in Western Sahara (MINURSO)	1991–present	Implement ceasefire and help promote referendum on the area's future
UN Mission in East Timor (UNAMET)	1999–1999	To carry out popular consultation (referendum) on political relation with Indonesia

[1] United Nations. (1945). *The United Nations and decolonization*. https://www.un.org/dppa/decolonization/en/about

Operation	Year	Purpose
UN Transitional Administration in East Timor (UNTAET)	1999–2002	Facilitating East Timor's transition to independence
United Nations Mission of Support in East Timor (UNMISET)	2002–2005	To ensure security and stabilize the nascent state during the post-Independence period
United Nations Office in Timor-Leste (UNOTIL)	2005–2006	To support the development of critical state institutions
United Nations Integrated Mission in Timor-Leste (UNMIT)	2006–2012	To support the government in consolidating stability, enhancing a culture of democratic governance and facilitating political dialogue among Timorese stakeholders in their efforts to bring about a process of national reconciliation and to foster social cohesion

Source: The author.

UN Security Force in West New Guinea or West Irian (UNTEA and UNSF): Did the UN Condone Manipulation of the Vote for Self-determination?

The UN's first mission in decolonization was carried out in the region now known as Papua (formerly West New Guinea or West Irian). At the time, the territory was under Dutch colonial rule. After Indonesia's independence, it claimed the territory as its part and the UN brokered an agreement in 1962. Under this agreement, UNTEA would administer the area till it was transferred to Indonesia. The UN deployed UNSF to assist UNTEA to carry out its tasks. The agreement stipulated that Indonesia would conduct an 'Act of Self-Determination' (vote) within seven years. The Indonesians conducted a vote with selected local leaders and announced that the majority had voted for joining Indonesia. The fairness and legitimacy of the vote are contested till now by opposition Papua groups.[2]

---

[2] Doherty, B. (2019). Why are there violent clashes in Papua and West Papua? *The Guardian.* https://www.theguardian.com/world/2019/aug/22/why-are-there-violent-clashes-in-papua-and-west-papua-explainer

UN Transition Assistance Group—Protracted Process That Led to Success

Namibia, formerly known as South West Africa, was a German territory before the First World War. Subsequently, South Africa assumed power over its administration as authorized by the League of Nations. After the UN came into existence, it recommended that the territory come under its Trusteeship System. South Africa refused and did not honour the judgement by ICJ, regarding its international obligations. The South-West Africa People's Organisation (SWAPO) engaged in an armed struggle against the South African regime. In 1978, the UN proposed a plan to South Africa for a ceasefire and for holding elections under its supervision. South Africa finally agreed to the proposal in 1988 and both the parties agreed to a ceasefire. In November 1989, the United Nations Transition Assistance Group (UNTAG), supervised the elections for the constitutional assembly. Namibia became an independent nation four months later when it adopted its constitution. UNTAG's success preceded protracted peace negotiations without which Namibia would not have attained independence.[3]

UN Mission for the Referendum in Western Sahara: The Unfinished Mission

Spain administrated the territory of Western Sahara till 1976. After 1976, both Morocco and Mauritania claimed control of the territory, prompting the Frente Popular para la Liberación de Saguia el-Hamra y de Río de Oro (Frente POLISARIO) to seek an independent state. Mauritania renounced its claims over Western Sahara in 1979, and the UN along with the AU (then OAU) made proposals for settlement that was accepted by Morocco and the Frente POLISARIO in August 1988. In 1990, the Security Council authorized the establishment of the UN Mission for the Referendum in Western Sahara (MINURSO). The mandate of the mission was to monitor the ceasefire and conduct a referendum to ascertain the wishes of the local population regarding independence or integration with Morocco. The ceasefire

[3] United Nations. (1989). *Namibia—UNTAG: Background*. https://peacekeeping.un.org/sites/default/files/past/untagS.htm

has generally held, but the referendum has not taken place due to differences over who qualifies to vote. Despite several UN initiatives, Morocco and the Frente POLISARIO are not able to come to an agreement on the registration of voters. After 30 years, MINURSO continues to remain in Western Sahara without completing its mandated task. Morocco is seen as intransigent, going to the extent of expelling more than 70 MINURSO civilian staff in 2016 because the UN Secretary-General Ban Ki-moon had termed Morocco's annexation of the territory as 'occupation'.[4]

UN Mission in East Timor and UN Transitional Administration in East Timor: A Success Story with Some Missteps

The Portuguese controlled East Timor since the early 16th century. The UN brought the territory under its decolonization enterprise in 1960. In 1975, the Portuguese abandoned the territory's control without arranging for its transition towards independence. The East Timorese political parties that emerged during this period were unable to come to a consensus on the transition. Among these parties, the Revolutionary Front of Independent East Timor or Fretilin had emerged as the most popular and powerful.

Indonesia, despite sharing a border with East Timor, historically had no political or economic association with it. In 1975, Indonesia was governed by Suharto who had assumed power 10 years ago in 1965 after purging the Indonesian Communist Party and its supporters. More than 500,000 people were killed during the violent liquidation of the communists. In 1975, the Suharto government sent its military and occupied East Timor in December under the pretext of preventing assumption of power by a Marxist Fretilin government. The UN continued to keep the issue under its decolonization agenda and engaged with Indonesia and Portugal to find a settlement regarding the status of the territory. The East Timorese suffered under Indonesian occupation, and there was widespread poverty and hunger. The Indonesian troops also committed gross violations of human rights. Indonesia armed and supported

[4] United Nations. (2015). *United Nations mission for the referendum in Western Sahara.* https://minurso.unmissions.org/background

East Timorese paramilitary groups as part of its occupation strategy and condoned crimes committed by these groups against the population.

In 1998, the Asian financial crisis severely impacted Indonesia, and the ensuing protests led to the fall of Suharto. President Habibie who succeeded Suharto conveyed to the UN negotiators that his government was willing to offer East Timor a choice between autonomy within Indonesia or independence. His government's proposal included the UN conducting a ballot to ascertain the wishes of the East Timorese. While the negotiations were taking place, the Indonesia-supported militia unleashed violence against the East Timorese as a way of opposing the talks. On 5 May 1999, Indonesia and Portugal signed an agreement in the presence of the UN Secretary-General on the modalities of ascertaining the wishes of the East Timorese population. The Indonesians wanted to avoid the word 'referendum' and used the phrase 'popular consultation' instead.[5] The date for the ballot was set for 8 August 1999 and the question to be put before the East Timorese was phrased, such as 'Do you *accept* the proposed special autonomy for East Timor within the Unitary State of the Republic of Indonesia'? or 'Do you *reject* the proposed special autonomy for East Timor, leading to East Timor's separation from Indonesia'?[6]

The Indonesian government refused the deployment of the UN Peacekeepers and insisted that its police and army would be responsible for maintaining law and order during the conduct of the 'popular consultation'.[7] The UN Police (CIVPOL) would play an advisory role. The East Timorese political leadership expressed apprehensions about the Indonesian security forces and the militias' potential to undermine the ballot. The UN accepted that there was no possibility of Indonesia allowing it to deploy peacekeeping forces to provide security to the mission and the population.

---

[5] United Nations. (1999, 25 October). *Security Council establishes United Nations transitional administration in East Timor for initial period until 31 January 2001*. Meeting Coverage and Press Releases.

[6] Martin, I. (2001). *Self-determination in East Timor: The United Nations, the ballot, and international Intervention*. Lynne Reinner Publishers.

[7] United Nations. (1999, 25 October). *Security Council establishes United Nations transitional administration in East Timor for initial period until 31 January 2001*. Meeting Coverage and Press Releases.

The Security Council authorized the deployment of the UN Mission in East Timor (UNAMET) which was established on 1 June 1999 in Dili. The Indonesian military, despite its assurances to the UN, gave a free hand to the militia to not only intimidate but also kill people to spread fear about the consequences of voting for independence. The Secretary-General decided that the mission should persist with its plans and not postpone the ballot despite the violence perpetrated by the militia. If the ballot had been postponed, UNAMET would have become like MINURSO in Western Sahara. Within four months and with only three weeks' delay, UNAMET successfully conducted the ballot on 30 August. This was done despite challenges of functioning in a country with mountainous terrain, poor infrastructure including bad roads and poor communication facilities.

The UN Secretary-General and UNAMET head Ian Martin announced the results on 4 September simultaneously in New York and Dili. The East Timorese had overwhelmingly (78.5%) voted for independence.

Starting from 30 August, the militia had gone on a rampage, and after the announcement of the results, both the militia and the Indonesian Army resorted to widespread violence and destruction.[8] The extent of violence and the damage to property led to the UN pressuring the Indonesians to accept the deployment of an international force. On 20 September, a UN-mandated and Australia-led multinational force for East Timor (International Force East Timor [INTERFET]) was deployed to restore order in the territory.[9]

Scholars criticized the UN Security Council for agreeing to a flawed security arrangement with the Indonesians and thereby exposing East Timorese and UN staff to violence. However, UNAMET

---

[8] The author spent three months between October and December 1999 in East Timor as the Secretary of the UN Commission of Inquiry on East Timor and saw first-hand the violence and destruction caused by the Indonesian army and the militia after the ballot.

[9] Martin, I. (2001). *Self-determination in East Timor: The United Nations, the ballot, and international intervention.* Lynne Reinner Publishers; Martin, I., & Mayer-Reickh, A. (2005). The United Nations and East Timor: From self-determination to state-building. *International Peacekeeping, 12*(1), 125–145.

achieved what many considered an impossible task since, till 1998, the Indonesians had vehemently opposed the idea of an independent East Timor.[10]

UN Transitional Administration in East Timor

After the Indonesian parliament formally recognized the result of the East Timor ballot, the Security Council on 25 October 1999 adopted a resolution establishing the United Nations Transitional Administration in East Timor (UNTAET). In February 2000, INTERFET transferred its operations to the United Nations Peacekeeping Force, and UNTAET was set up as a multidimensional peacekeeping operation with responsibility to administer East Timor during its transition to independence. Its tasks included providing security, maintaining law and order, establishing an effective administration, assisting in the development of civil and social services and ensuring the coordination of humanitarian assistance. UNTAET initiated steps to establish a functioning judicial and legal system.

Two years after the popular consultation, the East Timorese population went to the polls again to elect an 88-member Constituent Assembly to write and adopt a new constitution. The Constituent Assembly on 22 March 2002 signed into force the country's first constitution. On 20 May 2002, the UN handed over its powers when the Constituent Assembly transformed itself as the country's parliament.

UNTAET's mandate was unprecedented and complex. Several academic writings and other reports have identified UNTAET's challenges, achievements and failures. UNTAET ensured smooth transition to independence but did not contribute to creating a democratic political environment.[11]

---

[10] Robinson, G. (2000). With Unamet in East Timor: A historian's personal view. *Bulletin of Concerned Asian Scholars, 32*(1), 23–26. https://www.researchgate.net/publication/295388252_With_Unamet_in_East_Timor_A_historian's_personal_view/link/5939d9f9a6fdcc58aea31b69/download

[11] Martin, I., & Mayer-Reickh, A. (2005). The United Nations and East Timor: From self-determination to state-building. *International Peacekeeping, 12*(1), 125–145.

United Nations Mission of Support in East Timor

The Security Council on 20 May 2002 authorized the establishment of the United Nations Mission of Support in East Timor (UNMISET) to replace UNTAET.

The mission's focus was on stability, democracy and justice; public security and law enforcement; and external security and border control. UNMISET retained the interim law enforcement duties while the other functions were transferred to the Timorese government. The mission maintained a presence of 5,000 troops to counter the threats from militias based in West Timor.[12] UNTAET had previously assisted in political transition, but the country still faced tremendous challenges in setting up a functioning government with its limited local human resources. The mission deployed 100 'stability advisers' to assist the Timorese civil servants in the areas of finance, justice system and general administration. Recruitment of Timorese civil servants was a major challenge. In some cases, there was a mismatch between available talent and the job. In other cases, the UN-recruited advisers were not able to effectively mentor the Timorese due to the lack of experience in building a system from the scratch. The delay in recruitment of civilian advisers had a negative impact on the building of public administration. The administration of justice was struggling to function effectively. The 4 December 2002 rioting and excessive force used against the demonstrators revealed the shortcomings of both the East Timorese police and the UN police.[13]

The mission ended in May 2005.

United Nations Office in Timor-Leste and United Nations Integrated Mission in Timor-Leste

When UNMISET ended its operations, Security Council members were reluctant to deploy another mission particularly with the presence of

---

[12] United Nations. (2005). *East Timor—UNMISET—Mandate*. United Nations Mission of Support in East Timor. https://peacekeeping.un.org/mission/past/unmiset/mandate.html

[13] The author worked with UNMISET as the Director of the Human Rights Unit from October 2003 to February 2005 and witnessed first-hand the functioning of the mission.

peacekeepers. As a compromise, the Security Council agreed to replace UNMISET with a downsized mission for one year. The UN Office in Timor-Leste (UNOTIL) was established in May 2005 with the following mandate: support for public administration and justice system and for justice in the area of serious crimes, support for the development of law enforcement in Timor-Leste and support for the security and stability of Timor-Leste.[14]

In April–June 2006, the country faced a serious political and security crisis. The conflict began with dissatisfied elements of the military alleging discrimination, followed by a coup attempt, and it ended in widespread violence across the country. The Timor-Leste leadership requested urgent police and military assistance from Australia, New Zealand, Malaysia and Portugal. The international forces stabilized the situation by May 2006. In June 2006, the President of Timor-Leste, the Prime Minister and the President of the National Parliament requested the UN Secretary-General to re-establish a UN police force in Timor-Leste to maintain law and order in the country until the country's police was reorganized.

The Secretary-General sent Ian Martin, former head of UNAMET, as his special envoy to assess the situation and identify the scope of the proposed mission. In his report, Martin cautioned against viewing Timor-Leste as a failed state, but as a state in the initial stages of achieving democratic governance. Similarly, the UN Secretary-General in his presentation to the Security Council acknowledged that building institutions is a complex process that cannot be achieved within a few years.[15]

In August 2006, the Security Council authorized the deployment of the United Nations Integrated Mission in Timor-Leste (UNMIT).

---

[14] United Nations. (2005, 28 April). *Security council establishes one-year political mission in Timor-Leste, Unanimously adopting resolution 1599 (2005)* (Meeting Coverage and Press Release, Security Council, SC/8371). https://www.un.org/press/en/2005/sc8371.doc.htm

[15] United Nations. (2006). *United Nations determined not to abandon Timor-Leste at critical time of need says Secretary-General, as Security Council meets following recent violence* (Meeting Coverage and Press Releases, Security Council, SC/8745). https://www.un.org/press/en/2006/sc8745.doc.htm

The mandate of UNMIT was to support the government in consolidating stability, enhancing a culture of democratic governance and facilitating political dialogue among Timorese stakeholders in their efforts to bring about a process of national reconciliation and to foster social cohesion. The mission included military liaison and staff officers, police officers and civilian staff. UNMIT contributed to stabilizing the security situation and in the conduct of presidential and parliamentary elections in June 2007. In February 2008, another crisis engulfed the country with a separate armed attack against the Prime Minister and the President by a former and fugitive Military Police Commander. Fortunately, both the President and the Prime Minister survived the attack. UNMIT continued to assist the Timorese government and ended its operation in December 2012.[16]

An International Crisis Group report, published after the 2006 events, considered that the crisis was about the challenges involved in a guerrilla group's move from war to peace and the building of security institutions where they did not previously exist. The report was critical of UNTAET, UNMISET and UNOTIL's leadership. The report blamed the UN leadership for its passivity. The Crisis Group report singled out Sukehiro Hasegawa, the Special Representative of the Secretary-General (SRSG of UNOTIL), as 'widely seen as a well-meaning man, eager to avoid conflict, but put in a position beyond his depth and an uncomprehending bystander as the forces that erupted in 2006 gathered strength'.[17]

RESPONDING TO POST-INDEPENDENCE CRISIS

Several newly independent countries witnessed numerous crises in the initial years of their independence. The following table illustrates the UN's role in various such conflicts and situations.

[16] United Nations. (2012). *Background: United Nations mission in Timor-Leste*. https://unmit.unmissions.org/background

[17] International Crisis Group. (2006). *Resolving Timor-Leste's crisis* (Asian Report No. 120). https://www.crisisgroup.org/asia/south-east-asia/timor-leste/resolving-timor-leste-s-crisis

Operation	Year	Purpose
UN Military Observer Group in India and Pakistan (UNMOGIP)	1949	To monitor India–Pakistan ceasefire in Kashmir
UN Operation in the Congo (ONUC)	1960–1964	To prevent foreign intervention in and preserve the territory of Congo
UN Yemen Observation Mission (UNYOM)	1963–1964	Supervise disengagement of Saudi Arabia and Egypt from Yemen's Civil War (Disengagement of external actors and not for observation of ceasefire)
UN Peacekeeping Force in Cyprus (UNFICYP)	1964–present	Prevent conflict between the Greek and the Turkish Cypriots. Since the de facto division of the island in 1974, UNFICYP has served as a buffer force between the Turkish and Turkish Cypriot forces on one side and the Greek Cypriot National Guard and Greek troops on the other.
UN Mission in the Republic of South Sudan (UNMISS)	2011–present	Support for peace consolidation and thereby fostering longer-term state-building and economic development; conflict prevention, mitigation and resolution along with civilian protection; to establish rule of law; and to strengthen the security and justice sectors.

Source: The author.

UN Military Observer Group in India and Pakistan: The Never-ending Conflict

The British colonial regime's partition of India in 1947 while conferring independence to India and Pakistan remains the most horrendous crisis that engulfed the two newly independent nations. The partition also led to the conflict between India and Pakistan over Kashmir. In 1949, UNMOGIP was deployed to monitor India–Pakistan ceasefire in Kashmir.

The peacekeeping operation continues to remain after 71 years with no end to the dispute between the two countries.

UN Operation in the Congo: UN's First Foray into an Intrastate Conflict

This operation was the UN's first intervention in an internal conflict arising in the immediate aftermath of Congo's independence. In 1960, the Security Council deployed ONUC. The Congolese government requested the UN's intervention after the separatists in the wealthy province of Katanga declared independence. The Belgian troops and European mercenaries supported the secessionists. Secretary-General Dag Hammarskjöld sought a restricted mandate limiting the use of force only for purposes of self-defence. However, the intensity of the conflict soon increased, and the Security Council, in February 1961, authorized the UN forces to 'take all appropriate measures to prevent the outbreak of civil war in the Congo including arrangements for ceasefire … if necessary, to use force as a last resort'.[18] In September 1961, Dag Hammarskjöld died in an air crash in the region while travelling to negotiate ceasefire in Congo. After his death, the Security Council authorized the use of mass force against the Katanga secessionists and foreign troops.[19] In 1964, the UN withdrew from Congo after its intervention prevented the break-up of the country and for Congo to cope with the post-independence crisis.

UN Peacekeeping Force in Cyprus: UN Caught in a Communal Conundrum

In 1960, Cyprus attained independence. Post Independence, the conflict between the Turkish Cypriots and Greek Cypriots intensified.

---

[18] Shagalov, V. A., Letyaev, V. A., Grishin, Y., & Vladimirova, M. M. (2018). Dag Hammarskjold's role in the development of peacekeeping. *Revista Publicando 5*, 16(1), 606–616. https://pdfs.semanticscholar.org/41df/60a0c1372dfdbe07e3cec07 885a0eb1f3f76.pdf

[19] United Nations. (2001). *Republic of the Congo: ONUC background*.https://peace-keeping.un.org/sites/default/files/past/onucB.htm

In 1964, the Security Council established UNFICYP to deescalate the tensions between the two communities. In 1974, following the Greek Cypriot coup and the Turkish invasion of Cyprus, UNFICYP's mandate also included prevention of war, maintenance of military status quo and patrolling of the UN Buffer Zone in Cyprus.[20]

The mission continues to exist despite efforts by several UN Secretary-Generals to resolve the dispute and end the operation.

UN Mission in the Republic of South Sudan: Liberation That Got Messy

Several decades of war between the Government of Sudan and Sudan People's Liberation Movement/Army (SPLM/A) ended in 2005 with the signing of a Comprehensive Peace Agreement (CPA) by the parties.

The United Nations Assistance Mission in Sudan (UNMIS) supported the implementation of the peace accord. UNMIS, as per the accord, conducted a referendum in which the South Sudanese overwhelmingly voted for independence in July 2011. The Security Council authorized the UN Mission in the Republic of South Sudan (UNMISS) to assist the newly established government in the areas of development, security, institution building and rule of law.

During the long war of independence, SPLM/A faced internal strife and even armed conflict between factions identified with the majority Dinka and Nuer tribes. The political arrangement that emerged after the independence reflected SPLM/A's internal divisions with Salva Kiir from the Dinka tribe becoming president and Riek Machar from the Nuer tribe assuming office as his deputy. In December 2013, a civil war broke out in South Sudan arising from a political dispute between President Salva Kiir and his former deputy Riek Machar. This conflict between the two rapidly grew into a vicious inter-ethnic conflict.

---

[20] United Nations. (1964, March). *UNFICYP fact sheet: United Nations peacekeeping force in Cyprus.* United Nations Peacekeeping. https://peacekeeping.un.org/en/mission/unficyp

In the last seven years, about 400,000 people are estimated to have been killed in the civil war. About 1.8 million became internally displaced and another 2.5 million fled to the neighbouring countries. In March 2020, the UN Inquiry Commission on Human Rights in South Sudan submitted a damaging report to the UN Human Rights Council. It stated that the conflict had intensified at the local levels and that it had bitterly divided the country along ethnic lines. The Commission found that both parties to the conflict used intentional starvation as a method of warfare. It also documented recruiting of child soldiers and large-scale sexual violence. Nearly half the population, particularly women and children, faced acute food insecurity.[21]

UNMISS, deployed to assist in state-building, was faced with an internal conflict and rising demands to protect the civilians. The nature of the conflict with mobilization of local armed groups and lack of command posed a grave challenge to the mission. Responding to the plight of civilians who were caught in the conflict, the Security Council adopted a resolution in May 2014 prioritizing their protection and diminishing UNMISS' role in state-building activities. The resolution also reaffirmed UNMISS' role in documenting human rights violations and in delivery of humanitarian assistance. It further increased its troop strength. UNMISS gave refuge to civilians fleeing the conflict by opening civilian protection sites. These sites posed political, legal and practical challenges, including a few site attacks by the forces loyal to the government. The truce signed in 2015 between the President and his former deputy failed to hold.

On 20 February 2020, the President and Riek Machar finally agreed to a peace deal and formed a national unity government.

UNMISS is praised for its efforts in protecting the civilians. However, UNMISS demonstrates that a well-funded and ambitious

---

[21] United Nations Human Rights Council. (2020). *UN experts say pattern of years of extreme violations in South Sudan must be reserved*. UN Commission on Human Rights in South Sudan. https://www.ohchr.org/EN/HRBodies/HRC/Pages/NewsDetail.aspx?NewsID=25686&LangID=E

mandate does not necessarily contribute to resolving the complex issues of state-building after a prolonged war, internal divisions and devastation.[22] The South Sudan case demonstrates that state-building is a complex process, and there is no guarantee of success despite the presence of a large UN mission.[23]

[22] Zambakari, C., Kang, T. K., & Sanders, R. (2018). The role of the UN Mission in South Sudan (UNMISS) in protecting civilians. In S. C. Roach & Hudson (Eds.), *The challenge of governance in South Sudan: Corruption, peacebuilding, and foreign intervention* (1st ed.). Routledge. https://papers.ssrn.com/sol3/papers.cfm?abstract_id=3128701

[23] Stern, J. (2015). *Establishing safety and security at protection of Civilians sites: Lessons from the United Nations peacekeeping in South Sudan* (Civilians in Conflict, Policy Brief No. 2). Stimson Centre. https://www.stimson.org/wp-content/files/file-attachments/CIC-Policy-Brief_2_Sept-2015.pdf

Operations Deployed in Conflicts Arising from the Cold War and Its Aftermath

According to Hobsbawm, the period from the end of the Second World War to the end of the Soviet Union was marked by confrontation between two superpowers known as 'Cold War'. It involved efforts by the two superpowers to retain their sphere of interest, leading at times to armed conflict in the zones where they confronted each other through their proxies.[1]

In some countries, conflict emerged during the Cold War, and in others, it erupted after it ended. The UN was engaged in these countries through its peacekeeping operations.

Operation	Year	Purpose
UN Angola Verification Mission I (UNAVEM I)	1989–1991	Supervise withdrawal of Cuban troops from Angola
UN Angola Verification Mission II (UNAVEM II)	1991–1995	Enforce ceasefire in the Angolan Civil War
UN Angola Verification Mission III (UNAVEM III)	1995–1997	Monitor ceasefire and disarmament

[1] Hobsbawm, E. J. (1994). *Age of extremes: The short twentieth century, 1914–1991.* Michael Joseph; Viking Penguin.

Operation	Year	Purpose
UN Protection Force (UNPROFOR)	1992–1995	Protect areas of Croatia, Bosnia and Herzegovina and the Republic of Macedonia
UN Confidence Restoration Operation in Croatia (UNCRO)	1995–1996	To implement ceasefire
UN Preventive Deployment Force (UNPREDEP)	1995–1999	Replace UNPROFOR in Macedonia and monitor border with Albania.
UN Transitional Administration for Eastern Slavonia, Baranja and Western Sirmium (UNTAES)	1996–1998	Supervise and facilitate demilitarization, monitor return of refugees, contribute to the maintenance of peace and security, establish a temporary police force, undertake tasks relating to civil administration and public services and organize elections.
United Nations Interim Administration Mission in Kosovo (UNMIK)	1999–present	To provide interim administration in Kosovo with all legislative and executive powers and administration of judiciary. Following the declaration of independence by the Kosovo authorities in 2008, the mission's mandate was modified to focus on the promotion of security, stability and respect for human rights.
UN Civilian Support Group (UNPSG)	1998–present	Monitor Croatian police
UN Mission of Observers in Prevlaka (UNMOP)	1996–2002	Monitor demilitarization of the Prevlaka peninsula, Croatia
UN Mission in Bosnia and Herzegovina (UNMIBH)	1995–2002	Monitor human rights, demining and relief
UN Transitional Authority in Cambodia (UNTAC)	1992–1993	Assist Cambodia in its transition from war to a democratic state

Operation	Year	Purpose
UN Operation in Somalia I (UNOSOM I)	1992–1993	Enforce ceasefire, reorganized as the Unified Task Force (UNITAF)
UN Operation in Somalia II (UNOSOM II)	1993–1995	Stabilize Somalia and assist humanitarian efforts
United Nations Political Office for Somalia (UNPOS)	1995–2013	Advance peace and reconciliation
United Nations Assistance Mission in Somalia (UNSOM)	2013–present	Provision of policy advice to the Federal Government and the African Union Mission in Somalia (AMISOM) on peacebuilding and state-building in the areas of governance, security sector reform and rule of law (including the disengagement of combatants), development of a federal system (including state formation), constitutional review and democratization

Source: The author.

UN TRANSITIONAL AUTHORITY IN CAMBODIA: A JEWEL IN THE PEACEKEEPING OPERATION THAT LOST ITS SHINE

Background

In 1863, the Cambodian (Kampuchea) King Norodom placed the kingdom under the French protectorate. After Norodom and his successor Monivong, the French in 1941 appointed the 18-year-old Prince Sihanouk as the King on the assumption that he would be more accommodating of their interests. In 1945, the Japanese occupied Cambodia, and Sihanouk, encouraged by the Japanese, proclaimed an independent Kampuchea. The French returned after the Second World War and faced Kampuchean demand for independence. Kampuchea became independent in November 1953. Sihanouk, who now assumed power, did not tolerate any opposition; he believed that he was performing the role of a father figure to the Cambodians. The country was poverty-stricken, and inequalities were visible. In the decade after independence, some Khmer intellectuals established the clandestine Communist Party of Kampuchea known as 'Khmer Rouge' (Red Khmers). By the 1960s, Khmer Rouge had expanded their presence in the rural areas.

In the mid-1960s, in the Vietnam War, Sihanouk played a neutral card by refusing the Americans to use Cambodian territory for military purposes. The Americans doubted Sihanouk's sincerity and suspected that he was supporting the Viet Cong. Sihanouk increasingly withdrew from day-to-day running of the government and was engaged in pursing his hobbies like music and film-making. Consequently, dissatisfaction with his government grew. In March 1970, he was overthrown in a coup by Prime Minister General Lon Nol. The United States got directly involved in Cambodia with extensive bombing of the North Vietnamese bases inside the country. The bombings inflicted misery on the rural population and drove them to support Khmer Rouge. The North Vietnamese too overran vast parts of Cambodia and handed over them to Khmer Rouge. Sihanouk urged the population to overthrow the Lon Nol government which, in turn, increased the support for Khmer Rouge. Khmer Rouge became increasingly independent from the Vietnamese and more fanatical as they attacked ethnic Vietnamese living in Cambodia. Meanwhile, the Lon Nol government was tottering and eventually collapsed with the capture of Phnom Penh by Khmer Rouge in April 1975. The leader of Khmer Rouge, Pol Pot launched his rapid march to socialism to confront their hereditary enemy Vietnam.[2]

Pol Pot's policy led to the evacuation of all cities and towns as part of his plans to completely restructure the Cambodian society. He abolished the banking system and currency. It is estimated by various scholars that between 1.5 million and 2 million Cambodians died due to hunger, starvation and killings during the Pol Pot regime. The

[2] Chanda, N. (1986). *Brother enemy: The war after the war. A history of Indochina since the fall of Saigon.* Harcourt Brace Jovanovich.

regime tortured its alleged opponents and developed various torture methods which became known after the overthrow of his regime. By 1977, the Pol Pot regime had begun cross-border raids against the Vietnamese border villages and committed atrocities against the villagers. The increasing tension between Vietnam and the Pol Pot regime came to a boil on 25 December 1978 when more than 100,000 Vietnamese troops and a few thousands of Cambodian rebels launched an attack against the Pol Pot regime. In January 1979, the new People's Republic of Kampuchea was established.

After the Vietnam War, Cambodia was caught in another global and regional power struggle. This conflict became part of the Soviet-American rivalry, China-Vietnamese conflict and Sino-American alliance. These dynamics impacted on the next chapter of the Cambodian history. The Khmer Rouge leadership including Pol Pot fled to the Thai border, leaving evidence of his torture chambers and other cruelties. By the end of 1979, Khmer Rouge settled near the Thai border with 100,000 former cadres and supporters. China, the United States and the members of the Association of Southeast Asian Nations (ASEAN) condemned the Vietnamese incursion and the overthrow of Pol Pot's Democratic Kampuchea (DK) regime. The Chinese backed Pol Pot and provided arms and other material assistance to his supporters. Due to the Chinese and the US support, the UN recognized Pol Pot's DK as legitimate government of Cambodia. The international community provided relief to refugees along the Thai border that sustained Khmer Rouge and its supporters. The support provided to the Pol Pot's DK, its recognition by the UN and the isolation of the new regime in Cambodia was a 'full-blown moral farce'.[3]

In 1984, Hun Sen became the Prime Minister of People's Republic of Kampuchea (PRK). He had defected from Khmer Rouge and was fighting them along with the Vietnamese. When Vietnam invaded Cambodia, he was made Deputy Prime Minister and Foreign Minister. Under Hun Sen, PRK became the State of Cambodia (SOC) and gradually distanced itself from Vietnam.

---

[3] Strangio, S. (2014). *Hun Sen's Cambodia*. Yale University Press.

On the Thai border, along with Khmer Rouge, two other groups initiated by Son Sann and Sihanouk, respectively, had emerged to fight against the Vietnamese. The three groups with the active prodding of foreign backers formed a unified coalition called the Coalition Government of Democratic Kampuchea (CGDK). However, Khmer Rouge's new avatar, the Party of Democratic Kampuchea (PDK), remained the strongest among the coalition partners. The war waged by the coalition against the Vietnamese caused untold misery to the Cambodians inside the country and in the refugee camps along the Thai border. The war had reached a stalemate with both sides not able to force the issue.

In the late 1980s, ASEAN along with Australia made efforts to find a solution to the Cambodian conflict. The changing dynamics between the Soviet Union and the United States, and Soviet Union's willingness to normalize relations with China, provided further impetus to resolve the conflict. Gradual rapprochement between Vietnam and China also created conditions for negotiations for ending the conflict. In September 1989, the Vietnamese withdrew from Cambodia. In October 1991, the Cambodian factions and 18 other nations signed the Paris Peace Agreement. The agreement led to the deployment of the UN Transitional Authority in Cambodia (UNTAC) in 1992.

UN Transitional Authority in Cambodia

UNTAC had an ambitious mandate to coordinate the withdrawal of all foreign forces, disarming and demobilization of Cambodian armed factions, facilitating the return of refugees and organizing the elections. The changing geopolitical dynamics brought the warring Cambodian parties to the table, but they were not committed to working together. None of them was interested in reconciliation—only using an 'indecent peace' to prosecute the old war by new means.[4]

UNTAC was the first large peacekeeping operation in the post-Cold War period. The divisions within the parties that signed the peace agreement impacted on the mission's ability to implement its mandate.

---

[4] Ibid., p. 45.

Pol Pot and the Hun Sen government refused to disarm. Similarly, UNTAC was mandated to take charge of the SOC administrative apparatus which did not happen. UNTAC was not able to implement two of its major mandated tasks. It began to focus on organizing the elections. Hun Sen's Cambodian People's Party (CPP) used the government's machinery to campaign and had an undue advantage over other parties. Pol Pot refused to participate in the elections. Khmer Rouge unleashed violence again which included the kidnapping of UN peacekeepers. Pol Pot's PDK soldiers massacred 33 unarmed Vietnamese civilians in Siem Reap, and UNTAC was unable to respond adequately to the violence and protect the civilians.

Between 23 and 28 May 1993, the elections were conducted, and the polling was surprisingly peaceful. Despite previous threats, PDK did not sabotage the polls. CPP, the Buddhist Liberal Democratic Party (BLDP) and FUNCINPEC were the main contenders. CPP was confident that it would win the elections. On the contrary, FUNCINPEC won 45.5 per cent vote, and CPP managed to get only 38.2 per cent. Hun Sen accused the UN of manipulating the results. He announced secession of six provinces from the country. In the secession areas, CPP attacked the UN offices and members of the opposition party. FUNCINPEC's leader Prince Ranariddh agreed to share power with Hun Sen. The Royal Government of Cambodia came into existence with Prince Ranariddh as the 'first prime minister' and Hun Sen as the 'second prime minister'. UNTAC was complicit in the making of the new power arrangement. Despite the power-sharing arrangement, CPP was the dominant partner with the control of army, police and militias. UNTAC, despite the challenges it faced, was instrumental in bringing a modicum of peace and stability after many years of war and strife. The international community hailed UNTAC as a remarkable success story.

In 1997, the power-sharing arrangement broke down. Between 5 and 6 July, Hun Sen mounted a violent coup against FUNCINPEC's military positions. Hun Sen's forces engaged in targeted killing of FUNCINPEC's military and police figures. The fighting resulted in the killing of hundreds of people. The scale of violence undid all the achievements of the past five years, and 'UNTAC, the jewel in the peacekeeping crown, lay shattered'.[5] Twenty-seven years after UNTAC left, Hun Sen continues to rule Cambodia with an iron grip using violence and patronage to maintain his power. He is credited for bringing peace and economic growth to a war-ravaged country. Despite UNTAC's success, the political arrangement that emerged at the end of its mission continues to haunt the international community with regard to ensuring democracy and human rights in Cambodia.

Angola: UN Peacekeeping Operations— UNAVEM I, UNAVEM II, UNAVEM III and MONUA

In January 1975, Portugal signed an agreement granting independence to Angola. The Angolan side was represented by the Popular Movement for the Liberation of Angola (MPLA), the National Union for the Total Independence of Angola (UNITA) and the National Liberation Front of Angola (FNLA). During the transition, UNITA and FNLA fought against the MPLA. FNLA lost its importance, and UNITA, led by Jonas Savimbi, withdrew to its stronghold in the South and waged a war against MPLA. On 11 November 1975, MPLA established the People's Republic of Angola. The rift between MPLA and UNITA was considered an ideological division, with the former associated with Marxist ideology and the latter opposing it. However, as in many other postcolonial societies, in Angola too, the mobilization against the new regime was based on ethnic loyalties. The Cold War added another dimension to it, with the Soviet Union and Cuba supporting the MPLA and the United States and Apartheid South Africa supporting UNITA. The Angolan Civil War was one of the longest and brutal that caused untold misery to the civilians. Between 1975 and 2002, more than 500,000 people had died and over one million had been internally displaced. The use of child soldiers was rampant.[6]

---

[5] Adams, B. (1998). UN Human Rights work in Cambodia: Efforts to preserve the jewel in the peacekeeping crown. In A. H. Henkin (Ed.), *Honoring human rights from peace to justice*. Kluwer Law International.

[6] South African History Online. (2015). *The Angolan civil war (1975–2002): A brief history*. https://www.sahistory.org.za/article/angolan-civil-war-1975-2002-brief-history

UNAVEM I, UNAVEM II, UNAVEM III and MONUA: Failure that Costed US$1.5 Billion

The US-led mediation resulted in a tripartite agreement between Angola, Cuba and South Africa that led to an arrangement between Angola and Cuba for the withdrawal of 50,000 Cuban troops. The UN Security Council in December 1988 established the United Nations Angola Verification Mission (UNAVEM), later known as United Nations Angola Verification Mission I (UNAVEM I), to monitor the withdrawal of the Cuban troops. UNAVEM, implementing a pact between two friendly countries, succeeded in its task and ended its mission earlier than planned.[7]

In May 1991, peace accord between the Angolan government and UNITA led to the deployment of United Nations Angola Verification Mission II (UNAVEM II). The mandate was to observe ceasefire, confinement of troops in assembly areas and disarmament and demobilization of forces. The mission's role was limited to observance of the truce and not enforcing it. The UN monitors went beyond their limited role and engaged in humanitarian activities like providing food and clothing to the troops in assembly areas. In March 1992, the UN Security Council expanded UNAVEM II's mandate to include the observation of elections. The mission thereby expanded to include an electoral division, but its role was limited to observing the elections and not organizing it.

UNAVEM II became a contrary model for deployment of a peace-keeping operation. It remained a spectator when both parties did not comply with the demobilization plan agreed by them. Both parties maintained their own secret armies in violation of the accords.[8]

After a short period of relative peace, the fight between the Angolan government and UNITA resumed. The 1992 election was not conclusive, and before the second ballot, UNITA launched an attack against the government forces. In 1994, due to the pressure exerted by the

---

[7] United Nations. (2000). *Angola-UNAVEM II: Background*. https://peacekeeping.un.org/mission/past/Unavem2/UnavemIIB.htm

[8] Human Rights Watch. (1999). *The United Nations*. https://www.hrw.org/reports/1999/angola/Angl998-10.htm

United States, UN and other states, both parties signed a ceasefire agreement. The agreement included the UN's role in the implementation of the plan.

Despite the deteriorating situation, the Security Council authorized UNAVEM III in February 1995. The new mission had an expanded mandate that included military, political, civilian police, humanitarian and electoral duties. Importantly, it included a human rights component with offices throughout the country.[9]

In June 1997, UNAVEM III ended its operation and was replaced by the United Nations Observer Mission to Angola (MONUA). The security situation had deteriorated, and neither side was amenable to the pressure from the UN or other countries. They preferred the option of war over peace. The Security Council imposed sanctions against UNITA and repeatedly reiterated that the UNITA leadership was responsible for the deadlock in the peace process. With violence persisting, including the downing of two UN planes, the Secretary-General in January 1999 reported to the Security Council that the peace process had collapsed and proposed drawing down of MONUA with the aim to end its mission.[10]

UNAVEM and MONUA created conditions for the parties to find a peaceful solution and pursue reconciliation. However, despite UN spending US$ 1.5 billion, peace was not achieved, and the leaders must assume responsibility for the suffering of their people.[11]

SOMALIA: UNOSOM, AMISOM, UNPOS AND UNSOM—EXPERIENCING THE PITFALLS OF PEACEKEEPING

During the Cold War, thanks to the superpowers, numerous countries got militarized and had abundance of arms at their disposal. Somalia was one such country that benefitted from the generosity of both

[9] United Nations. (1997). *Angola-UNAVEM III*. https://peacekeeping.un.org/en/mission/past/unavem3.htm

[10] United Nations. (2001). *Angola-MONUA: Background*. https://peacekeeping.un.org/en/mission/past/monua/monuab.htm

[11] Human Rights Watch. (1999). *The United Nations*. https://www.hrw.org/reports/1999/angola/Angl998-10.htm

superpowers. It received arms worth US$ 1 billion during the eight years when it was under the Soviet influence. When it switched sides, the United States gave nearly US$ 403 million worth of arms.[12]

Somalia gained independence on July 1960, formed by the integration of British Somaliland and Italian Somaliland. In 1969, Major General Mohamed Siad Barre assumed power after a coup. Siad Barre was with the Soviet Camp during the first decade, then switched sides, and was supported by the United States till 1989. His rule was oppressive. Human Rights Watch called Somalia a country with 'a government at war with its own people'.[13]

In 1991, a coalition of rebel groups ousted Siad Barre and he fled the country. After his overthrow with the end of Cold War and without any major backers, the country slid into anarchy. In the absence of a central government, various war lords created chaos. It was an unprecedented humanitarian disaster; an estimated 300,000 Somalis died and about two million fled the country with similar numbers internally displaced.[14]

UN Intervention in Somalia

In April 1992, the Security Council authorized the deployment of the United Nations Operation in Somalia (UNOSOM). The deployment was based on an agreement made between the two main Somali factions. The mission's focus was on delivering humanitarian assistance. However, looting by the armed groups, along with attacks against docked ships and airstrips, prevented the delivery of humanitarian assistance. On 24 November 1992, the Secretary-General informed the Security Council that the lack of government in Somalia and repeated attacks against the UN personnel and equipment prevented UNOSOM from implementing its mandate. The Security Council

---

[12] See https://www.chicagotribune.com/news/ct-xpm-1992-12-13-9204230505-story.html

[13] Africa Watch Committee. (1990). *Somalia: A government at war with its own people* (An Africa Watch Report). Human Rights Watch. https://www.hrw.org/sites/default/files/reports/somalia_1990.pdf

[14] Study.com. (2017). *Humanitarian intervention in Somalia*.https://study.com/academy/lesson/humanitarian-intervention-in-somalia.html

requested the Secretary-General to submit specific recommendations to remedy the situation.[15]

International Intervention Led by the United States

The Secretary-General among others proposed the deployment of a force led by a group of Member States to ensure the delivery of humanitarian assistance. On 3 December 1992, the Security Council unanimously adopted authorizing the Secretary-General and Member States to take steps to establish a secure environment for humanitarian relief operations. The Secretary-General's proposal was based on the United States' willingness to lead an operation if approved by the Security Council. On 9 December 1992, the US-led Unified Task Force (UNITAF) was deployed, and it included participating forces from 23 countries. In March 1993, based on the Secretary-General's report, the Security Council adopted a resolution expanding the mandate and size of UNOSOM. In October 1993, in a battle with Somali armed groups, 19 US troops were killed, and more than 80 others were injured. In 1994 and 1995, with no end to violence by the Somali groups and after suffering numerous casualties, the United States and the UN withdrew in 1994 and 1995, respectively.[16]

African Union and Neighbouring Countries Intervention

The 1995–2000 period witnessed continued chaos, and no stable government assumed power in Somalia. Between 2000 and 2006, the Intergovernmental Authority on Development (IGAD) facilitated the setting up of a Transitional National Government (TNG). In October 2004, the TNG was replaced by Transitional Federal Government (TFG) that emerged from IGAD's Peace and Reconciliation Conference. During 2006–2011, Somalia witnessed intervention by Ethiopia to oust the Islamic Court group which was then replaced by the al-Shabaab militants. In 2007, the AU with the approval of the UN Security Council established the African Union

---

[15] United Nations. (1992). *Somalia-UNOSOM I: Background.* https://peacekeeping. un.org/mission/past/unosom1backgr2.html

[16] Ibid.

Mission in Somalia (AMISOM).[17] In 2011, the Kenyan government in conjunction with AMISOM launched an attack against al-Shabaab that continued to operate in parts of southern Somalia. In the same year, TFG recaptured Mogadishu from al-Shabaab.

Return of the UN

Between 1995 and 2013, the UN functioned in Somalia through its United Nations Political Office for Somalia (UNPOS). It was a special political mission and was involved in supporting various initiatives aimed at promoting peace and national reconciliation in Somalia. It supported the efforts by the Government of Djibouti that led to the formation of the TNG of Somalia in 2000. The TFG began functioning from Somalia in February 2009. The election of a new President in September 2012 ended the role of TFG. Subsequently, the National Constituent Assembly adopted a Provisional Constitution and selection of members of the new Federal Parliament of Somalia.

In June 2013, the UN Security Council authorized the establishment of the United Nations Assistance Mission in Somalia (UNSOM). The mission continues to function till now with the mandate to peace and state-building, security sector reform, preparation for political transition, promoting respect for human rights, preventing sexual and gender-based violence and strengthening justice institutions. The mandate also includes investigation and reporting on violations of human rights and humanitarian laws committed in Somalia.[18]

The emergence of al-Shabaab complicated the political and security situation in Somalia. It was brutal and it mounted numerous bombings against AMISOM and other international actors. After the Kenyan operation, al-Shabaab's control is now much reduced, but it is still capable of launching attacks with devastating effects.[19]

---

[17] African Union Mission in Somalia. (2007). *AMISOM Background.* https://amisom-au.org/amisom-background/

[18] United Nations. (2013). *Mandate: United Nations Assistance Mission in SOMALIA.* https://unsom.unmissions.org/mandate

[19] *BBC News.* (2017). *Who are Somalia's al-Shabab?* https://www.bbc.com/news/world-africa-15336689

After a disastrous beginning in the 1990s, it is remarkable that UNSOM and AMISOM have survived in Somalia and have contributed to creating conditions for the country's political transition to resume. The Secretary-General in February 2020 reported to the Security Council that preparations for the 2020 national elections were in process and underlined that the security situation remains volatile.[20]

According to a briefing note by the Brookings Institution in Washington, DC, tension between the federal government and the federal state remains, making the political context 'fraught and fractured as the military battlefield'.[21] The same briefing note also cautioned that in the absence of an inclusive and accountable governance, vested powerbrokers would undermine the stabilization of Somalia for maintaining their control. Crackdown on selected vested groups would not help instead might exacerbate the conflict.[22]

FORMER YUGOSLAVIA: UNPROFOR—DIPLOMATIC DANCE THAT ENDED IN HORROR

The end of Cold War saw the break-up of Yugoslavia which caused unimaginable violence and misery to the people of the territory. Yugoslavia had emerged as a nation in 1945, consisting of six republics: Bosnia and Herzegovina, Croatia, Macedonia, Montenegro, Serbia and Slovenia. Serbia also had two autonomous provinces: Kosovo and Vojvodina. During the 1970s, Yugoslavia was considered a model of federalism for newly independent countries. Religious and ethnic divisions and the emergence of nationalism in the narrow sense contributed to the breaking up of the country. The collapse of communism in Eastern Europe in 1989 and the beginning of the end of the Soviet Union added to the destabilization of the federation. Slobodan Milosevic, Serbia's president from 1989, articulated

---

[20] United Nations. (2020, 13 February). *Situation in Somalia: Report of the Secretary-General*. Security Council. https://undocs.org/S/2020/121

[21] Felbab-Brown, V. (2018, 14 November). *Developments in Somalia*. Brooking. https://www.brookings.edu/testimonies/developments-in-somalia/

[22] Ibid.

ultra-Serbian nationalism and hatred of other ethnic groups to consolidate his power.

In 1990, Slovenia and Croatia proclaimed independence, which was followed by Bosnia and Herzegovina in 1992. In Croatia, armed conflict erupted between the Croatians and the Croatian Serbs. Milosevic's army intervened and it led to the death of tens of thousands and displacement of hundreds of thousands. In Bosnia, the Serb population opposed its independence. The extremist groups inelgrade supported the Serbs in Bosnia to attack the Muslim population to drive them away from their homes. It was a planned attack which came to be known as 'ethnic cleansing'. Serb forces lay siege to Bosnian capital Sarajevo for three and a half years from April 1992, causing immense suffering to the people.[23]

International and UN Interventions

The UN Secretary-General through his personal envoy was engaged with the situation from October 1991. In February 1992, the Security Council authorized the United Nations Protection Force (UNPROFOR). Initially, it was set up to deal with the Croatian and Serbian conflict. The Security Council extended its operational mandate to cover Croatia, Bosnia and Herzegovina, Macedonia, Montenegro and Serbia.[24]

The humanitarian situation was dire, and any intervention lead to the complexity of war among three warring parties and numerous paramilitary units that remained outside of any regular chain of command. In April 1993, when the Serb forces captured large parts of eastern Bosnia and created a humanitarian crisis, the Security Council responded by declaring Srebrenica as a 'safe area' and free from any armed attack. In May, the Security Council extended the concept to

---

[23] *BBC News.* (2006). *Timeline: Break-up of Yugoslavia.* http://news.bbc.co.uk/2/hi/europe/4997380.stm; Office of the Historian. (1990). *The breakup of Yugoslavia, 1990–1992.* https://history.state.gov/milestones/1989-1992/breakup-yugoslavia

[24] United Nations. (1996). *United Nations Protection Force. Former Yugoslavia-UNPROFOR, United Nations: Department of Public Information.* https://peacekeeping.un.org/en/mission/past/unprof_b.htm

include Sarajevo, Tuzla, Žepa, Goražde and Bihać.[25] From the beginning, the operation of 'safe areas' created confusion. The role of the UN troops placed within these areas was unclear.

UNPROFOR, between 1992 and 1995, had an arduous journey and ultimately came to be associated with the July 1995 massacre of Bosniaks in Srebrenica 'safe area'. The Bosnian Serb forces under the command of Ratko Mladić killed more than 8,000 Bosniaks (mostly men and boys) when they overran Srebrenica under the protection of the UN Dutch forces. The International Criminal Tribunal for the Former Yugoslavia (ICTY) ruled that the killing of male inhabitants of the enclave constituted genocide.[26]

In reality, a few hundred lightly armed UN forces protected the Srebrenica area with the threat of NATO airstrikes as a ploy. The confusion and the lack of resources available to UNPROFOR reflected the ambiguity of the world powers who wanted to avoid waging war and used the UN mission to show the world that they were acting. The Security Council resolutions authorized peacekeepers to seek air power for self-defence but did not authorize them to defend or protect the safe areas. 'A masterpiece of diplomatic drafting, but very hard to implement as an operational directive'.[27]

The international community displayed the lack of concern and was ineffectual in dealing with the brutal crimes committed by the Serbians. The Bosnian situation threatened the international order.[28]

[25] Akashi, Y. (1995). The use of force in a United Nations peace-keeping operation: Lessons learnt from the safe areas mandate. *Fordham International Law Journal, 19*(2), 312–23. https://ir.lawnet.fordham.edu/cgi/viewcontent.cgi?referer=https://www.google.com/&httpsredir=1&article=2223&context=ilj

[26] Bowcott, O., & Borger, J. (2017). Ratko Mladić convicted of war crimes and genocide at UN tribunal. *The Guardian.* https://www.theguardian.com/world/2017/nov/22/ratko-mladic-convicted-of-genocide-and-war-crimes-at-un-tribunal

[27] Ashton, B. (1997). Making peace agreements work: United Nations experiment in the former Yugoslavia. *Cornell International Law Journal, 30*(3), 769–788. https://scholarship.law.cornell.edu/cgi/viewcontent.cgi?article=1417&context=cilj

[28] Lupis, I., & Pitter, L. (1995). *The fall of Srebrenica and the failure of UN peacekeeping: Bosnia and Herzegovina.* Human Rights Watch. https://www.hrw.org/report/1995/10/15/fall-srebrenica-and-failure-un-peacekeeping/bosnia-and-herzegovina

UN SECRETARY-GENERAL'S REPORT ON FALL OF SREBRENICA

In 1999, the Secretary-General submitted a report to the Security Council and the General Assembly on the 'fall of Srebrenica'.[29] The report explained 'in meticulous, systematic, exhaustive and ultimately harrowing detail the descent of Srebrenica into a horror without parallel in the history of Europe since the Second World War'.[30]

Some relevant sections from the report are reproduced here (the headings are the author's own).

On the Security Council and Member States

As the situation in Bosnia and Herzegovina deteriorated, the activity of the Security Council increased. During the 18-month period from the opening of full-scale hostilities in Bosnia and Herzegovina on 6 April 1992 to 5 October 1993, 47 Security Council resolutions were adopted and 42 statements of the President of the Council were issued on matters relating to the conflict in the former Yugoslavia.[31]

Despite this unprecedented flow of resolutions and statements, however, consensus within the Security Council was limited. There was general agreement on the need for action, but less agreement as to what action was appropriate.[32]

In this way, the efforts of Member States to find compromise between divergent positions led to the UNPROFOR mandate becoming rhetorically more robust than the Force itself.[33]

Prior to his departure in December 1993, the then Commander of UNPROFOR's forces in Bosnia and Herzegovina commented that his mission had been beset by 'a fantastic gap between the resolutions of the Security Council, the will to execute these resolutions, and the means

---

[29] United Nations. (1999, 15 November). *Report of the Secretary-General pursuant to general assembly resolution 53/35: The fall of Srebrenica*. A/54/549. https://www.refworld.org/docid/3ae6afb34.html

[30] Ibid.

[31] Ibid.

[32] Ibid.

[33] Ibid.

available to commanders in the field'. He added that he had stopped read-ing Security Council resolutions.[34]

On Safe Areas

One of the proposals which emerged during this search for compromise within the Security Council was to establish 'security zones', 'safe havens' and 'protected areas' for the Bosniac population.[35]

The Force Commander of UNPROFOR opposed the concept of establishing safe areas other than by agreement between the belligerents. He was con-cerned that the nature of the safe area mandate which was being proposed would be inherently incompatible with peacekeeping.[36]

The Secretary-General then noted the failure of the parties 'to understand or fully respect the safe area concept', and that 'UNPROFOR found itself in a situation where many safe areas were not safe, where their existence appeared to thwart only one army in the conflict, thus jeopardizing UNPROFOR's impartiality'. It must also be accepted, however, that the ability of a peacekeeping force such as UNPROFOR to enforce respect for the safe areas by unwilling parties is extremely limited, unless additional troops and the necessary weapons and equipment are made available.[37]

He also said that he did not believe that 'UNPROFOR should be given the mandate to enforce compliance with the safe area regime ... such a mandate would be incompatible with the role of UNPROFOR as a peace-keeping force'.[38]

ON THE GROUND: SREBRENICA

In contrast to the lightly armed Netherlands peacekeepers, the Serbs were prepared for war. They used 1,000 to 2,000 well-equipped soldiers from three brigades of the BSA Fifth 'Drina' Corps to maintain the siege around the enclave. The Serbs were armed with tanks, tracked armoured vehicles, artillery and mortars.[39]

[34] Ibid.

[35] Ibid.

[36] Ibid.

[37] Ibid.

[38] Ibid.

[39] Ibid.

The Commanding Officer of the Dutch battalion observed that this long-lasting and severe situation is no longer acceptable for the soldiers. Therefore, it is my strongest opinion that this Bosnian-Serb government should be blamed for it in the full extent as well as for the consequences in the future.[40]

Thousands of men and boys were summarily executed and buried in mass graves within a matter of days while the international community attempted to negotiate access to them. [...] Evidence of atrocities taking place gradually came to light but too late to prevent the tragedy which was unfolding.[41]

Conclusions by the Secretary-General

The tragedy that occurred after the fall of Srebrenica is shocking for two reasons. It is shocking, first and foremost, for the magnitude of the crimes committed. Not since the horrors of the Second World War had Europe witnessed massacres on this scale.[42]

The fall of Srebrenica is also shocking because the enclave's inhabitants believed that the authority of the United Nations Security Council, the presence of UNPROFOR peacekeepers, and the might of NATO air power, would ensure their safety. Instead, the Bosnian Serb forces ignored the Security Council, pushed aside the UNPROFOR troops, and assessed correctly that air power would not be used to stop them. They overran the safe area of Srebrenica with ease, and then proceeded to depopulate the territory within 48 hours. Their leaders then engaged in high-level negotiations with representatives of the international community while their forces on the ground executed and buried thousands of men and boys within a matter of days.[43]

Questions must be answered, and foremost among them are the following: how can this have been allowed to happen? and how will the United Nations ensure that no future peacekeeping operation witnesses such a calamity on its watch? In this assessment, factors ranging from the proximate to the overarching will be discussed, in order to provide the most comprehensive analysis possible of the preceding narrative.[44]

With the benefit of hindsight, one can see that many of the errors the United Nations made flowed from a single and no doubt well-intentioned effort:

[40] Ibid.

[41] Ibid.

[42] Ibid.

[43] Ibid.

[44] Ibid.

we tried to keep the peace and apply the rules of peacekeeping when there was no peace to keep.[45]

It soon became apparent that, with the end of the cold war and the ascendancy of irregular forces—controlled or uncontrolled—the old rules of the game no longer held. Nor was it sufficiently appreciated that a systematic and ruthless campaign such as the one conducted by the Serbs would view a United Nations humanitarian operation, not as an obstacle, but as an instrument of its aims.[46]

In the end, these Bosnian Serb war aims were ultimately repulsed on the battlefield, and not at the negotiating table. Yet the Secretariat had convinced itself early on that the broader use of force by the international community was beyond our mandate and anyway undesirable. There are occasions when Member States cannot achieve consensus on a particular response to active military conflicts, or do not have the will to pursue what many might consider to be an appropriate course of action. The first of the general lessons is that when peacekeeping operations are used as a substitute for such political consensus they are likely to fail.[47]

Peacekeepers must never again be told that they must use their peacekeeping tools—lightly armed soldiers in scattered positions—to impose the ill-defined wishes of the international community on one or another of the belligerents by military means. If the necessary resources are not provided—and the necessary political, military and moral judgments are not made—the job simply cannot be done.[48]

The international community as a whole must accept its share of responsibility for allowing this tragic course of events by its prolonged refusal to use force in the early stages of the war.

The cardinal lesson of Srebrenica is that a deliberate and systematic attempt to terrorize, expel or murder an entire people must be met decisively with all necessary means, and with the political will to carry the policy through to its logical conclusion.[49]

The United Nations experience in Bosnia was one of the most difficult and painful in our history. It is with the deepest regret and remorse that we have reviewed our own actions and decisions in the face of the assault on

[45] Ibid.

[46] Ibid.

[47] Ibid.

[48] Ibid.

[49] Ibid.

Srebrenica. Srebrenica crystallized a truth understood only too late by the United Nations and the world at large: that Bosnia was as much a moral cause as a military conflict. The tragedy of Srebrenica will haunt our history forever.[50]

DAYTON AGREEMENT AND THE END OF WAR

Following the Dayton Agreement, signed by the parties in November 1995, a NATO-led multinational force known as The Implementation Force (IFOR) took over the mandate from UNPROFOR. In December 1995, the Security Council authorized the deployment of a UN International Police Task Force (IPTF) and a UN civilian office under the United Nations Mission in Bosnia and Herzegovina (UNMIBH). UNMIBH's mandate was to contribute to the establishment of the rule of law, reform and restructure the local police and assessing the functioning of the existing judicial system. UNMIBH ended its operations in December 2002.

In January 1996, the Security Council authorized the establishment of United Nations Transitional Administration in Eastern Slavonia, Baranja and Western Sirmium (UNTAES). It was set up to reintegrate the region peacefully into Croatia's legal and constitutional system. In January 1998, UNTAES ended its operations having accomplished its mandate in reintegrating Eastern Slavonia, Baranja and Western Sirmium into Croatia.

[50] Ibid.

Operations Responding to Intrastate Conflicts

> The world which enters the third millennium is not a world of stable states or stable societies.[1]

The UN increasingly became involved in restoring normalcy in many countries after violent internal conflicts. In some countries, the internal conflicts were ideological (left vs right) even when the conflict was about marginalized ethnic or indigenous communities. In most others, they were based on ethnic identities. Both types of conflicts were often prolonged; they destroyed state institutions and caused immense suffering to the population.

UN Observer Mission in El Salvador (ONUSAL)	1991–1995	Enforce ceasefire in the El Salvador Civil War
UN Verification Mission in Guatemala (MINUGUA)	1997–1997	Monitor ceasefire in Guatemalan Civil War
United Nations Mission in Nepal (UNMIN)	2007–2011	To monitor the arms and cantonment of Maoist rebels and assist the preparations for Constituent Assembly elections

Source: The author.

INTRASTATE CONFLICTS BASED ON IDEOLOGY AND PEACEKEEPING OPERATIONS

In El Salvador, Guatemala and Nepal, intrastate conflict was between the state and its opponents pursuing a political ideology. The opponents

[1] Hobsbawm, E. J. (1994). *Age of extremes: The short twentieth century, 1914–1991.* Michael Joseph; Viking Penguin.

may have mobilized the poor and the marginalized, including indigenous or minority ethnic groups, but the pronounced aim was to offer an alternative political system. Focus on human rights during the transition was another characteristic of the conflict in these three countries.

EL SALVADOR: ONUSAL—LEFT SOUGHT PEACE AND RIGHT OPPOSED IT

During the colonial period, El Salvador's economy was predominantly dependent on cash crops produced in large estates. In the post-colonial period too, it continued in the same path with a small number of Salvadoran landholders of European ancestry controlling the plantations. The landlords brutally exploited the labour force belonging to the indigenous population which comprised 95 per cent of the population. The landlords effectively controlled the government that was run by military dictators from the same class as that of them. In the 1970s, the country witnessed a brutal war between the left-wing guerrillas and government troops. The government extensively used vigilante death squads to kill the guerrillas and their supporters. In 1980, five major left-wing guerrilla groups merged to form the Farabundo Martí National Liberation Front (FMLN) and intensified their guerrilla war against the government troops.

In 1980, the assassination of Archbishop Romero and the killing of 42 mourners at his funeral escalated the civil war. The violence spiralled with the government forces and their proxies committing torture, extrajudicial executions, involuntary disappearances and mass rape. In the 1980s, about 75,000 Salvadorans were killed due to executions, indiscriminate bombings and landmines. In 1989, a government's counter-insurgency force killed six prominent Jesuit priests and their housekeeper. The incident brought the situation in El Salvador to the world's attention and condemnation.

To prevent the left-wing guerrillas from winning the war, the US administration had supported the Salvadoran governments. After the killing of the Jesuits, the US Congress appointed a task force to investigate the incident. The task force concluded that the act was perpetrated by high-ranking military officers. After the end of the Cold War, the

United States changed its policy and pushed for a peace agreement. The UN-mediated peace talks led to an agreement on peace and human rights signed by both parties in July 1990. The agreement included deployment of a UN mission to monitor the accord. In May 1991, the UN Security Council approved the United Nations Observer Mission in El Salvador (ONUSAL). ONUSAL's tasks included monitoring ceasefire, reforming the armed forces and the police and actively monitoring human rights situation and promoting human rights in the country.

In January 1992, the parties signed a final peace settlement in Mexico City, which included a UN-appointed Truth Commission to investigate the abuses committed during the war. Based on a meticulous collection of information from a vast number of victims, the Truth Commission attributed 85 per cent of violence to government forces. The El Salvador government rejected it and passed an amnesty law covering all crimes related to the civil war. In April 1995, ONUSAL's mandate ended and a small, follow-up mission called the United Nations Mission in El Salvador (MINUSAL) was deployed.[2]

The Independent Expert on El Salvador appointed by the UN Commission on Human Rights, in his 1995 report, acknowledged ONUSAL's achievements. These achievements included initiating the process for ensuring the independence of the judiciary, holding general elections, beginning the process for electoral reforms and disbandment of the national police and creation of a new police force.[3]

The El Salvador experience led to the making of human rights central to peacekeeping operations. ONUSAL, and in particular the UN Truth Commission, contributed to the development of concepts and tools that later became integral to the transitional justice process.

---

[2] *BBC News*. (2018). *El Salvador Profile—Timeline*. https://www.bbc.com/news/world-latin-america-19402222; The Centre for Justice & Accountability. (2010). *El Salvador*. https://cja.org/where-we-work/el-salvador/; United Nations. (1995). *El Salvador—ONUSAL: Mandate*. https://peacekeeping.un.org/en/mission/past/onusalmandate.html; United States Institute of Peace. (1992). *Truth commission: El Salvador*. https://www.usip.org/publications/1992/07/truth-commission-el-salvador

[3] United Nations Economic and Social Council. (1994). *Advisory services in the field of human rights*. Commission of Human Rights. http://hrlibrary.umn.edu/commission/country51/88.htm

GUATEMALA: MINUGUA—CONFLICT THAT KILLED 200,000 PEOPLE

In Guatemala, the exclusion and exploitation of the Mayan dated back to the colonial period, and it continued with the same intensity after independence. In 1944, a civilian government was elected with an agenda to bring about land and other reforms. Subsequent governments too continued to implement the reforms which impacted the powerful multinational corporations. In 1954, the US Central Intelligence Agency (CIA) assisted in organizing a coup that brought to power a right-wing military dictator. For the next 40 years, the country was plummeted into civil war pitting the right-wing governments against the left-wing rebels who were supported by the indigenous population. Successive military governments unleashed violence against the indigenous people as a means to contain the rebels. The 1970s and the 1980s saw an escalation of conflict in which the government forces killed more than 100,000 people and displaced 50,000.

In March 1994, the UN-sponsored peace talks led to an agreement between the government and the Guatemalan Revolutionary National Unity (URNG) representing the rebels. The agreement was called the Comprehensive Agreement on Human Rights as an interim measure pending the final peace agreement. The pact provided a structure for promoting human rights in Guatemala. It proposed a UN-led verifying mission that would receive, consider and follow-up complaints regarding possible human rights violations and determine whether such violations have indeed occurred.[4]

Based on the agreement, the Security Council authorized the United Nations Mission for the Verification of Human Rights and of Compliance with the Comprehensive Agreement on Human Rights in Guatemala (United Nations Verification Mission in Guatemala [MINUGUA]). Subsequently, between 1994 and 1996, several agreements were made on concerns like the resettlement of the population groups uprooted by the armed conflict, social and economic aspects and agrarian situation,

[4] United Nations. (1994). *Document retrieval: Comprehensive agreement on Human Rights.* United Nations Peacemaker. https://peacemaker.un.org/guatemala-humanrightsagreement94

civilian power and the role of the army and identity and rights of indigenous persons. In December 1996, the Guatemalan government and URNG reached an agreement on details of ceasefire and a final peace accord. In January 1997, the Security Council authorized the addition of military observers to MINUGUA and the name of the mission was changed to United Nations Verification Mission in Guatemala.[5]

In June 1994, the parties agreed to establish the Guatemala's Commission for Historical Clarification. The Commission functioned from 1997 to 1999 with a mandate to clarify human rights violations committed between 1960 and 1996 and to foster tolerance and preserve the memory of victims. The Commission was established not to judge but to clarify the past. The Commission established that more than 200,000 thousand people were killed or had disappeared, and 83 per cent of the victims were Mayan. Paramilitary groups were responsible for 93 per cent of the violations. Former officials resisted prosecution based on the Commission's findings. A decade later, some progress was made with the UN assisting in the establishment of the International Commission against Impunity in Guatemala (CICIG). The CICIG's mandate was to conduct independent investigations, present criminal cases to the Public Prosecutor and function as a complementary prosecutor in criminal proceedings. In 2009, a retired colonel and three paramilitaries were successfully convicted for disappearances during the civil war.[6]

Similar to El Salvador, in Guatemala, human rights became the major aspect of the peace process. The Guatemalan agreement's scope is unique. The pact, in addition to ceasefire and other essential elements of a peace process, dealt also with the country's economic, social and political structures. It engaged with the inter-ethnic relations that had contributed to the conflict since the country's colonization.[7]

---

[5] Wikipedia: The Free Encyclopedia. (1997). *United Nations verification mission in Guatemala (MINUGUA)*. From Wikipedia, The Free Encyclopedia. https://en.wikipedia.org/wiki/MINUGUA

[6] United States Institute of Peace. (1997). *Truth commission: Guatemala*. https://www.usip.org/publications/1997/02/truth-commission-guatemala

[7] Peralta, G. A. (2005). *Anatomy of the accords and levels of compliance*. Irenees.net a Website of Resources for Peace. http://www.irenees.net/bdf_fiche-analyse-797_en.html

NEPAL: UNMIN—PEACE AND END OF ROYALTY

In Nepal, in the 1990s, the struggle for democracy that was usurped by the monarchy entered a different phase with an armed insurrection adding to the crisis. In 1960, the King had abolished the constitution and multiparty politics, and in 1963, he had established a non-party system called 'Panchyat'. Beginning in 1980, the Nepali Congress Party (NCP) launched agitations for the restoration of multiparty democracy. In 1990, the agitation escalated, with NCP and other leftist groups organizing coordinated street protests. The King allowed the democratic elections to be held in 1991 and NCP came to power. However, the elections did not end the political instability. In 1995, the Communist Party of Nepal (Maoist) launched an armed revolt demanding political and economic changes. The state and the Maoists were engaged in an increasingly intense conflict.

In 2001, the King proclaimed a state of emergency and the army was tasked to crush the Maoists. Consequently, the war became even more brutal. In 2002, the King indefinitely postponed the elections. In 2004, following street protests, he dismissed the government. In 2005, he restored absolute monarchy. This move led to the Maoist rebels and mainstream opposition parties agreeing to jointly fight for the restoration of democracy and a new constitution. In 2005, amidst the ongoing political turmoil, the Office of the High Commissioner for Human Rights (OHCHR) established its presence in Nepal. In 2006, unable to contain the protests, the King reinstated the parliament. The government and the Maoists held peace talks, and in November 2006, they signed CPA.[8]

UN Mission in Nepal

CPA included finalization and promulgation of an interim constitution, forming an interim assembly, establishing an interim government and organizing the Constituent Assembly elections in June 2007.

---

[8] Reuters Staff. (2008, 28 May). TIMELINE: Milestones in political history of Nepal. *World News*. https://uk.reuters.com/article/us-nepal-chronology/timeline-milestones-in-political-history-of-nepal-idUKL281216020080528

The agreement also stipulated that the fate of the monarchy would be determined in the first meeting of the Constituent Assembly. The pact provided for arrangements for the cantonment of the Maoist army combatants, restriction of the Nepal Army to its barracks and storage of arms and ammunition of both sides. Both parties also committed to socio-economic transformation, promoting greater inclusion of marginalized groups and ensuring proportional representation for their participation in political structures.

In January 2007, the Security Council authorized the deployment of the UN Mission in Nepal (UNMIN). UNMIN was mandated to monitor the management of arms and armed personnel and advise the government of Nepal on holding elections for the Constituent Assembly.[9]

The Secretary-General appointed Ian Martin as his Personal Representative and to lead UNMIN. Ian Martin, since 2015, resided in Nepal as the Representative of the High Commissioner for Human Rights and was already engaged in dialogue with the government ministers, officials, political parties, civil society and the Maoist leadership. He and a small team of advisers on political, military, electoral and ceasefire monitoring assisted the parties during their negotiations in finalizing CPA. It was a unique situation in which the mission leadership was familiar with the context and the players involved in the conflict. The mission leadership's role in engaging with the senior officials of the Nepal Army and the Maoists contributed to creating a climate for negotiations between the parties.[10]

In 2007, the parliament abolished the monarchy. In April 2008, elections were held for the new Constituent Assembly, and in May, Nepal became a republic. In 2011, UNMIN concluded its mission in Nepal. After several setbacks, in 2015, the Constituent Assembly adopted a landmark constitution that defined Nepal as a secular country.

[9] United Nations Security Council. (2007). *Resolution 1740 (2007): Adopted by the security council at its 5622nd meeting on 23 January 2007*. https://www.un.org/ga/search/view_doc.asp?symbol=S/RES/1740(2007)

[10] Adhikari, A. (2008, 1 October). Shackled or unleashed UNMIN in Nepal's peace process. *Himal Southasian*. https://www.himalmag.com/shackled-or-unleashed-unmin-in-nepals-peace-process

In his briefing to the Security Council in 2009, Ian Martin stated that the peace agreement was based on mutual commitment by the parties to CPA. He feared that despite the progress made, the parties are now challenging the fundamentals of the agreement.[11]

In 2009, Ian Martin, after stepping down from leading UNMIN, reflected on the Nepal peace process. He identified the parties' lack of commitment to the five core aspects of CPA signed by them. The first was the power sharing between Maoists and major political parties, which was not pursued sincerely. The second was the Maoist commitment to a democratic state and multiparty politics. The Maoists did not fully demonstrate their commitment to it, but the other parties also were not different. The third element was about the two armies that fought the civil war. It included democratizing the Nepalese army and integration and rehabilitation of the Maoist combatants. The Maoists and the Nepalese army disregarded the procedures agreed upon under CPA and made it difficult to fully implement a vital element of the agreement. The fourth and fifth elements were about bringing a socio-economic transformation and a commitment to address the needs of the victims of the conflict, respectively. The parties made least efforts on pursuing these two elements.[12]

The Crisis Group in 2011 commented that the peace process has narrowed down to deal with the Maoist fighters and not engage with structural issues such as democratization of the Nepal Army or justice for crimes committed by both parties during the war.[13]

UNMIN was a small mission with a narrow technical mandate. India opposed the idea of a full-fledged UN mission in its backyard and was closely monitoring UNMIN's functioning. UNMIN's mandate

---

[11] United Nations. (2009, 16 January). *Nepal special representative describes 'Important Achievements' in peace process, hopes world community understanding long-term stability far from being achieved.* Press release: Security Council, S/9575. https://www.un.org/press/en/2009/sc9575.doc.htm

[12] Martin, I. (2010). *Nepal's peace process at the United Nations* (Vol. 1). Himal Books.

[13] International Crisis Group (2011, 13 December). *'Nepal's peace process: The end-game nears'* (Briefing No. 131). Crisis Group Asia.

did not include supervisory or enforcement capability with regard to the security issues, particularly in managing the two armies that had fought a bitter war. UNMIN had less than 200 unarmed UN monitors. It also provided technical support for conducting the election. Despite its limitations and challenges, it succeeded in bringing an insurgent group into the democratic process and contributed to the transition of a political system stymied by the monarchy to become a republic. The uniqueness of the Nepal peace process was that it was managed by the parties without any third party intervention. The UN encouraged and facilitated the process.[14]

INTRASTATE CONFLICTS BASED ON ETHNIC AND OTHER IDENTITIES

In the post-Second World War period, the world has witnessed numerous conflicts based on the assertion of ethnic or other identities. The emergence of identity politics challenged the recognition of an individual based on universal ideas and sought recognition based on nation, religion, sect, race ethnicity or gender.[15]

The UN deployed peacekeeping operations in response to some of the identity-based conflicts. These operations were often complex, intense and posed a challenge to the organization.

Operation	Year	Purpose
UN Assistance Mission for Rwanda (UNAMIR)	1993–1996	Monitor ceasefire and, after Rwanda genocide, promote relief efforts
UN Observer Mission in Liberia (UNOMIL)	1993–1997	Monitor ceasefire and elections in Liberia
United Nations Peace-Building Support Office in Liberia (UNOL)	1996–2003	Oversee ceasefire and train national police

[14] Martin, I. (2008, 28 August). Nepal: A remarkable peace. *The Guardian*. https://www.theguardian.com/commentisfree/2008/aug/28/nepal.humanrights

[15] Fukuyama, F. (2018). *Identity: The demand for dignity and the politics of resentment*. Profile Books.

Operation	Year	Purpose
United Nations Mission in Liberia (UNMIL)	2003–2018	To support the National Transitional Government of Liberia and the other parties in the effective and timely implementation of the Comprehensive Peace Agreement; to monitor adherence to the ceasefire agreement of 17 June; to assist the National Transitional Government in extending State authority throughout Liberia; to facilitate the free movement of people, humanitarian assistance and goods; to support the safe and sustainable return of refugees and internally displaced persons; to report on human rights situation and assist in building institutions; and to protect civilians under imminent threat of physical violence
United Nations Mission in the Sudan (UNMIS)	2005–2011	To support implementation of the Comprehensive Peace Agreement, perform certain functions relating to humanitarian assistance and protection and promotion of human rights
United Nations–African Union Mission in Darfur (UNAMID)	2007–present	Protect civilians, facilitate the delivery of humanitarian assistance and ensure the safety of humanitarian personnel; mediate between the Government of Sudan and non-signatory armed movements on the basis of the Doha Document for Peace in Darfur; support the mediation of community conflict, including measures to address its root causes
UN Mission in the Central African Republic (MINURCA)	1998–2000	To restore a climate of stability and security as well as facilitate dialogue among political actors
United Nations Peacebuilding Support Office in the Central African Republic (BONUCA)	2000–2008	To assist in peacebuilding efforts

Operation	Year	Purpose
United Nations Integrated Peacebuilding Support Office in the Central African Republic (BINUCA)	2008–2014	To support stabilization efforts, ensure humanitarian assistance and protection of human rights
United Nations Multidimensional Integrated Stabilization Mission in the Central African Republic (MINUSCA)	2014– present	Protection of civilians, support for the transition process, facilitating humanitarian assistance, promotion and protection of human rights, support for justice and the rule of law and disarmament, demobilization, reintegration and repatriation processes
United Nations Mission in Côte d'Ivoire (MINUCI)	2003–2004	To facilitate the implementation of the Linas-Marcoussis Agreement by the Ivorian parties
United Nations Operation in Côte d'Ivoire (UNOCI)	2004–2017	Protection of civilians
The United Nations Multidimensional Integrated Stabilization Mission in Mali (MINUSMA)	2013– present	To support the political process and carry out security-related stabilization tasks, protecting civilians, human rights monitoring, the creation of conditions for the provision of humanitarian assistance and the return of displaced persons, the extension of State authority and the preparation of free, inclusive and peaceful elections

Source: The author.

RWANDA: UNAMIR—GENOCIDE AND APOLOGY BY THE UN

'Approximately 800,000 people were killed during the 1994 genocide in Rwanda. The systematic slaughter of men, women and children which took place over the course of about 100 days between April and July of 1994 will forever be remembered as one of the most abhorrent events of the twentieth century'.[16]

---

[16] Carlsson, I., Sung-Joo, H., & Kupolati, R. M. (1999). *Report of the independent inquiry into the actions of the United Nations during the 1994 genocide in Rwanda.* United Nations.

The Rwandan tragedy was also the result of the colonial legacy that strengthened the ethnic divides and the nationalist project that failed to provide an alternative to it.[17]

After Rwanda became an independent country in 1962, the majority Hutus asserted themselves over the minority Tutsis who had historically held power in the territory. By 1964, more than 300,000 Tutsis fled to neighbouring countries.[18] The post-colonial nation state boundaries made the Tutsis refugees in these countries for the next three decades. They began to wage armed incursions into Rwanda particularly from Uganda. In 1990, the Tutsi Rwandan Patriotic Front (RPF) invaded Rwanda from Uganda. In 1993, in Arusha, Tanzania, the Hutu President Habyarimana and the Tutsis signed a peace deal and agreed to share power.[19]

The Arusha Agreement was 'still born'.[20] A week after the signing of the agreement, between 8 and 17 April 1993, the Special Rapporteur of the UN Commission on Human Rights on Extrajudicial, Summary or Arbitrary Executions visited the country. In his report, he indicated a serious risk of genocide in Rwanda with Tutsis as the target because of their ethnic identity.[21] His report was not considered while planning the peacekeeping operation in Rwanda. Both parties pressed the UN Secretary-General to deploy a mission to monitor the implementation of the Arusha Agreement. In October 1993, the Security Council authorized the deployment of the United Nations Assistance Mission for Rwanda (UNAMIR). The mission had a limited mandate and did not include recovery of arms as proposed by the Secretary-General.[22]

---

[17] Mamdani, M. (2001). *When victims become killers: Colonialism, nativism and the genocide in Rwanda.* Fountain Publishers.

[18] History.com Editors. (2009). *Rwandan genocide.* A & E Television Networks. https://www.history.com/topics/africa/rwandan-genocide

[19] *BBC News.* (2018). *Rwanda profile—Timeline.* https://www.bbc.com/news/world-africa-14093322

[20] Mamdani, M. (2001). *When victims become killers: Colonialism, nativism and the genocide in Rwanda.* Fountain Publishers.

[21] Carlsson, I., Sung-Joo, H., & Kupolati, R. M. (1999). *Report of the independent inquiry into the actions of the United Nations during the 1994 genocide in Rwanda.* United Nations.

[22] Ibid.

The Denmark-initiated Joint Evaluation Report in 1994 stated that the Security Council based its actions on Chapter VI versus Chapter VII dichotomy and did not provide for options that would have prevented the genocide.[23]

In April 1994, the plane in which the Hutu President Habyarimana and the Burundian President were travelling was shot down over the Rwandan capital Kigali. RPF launched a major offensive. The extremist Hutu elements embarked on a systematic massacre of Tutsis and moderate Hutus in Rwanda leading to a genocide.[24]

Boutros Boutros-Ghali, commenting on the Security Council process, bemoaned that his request to the international community to prevent the genocide was not heeded and it is a scandal.[25]

In March 1999, the UN set up an independent inquiry commission to investigate the actions of the UN during the 1994 genocide in Rwanda. The inquiry commission submitted its report in December 1999 in which it found that the UN failed in a number of fundamental aspects. The Secretary-General, the Secretariat, the Security Council and UNAMIR are responsible for the failure to prevent the genocide. It identified the lack of resources and lack of will as the overriding reasons for the failure to prevent the genocide. The UN Security Council did not plan or deploy UNAMIR with the aim to be proactive in dealing with the peace process that was in crisis. The mission was not functioning in a cohesive manner particularly when the killing started. When it mattered, the mission lacked military capacity, coordination and discipline. The report also stated that the organization must apologize to the Rwandese people, and the perpetrators must be brought to justice.[26] In March

---

[23] Eriksson, J., Adelman, H., Borton, J., Christensen, H., Kumar, K., Suhrke, A., Tardif-Douglin, D., Villumstad, S., & Wohlgemuth, L. (1996). *The international response to conflict and genocide: Lessons from the Rwanda experience: Synthesis report*. Joint Evaluation of Emergency Assistance to Rwanda.

[24] *BBC News*. (2018). *Rwanda profile—Timeline*. https://www.bbc.com/news/world-africa-14093322

[25] United Nations. (1996). *The United Nations and Rwanda 1993–1996*. UN Department of Public Information.

[26] Carlsson, I., Sung-Joo, H., & Kupolati, R. M. (1999). *Report of the independent inquiry into the actions of the United Nations during the 1994 genocide in Rwanda*. United Nations.

1996, the UN ended UNAMIR's operations due to Rwandese government's lack of cooperation based on its assertion that UNAMIR failed in preventing the genocide. For another decade or so, the Rwandan genocide continued to impact the region and contributed to immense humanitarian crisis.[27]

SUDAN: UNMIS—MISSIONS MUSHROOMED WHILE PEACE WAS A MIRAGE

In Sudan, hegemony of the Arab—Islamic elite from the North—was challenged initially by the non-Muslim in the South and later by Muslim Africans in other regions. These groups demanded secession and or restructuring of the political system to make it more equitable.[28]

North–South Conflict

The war between the Muslim North and the Christian/Animist South began in 1955 and continued till 1972. It resumed again in 1983 when John Garang, leader of SPLM/A, intensified the war against the Sudanese government forces. It spread from South to the Nuba Mountains and the Blue Nile territory. Since its inception, the conflict had contributed to the death of nearly two million people due to war, famine and disease. About four million people were displaced. Both sides violated with impunity the international human rights law and humanitarian law.[29]

In the 1990s, concerned about the humanitarian crisis, the UN, along with regional and international communities, made efforts to bring an end to the conflict. Assisted by the UN, the African regional group IGAD led the talks between the Sudanese government and SPLM/A. In July 2002, both parties signed the Machakos Protocol on governance, transitional process and the principle of self-determination

[27] Mamdani, M. (2001). *When victims become killers: Colonialism, nativism and the genocide in Rwanda*. Fountain Publishers.

[28] Mosely, A. L. (1998). *Sudan's contested national identities*. Indiana University Press.

[29] News and Resources. (2001). *Crisis in Sudan*. https://web.archive.org/web/20041210024759/; http://www.refugees.org/news/crisis/sudan.htm

for the people of South Sudan. Subsequently, in 2003 and 2004, both parties signed several agreements clarifying various contested issues like wealth sharing and power sharing. Building on these pacts, in January 2005, the Government of Sudan and SPLM/A signed CPA. Acknowledging that the unity of Sudan was a priority under CPA, they agreed to set up a six-and-a-half-year interim period, following which the South Sudanese would, through a referendum, exercise their option to either remain within Sudan or secede.

The 2005, CPA was an ambitious political agreement and set the process for deciding by a referendum whether the country would remain one nation or become two.[30]

In March 2005, the Security Council established UNMIS. It was a large (with 10,000 military personnel) and complex mission with wide-ranging tasks. The tasks included monitoring the implementation of the ceasefire and redeployment of forces under the agreement; assisting in the setting up of voluntary disarmament and demobilization programme; assisting the parties in pursuing a national inclusive approach including the role of women in peacebuilding; assisting in the training of police and restructuring the police service in Sudan; assisting in promoting the rule of law and protection of human rights; providing humanitarian demining assistance, technical advice and coordination; and supporting the preparations for and conducting elections and referenda as stipulated under CPA.

As per CPA, both parties adopted an Interim National Constitution, and in July, they established the Government of National Unity (GoNU) in Khartoum. In October, SPLM established the Government of South Sudan (GOSS) in Juba, and the interim constitution was adopted in December.

In the first few months, two important factors affected the functioning of UNMIS. The first was the death of John Garang in a helicopter crash on 31 July 2005, which deprived UNMIS of an important partner in the peace process. The second was the escalation of

---

[30] De Waal, A. (2010). Sudan's choices: Scenarios beyond the CPA. In Heinrich Böll Foundation (Ed.), *Sudan—No easy ways ahead* (Vol. 18, pp. 9–30, English ed., Publication Series on Democracy). Heinrich Böll Foundation.

Darfur conflict that erupted in 2003. It diverted the mission's attention from focusing on CPA and complicated its relationship with the Government of Sudan. The relationship between SRSG Jan Pronk and the Sudanese government deteriorated to the extent that he was declared persona non grata in October 2006.[31]

The mission was faced with delays in the deployment of military forces and civilian personnel. Only by the middle of 2007, UNMIS was fully deployed. Both the South Sudanese and the Sudanese governments at various times created considerable obstacles to UNMIS which impacted the CPA implementation schedule. UNMIS was not able to contribute adequately to the democratization of Sudan and support the establishment of institutions in South Sudan. In the end, however, despite all the challenges and its limitations, UNMIS managed to successfully conduct the referendum in January 2011, with the majority, at 98.83 per cent, voting for independence. The Government of Sudan informed the Secretary-General that UNMIS' presence would terminate on 9 July 2011.[32]

Conflict in Three Areas: Abyei, South Kordofan and Blue Nile State[33]

In May–June 2011, full-scale conflicts erupted in Abyei, South Kordofan and the Blue Nile state. These territories are officially known as the 'three areas'. As a buffer zone, these areas witnessed intense conflict during the North and South civil war. The areas were populated by both Black African and Arab groups. The conflict was also about the oppression and discrimination faced by the Black African population from the Arab-controlled central government. The vast mineral wealth in these areas made them strategic, and the central government's exploitation of the resources without much benefit to the local

---

[31] The author was with UNMIS from 2005–2008 as the Director of Human Rights Division.

[32] United Nations. (2011). *Background: United Nations mission in Sudan*. https://unmis.unmissions.org/background-0

[33] In 2010–2011, the author as the Regional Coordinator (North) was responsible for the coordination of Abeyi, South Kordofan and the Blue Nile state.

population aggravated the conflict. The Machakos Protocol defined the South Sudan territory as it was during Sudan's independence in 1956. Accordingly, the three areas were not included as forming part of the South Sudan territory. CPA proposed a referendum for Abyei to exercise the option of joining South Sudan or remaining with the North under a special status. As for South Kordofan and the Blue Nile state, CPA proposed a popular consultation process.[34]

Abyei

Ngok Dinka (a subgroup of the Southern Sudanese Dinka) claimed traditional ownership of the Abyei area. The nomadic Arab Misseriya would annually graze their cattle in the Abyei region. The Ngok Dinka, while claiming ownership of the land, historically acknowledged the grazing rights of Misseriya. Despite occasional conflicts, the arrangements between them held. After Sudan's independence, when the civil war broke out between the North and the South, the Ngok Dinka fought with the South and the Misseriya sided with the North. During the civil war, the Misseriya attacks displaced the Ngok Dinka and the Misseriya expanded their territory to include large parts of Abyei. Thus, during the CPA negotiation, both the South and the North contested the definition of Abyei's area. As a compromise, the Abyei Border Commission was established to define the precise borders of the area. The Abyei area was given a special administrative status and brought directly under the supervision of the presidency. CPA provided for a referendum that would allow Abyei residents to either join South Sudan or become a part of the North while retaining the area's special administrative status. Once the border was defined, a referendum commission would identify the Misseriyas who were eligible to vote in the referendum, which made the demarcation process a contentious issue. The Sudanese government at the behest of the Misseriya rejected the Abyei Boundary Commission's report. In 2008, tensions

---

[34] Cook, T. D. (2007). *Lost in the middle of peace: An exploration of citizen opinion on the implementation of the CPA in the three areas of Abyei, Southern Kordofan and Blue Nile.* Findings from Focus Groups with Men and Women in the Three Areas: Conducted 26 April 26–2 July 2006. National Democratic Institute for International Affairs.

over the boundary and Ngok Dinka's obstruction of Misseriya grazing rights during the dry season escalated into a major conflict. In response to the tensions, the Sudanese government deployed its army in Abyei town. In March 2008, despite UNMIS' presence, clashes between the Sudanese troops and the Ngok Dinka armed elements resulted in widespread destruction and displacement of several thousand Ngok Dinka civilians. The Sudanese army committed serious human rights violations during the conflict.[35]

In June 2008, Sudanese President Bashir and the Government of South Sudan President Salva Kiir agreed to refer the Abyei Boundary Commission's report for arbitration at the Permanent Court of Arbitration (PCA) in The Hague. In 2009, the PCA award redrew the boundaries and decreased the size of Abyei. Most of the Misseriyas remained outside the redrawn borders which made them ineligible to vote in the referendum. Both the governments of Sudan and the South Sudan accepted the award avoiding further disagreements at their level. The boundary as defined by PCA was not demarcated. The Abyei referendum that was to take place along with the South Sudan referendum in January 2011 was postponed.

The postponement of the referendum angered the Ngok Dinka and the simmering tension escalated again. In January, in a clash between the Ngok Dinka and Misseriya, three Sudanese soldiers were killed. SRSG Haile Menkerios encouraged the UNMIS staff to facilitate talks at the local level.[36] A series of initiatives at Abyei and Kadugli (Misseriya) created a forum for both the Ngok Dinka and Misseriya leadership to discuss ways to reduce tensions. On 13 January, SRSG chaired a meeting of both parties that did not involve Khartoum or Juba. The Kadugli Governor Ahmed Haroun representing NCP provided facilities for the meeting. In this meeting, the parties agreed on the compensation to be paid for those killed during the recent clashes. It also provided for removing Misseriya-imposed restrictions on the movement of goods to

---

[35] UNMIS Human Rights Section. (2011, 5 July). *Report on the human rights situation during the SAF military offensive and control of Abyei.*

[36] The author was involved in coordinating the work of the sector heads, Civil Affairs and other departments involved in facilitating talks between the Ngok Dinka and the Misseriya.

Abyei. The Ngok Dinka, in return, allowed the Misseriya the access to Abyei for grazing purposes. On 17 January, South Kordofan Governor Ahmed Haroun and Abyei's administrator Deng Arop endorsed the 13 January agreement and consented to the withdrawal of unauthorized armed elements from the Abyei area. The agreement stipulated redeployment of Joint Integrated Units (JIUs) consisting of Sudanese and South Sudanese forces.[37]

On 4 March, Haile Menkerios persuaded NCP and SPLM to agree for a joint meeting on Abyei to be held at the UNMIS sector headquarters in Abyei town. The NCP delegation included Sala Ghosh, Adviser to President Bashir and former head of the powerful Sudanese National Intelligence and Security Services (NISS). The SPLM delegation included senior leaders Deng Alor and Pagan Amum. The Governor of South Kordofan Ahmed Haroun and Abyei's Administrator Deng Arop also participated in the meeting. While the meeting was in progress, large crowds from the Ngok Dinka population gathered in front of the UNMIS gate and shouted slogans against the NCP delegation. They demanded that the meeting be aborted. Deng Alor met with the protesters and the crowd dispersed without causing any further problems. SRSG chaired the meeting that was difficult and at times unruly. Both parties agreed on steps to deescalate the situation in Abyei. The same evening, when delegates from the North and the UNMIS staff were returning to Khartoum, the crowd gathered again and threw stones at the helicopters. Fortunately, no one was injured, and the helicopters flew away without any major incident. Haile Menkerios decided not to return to Khartoum and stayed back with a few staff members.[38] The NCP delegation had signed the agreement before leaving for Khartoum. The next morning, Haile Menkerios had a meeting with the SPLM delegation, and after some discussion, they also signed the document.

Haile Menkerios' efforts to find a political solution and avoid a major armed conflict were not successful. The ground reality in Abyei

---

[37] Young, J. (2012). *The fate of Sudan: The origins and consequences of a flawed peace process*. Zed Books.

[38] Hua Jiang, UNMIS Public Information Officer, a political affairs officer, and the author stayed behind.

was not conducive for a negotiated settlement of a complex conflict. The local Ngok Dinka community had unrealistic expectations from the international community regarding political, humanitarian and development assistance. They felt betrayed by the postponement of the Abyei referendum. UNMIS and other international actors made efforts to facilitate the Misseriya migration to prevent conflict. The Ngok Dinka interpreted it as international community's bias towards the Misseriya. They considered blocking the Misseriya migration as a bargaining tool, but the Kadugli agreements made them abandon the idea. In addition, they also opined that withdrawal of their armed forces under the Kadugli agreement had compromised their security. They did not trust JIU since it included Sudanese armed forces.[39]

Abyei's administrator Deng Arop, a hardliner, was not interested in negotiation or mediation. Deng Arop had valid reasons to mistrust the Misseriya and the Sudanese government. However, he had unrealistic vision of Abyei becoming the next Dubai. He was not committed to finding a political solution to avoid the hardships faced by the people of Abyei. Contravening CPA that prohibited the armed forces' presence in Abyei, he deployed the so-called South Sudan Police Force which was a masquerade for the deployment of armed SPLA military forces.[40]

At the end of 2009, due to increasing tensions in the Abyei region, Haile Menkerios moved Gaung Cong, the head of Sector 5 (South Kordofan), to head Abyei (Sector 6). Gaung Cong was an able administrator and ensured coordination among the military, the police and the civilian staff. His main challenge was working with Deng Arop, who created numerous obstacles for UNMIS. To ensure smooth functioning of his sector, Gaung Cong did not develop a critical relationship and was unduly differential to Deng Arop. At times, Gaung Cong gave the impression that the functioning of his sector was more important than the mandate of the mission that required taking a more principled approach with the administrator.

[39] See Abyei JOC Assessment, 'Ngok Dinka Perceptions of UNMIS and Their Impact Upon Operations', April 2011. File with the author.

[40] Ibid.

In March, UNMIS made a contingency plan for Abyei due to continuing tensions that included the Abeyi administrator's restrictions on the movement of UNMIS forces. The UNMIS Strategic Planning Cell, in consultation with all the relevant UNMIS departments, including military and police, OCHA, UNDSS and the UN agencies, produced a document for consideration by SRSG. The Regional Coordinator North was tasked with the follow-up.[41] The contingency plan recommended high-level political engagement with SPLM/A and NCP/SAF to reduce tensions and reverse military buildup. The document also proposed human rights monitoring, engagement with the local community and humanitarian response. The document recommended that the military set up a Joint Situation Centre (JSC) in Abyei that would become an information hub for the area, send additional reinforcement in case of crisis to be pre-positioned in Kadugli, conduct robust and non-routine patrolling, rehearse UNMIS compound protection plan and identify possible humanitarian corridors/safe havens for civilian protection.

The intransigence of the Misseriya and Ngok Dinka and their sponsors in the North and South, respectively, meant that no short-term tangible political solution was possible to avoid the escalation of the conflict. The other option was to buy time. The UNMIS Force Commander was a crucial player in preventing the escalation of the conflict by engaging with the senior SAF and SPLM officials and in preparing the forces under his command to deal with the crisis as and when it happened. The Head of UN Peacekeeping Operations, Jean-Marie Guehenno, visited Abyei at the end of 2010. He conveyed a clear message to the Force Commander Major General Moses Obi that the UN did not want to see a repetition of 2008 violence against the civilians in Abyei. Despite that, the Force Commander did not demonstrate the required leadership to deal with the emerging situation. He did not take the steps to implement the proposals made in the March 2011 UNMIS contingency plan. Haile Menkerios, during senior management meetings, publicly admonished him for his lack of initiatives in dealing with the emerging crisis.

---

[41] File with the author.

On 1 May 2011, seven Sudan Armed Force (SAF) soldiers were killed in a firefight between the South Sudan Police Force and SAF.[42] On 10 May, some Misseriya armed elements attacked a Joint Monitoring Team patrol consisting of the UNMIS military observers, peacekeepers and the Sudanese Armed Forces National Monitor. In the attack, four Zambian peacekeepers were wounded and evacuated for medical assistance.[43] On 12 May, the UNMIS Force Commander, after attending an Abyei Joint Technical Committee meeting, stated that the mission will assist with redeployment of JIUs from the bases they have vacated. It would also assist in the withdrawal of all unauthorized forces from the Abyei area. He assured full support and resources such as water and regular liaison with the UNMIS forces to JIU to carry out their tasks.[44]

It was too little, too late. On 19 May, an SAF convoy under UNMIS escort was attacked. A UNMIS internal report identified SPLA forces as responsible for the attack, and it was confirmed by Abyei's Administrator Deng Arop. SAF initially claimed that 22 of its soldiers were killed but later revised the number to 197.[45] On the night of 21 May, SAF launched a full-scale military offensive using heavy weapons. The next morning, the Misseriya militia from the surrounding areas moved into Abyei and engaged in burning and looting of Abyei town. More than 100,000 Ngok Dinka civilians from Abyei town and the surrounding areas fled to the South. The UNMIS compound also came under attack. Two Egyptian peacekeepers sustained minor injuries, and a World Food Programme vehicle was destroyed.[46]

General Babacar, UN's Military Adviser in New York, acknowledged that the peacekeepers (Zambians) were wrong to stay in barracks

---

[42] See note 39.

[43] SRSG letter to the Sudanese Foreign Minister dated 16 May 2011. File with the author.

[44] United Nations. (2011, 12 May). *UNMIS to provide more assistance with Kadugli Agreements*. United Nations Mission in Sudan. https://reliefweb.int/report/sudan/unmis-provide-more-assistance-kadugli-agreements

[45] See note 39.

[46] See OHCHR's UNMIS Human Rights Section (2011).

during the recent fighting in Abyei. He also said that UNMIS forces should have had more visibility to deter violence against civilians.[47]

On 27 June 2011, the Security Council authorized the deployment of the United Nations Interim Security Force for Abyei (UNISFA). It was mandated to verify the redeployment of armed forces from the Abyei area, strengthen the capacity of the Abyei Police Service, assist in the delivery of humanitarian services and ensure the protection of civilians from imminent threat of physical violence. The mission run by Ethiopian troops continues to remain in Abyei with no end to the resolution of the dispute.[48]

BLUE NILE AND SOUTH KORDOFAN

People in Blue Nile and South Kordofan fought alongside SPLM during the civil war. However, the population in these states was mostly Muslims and did not have cultural ties to the South. SPLM did not contest the fact that both the territories were situated in the North and were part of the North. Under CPA, the South and Abyei were given an option to secede from the North. Both Blue Nile and South Kordofan were governed by a separate protocol that stipulated holding of a 'popular consultation' to enable the population to agree upon CPA as the final settlement or renegotiate its shortcomings[49]. CPA provided for legislatures in the respective states to conduct the popular consultation to ascertain the views of the population. The process included civic education to create awareness on CPA and consultations with the people facilitated by a commission established for that purpose.

---

[47] Smith, D. (2011, 6 June). UN admits peacekeepers dialed in Sudan clashes. *The Guardian*. https://www.theguardian.com/world/2011/jun/06/un-admits-sudan-peacekeepers-failure

[48] United Nations. (2019). *Mandate: Summary of UNISFA mandate*. https://unisfa.unmissions.org/mandate

[49] Rogier, E. (2005). *The (Un-) Comprehensive peace agreement. From the Report No More hills ahead? The Sudan's tortuous ascent to heights of peace* (Chapter 4). Clingendael Institute.

Blue Nile

In the April 2010 elections, Malik Agar, an SPLM (North) candidate, won the election for the governorship of the Blue Nile state. He was the only non-NCP candidate to win in Sudan. Despite his reservations regarding the popular consultation, he implemented it in the state. In October 2010, the Blue Nile Parliamentary Commission for Popular Consultation was established, comprising 13 members from NCP and 8 from SPLM (North). The Commission identified four broad themes—constitutional, administrative, political and economic—for seeking the views of the participants. In January and February 2011, the Commission conducted 116 public hearings with more than 60,000 participants. The hearings did not facilitate discussions on the broad themes. The participants made short statements expressing their support to autonomy or federalism.[50] Political parties mobilized participants for the hearings based largely on tribal lines, aggravating the existing tribal tensions in the state. It was a show put up by NCP and SPLM (North), and there was no interest in seeking the views of the population.[51] The Carter Center that observed the whole process undermined the goal and spirit of the popular consultations to seek citizens' views.[52] Both NCP and SPLM (North) contested the results of the hearings and the follow-up steps that had to be taken. The people wanted development such as schools, health care and infrastructure, but there was no consensus among the two parties on how to proceed with it. SPLM (North) persisted with its idea of self-determination or greater autonomy from Khartoum. The tensions between SPLM (North) and NCP continued and escalated after South Sudan became an independent country in July 2011.

---

[50] Based on the author's first-hand observation of the process in a few places.

[51] Cook, T. D. (2007). *Lost in the middle of peace: An exploration of citizen opinion on the implementation of the CPA in the three areas of Abyei, Southern Kordofan and Blue Nile*. Findings from Focus Groups with Men and Women in the Three Areas: Conducted 26 April 26–2 July 2006. National Democratic Institute for International Affairs.

[52] The Carter Center. (2011). *Carter center urges political parties and Blue Nile popular consultation commission to ensure genuine dialogue on key issues in Blue Nile state.* https://www.cartercenter.org/news/pr/sudan-032111.html

On 1 September, a conflict broke out in Blue Nile. Sudanese President Bashir declared a state of emergency, dismissed Malik Agar and appointed a new governor. SPLM in the North was formally banned. Malik Agar fled to the southern part of the state to fight against the central government. He is a founder member and president of the Sudanese Revolutionary Front that was set up in 2012 as an alliance of armed groups in Darfur and other parts fighting against the Government of Sudan.

South Kordofan

Post CPA, the South Kordofan state was formed by including West Kordofan. The state contains the ethnic fault line between the Arab and the African (mainly Nuba) tribes. During the North-South civil war and despite being located in the North, the Nuba joined SPLM and took up arms to oppose their marginalization. Their grievances included appropriation of their land and resources, imposition of language and undermining of their culture through Islamization and Arabization. The Nuba were disappointed that CPA did not offer a better deal for them. Post CPA, SPLM represented Nuba interests in the North, and they wanted the popular consultation process to address their grievances including the demand for self-determination. NCP opposed the idea of expanding the popular consultation process, and SPLM made threats that they would return to war if their grievances were not addressed adequately. Till 2009, the South Kordofan administration suffered due to frequent change in the governorship and disagreements between NCP and SPLM. In 2009, Bashir appointed Ahmed Haroun as the governor of the state.[53] Juba appointed Abdelaziz al-Hilu as the Deputy Governor of the state. Haroun worked closely with Abdelaziz, and their partnership worked well. Haroun's influence in Khartoum also brought funds to the state. The state witnessed peace, security and infrastructure development. The joint efforts of Haroun and Abdelaziz reduced the tensions between the Arabs and the Nuba. Among the states, South Kordofan seemed to have benefitted more from CPA's peace dividend.

---

[53] In 2007, the International Criminal Court indicted Ahmed Haroun as the Minister of Interior Affairs committing war crimes and crimes against humanity in Darfur.

Due to the objection raised by SPLM on the voters list, the CPA-stipulated April 2010 election was postponed. Without an elected legislature, the popular consultation was put on hold. SPLM agreed on holding the elections after the missing Nuba voters were included in the modified census. Between 2 and 4 May, elections were held for the governorship and the legislature. The state elections were significant for both NCP and SPLM. NCP was keen to win the election to control the popular consultation process and limit any demand for self-determination by the Nuba. SPLM wanted to win the election precisely to advance the interests of Nuba and to survive as a political party in the North. On 13 May, SPLM accused the National Election Commission (NEC) of systematic rigging of the elections and threatened to withdraw at this stage of the process. The Carter Center based on its election observation concluded that the elections were generally peaceful and credible.[54]

On 15 May, NEC announced that Ahmed Haroun was elected as the governor by a margin of 6,500 votes against Abdelaziz. In the legislature, NCP won 33 seats against SPLM's 22. SPLM was confident of winning the election and accused NCP of rigging the election with the help of NEC. According to John Young, the election was not rigged. SPLM lost because it did not include concerns of other marginalized groups and focused on narrow Arab-African discourse.[55]

The post-election tensions were complicated by the presence of the SPLM and SAF forces in the state. Lacking real political influence, SPLM in the North was unwilling to demobilize its forces. Similarly, SAF brought even larger troops into the state. Immediately after the announcement of the election results, Abdelaziz absconded and made provocative statements. It confirmed Khartoum's fears that SPLM was engaged in toppling the regime by joining forces within the country and outside, including the Government of South Sudan. On 4 June, SPLA took control of a police station in Kadugli and held it for three

---

[54] Uma, J. N. (2011, 30 March). S. Kordofan elections: Carter center concerned over low voter registration. *Sudan Tribune: Plural News and Views on Sudan.* https://sudantribune.com/S-Kordofan-elections-Carter-Center,38427

[55] Young, J. (2012). *The fate of Sudan: The origins and consequences of a flawed peace process.* Zed Books.

days. Both SAF and SPLM took positions in several parts of Kadugli and clashed in various parts of the city. SAF commenced aerial bombardments and indiscriminate shelling in the town and surrounding areas. Alongside its militias, it also looted and attacked civilian population, mainly targeting the Nuba.

The UN Security Council relocated all the UN agency staff from Kadugli town to the UNMIS compound situated outside the town. The UNMIS national staff, particularly Nuba, sought refuge in the UNMIS compound. By 8 June, about 6,000–7,000 civilians sought refuge near the UNMIS compound perimetre. Ahmed Haroun, learning from his Darfur experience, banned UN flights and entry of foreigners into South Kordofan. The influx of civilian staff into the UNMIS compound created a security situation and shortage of food and accommodation. The national staff were agitated and expected UNMIS to engage with the authorities on their behalf. I was in Khartoum when the fighting broke out. Haile Menkerios, known for his proactive leadership, instructed me to reach Kadugli the next day despite the ban imposed by the governor. I travelled from El Obeid as part of a food convoy bringing rations to UNMIS. An Indian Air Force officer returning to his base in Kadugli joined me. We passed several check points, but SAF was more interested in checking the food truck to verify if any weapons were being smuggled into South Kordofan. The 250 km distance took about 8 h to complete due to numerous checkpoints on the way.

The UNMIS compound was situated way outside Kadugli town and was not affected by the ongoing fighting or shelling. However, the lack of water created a major crisis. Everyday, tankers used to fetch water from the city to the UNMIS compound. Once the fighting started, SAF restricted access to water points. The UNMIS staff were upset with Mark Rutgers, Head of the Sector, for the deteriorating living conditions. In the morning next day, along with Mark Rutgers, I visited Ahmed Haroun mainly to find a solution for the water crisis faced by UNMIS. Ahmed Haroun's first question was how I reached Kadugli despite the lockdown. I understand that later, he imposed even severe restrictions on the movement of people and vehicle between Khartoum and Kadugli. He agreed to instruct SAF to provide safe passage for UNMIS water tankers to fetch water. On our return to the compound, when we instructed the water tankers to fetch water, the drivers sought armed protection to drive into the city. The Egyptian contingent based in Kadugli refused to provide armed security to the tankers. I realized that among other things, the refusal was also to do with the lack of communication between the Egyptian contingent Commander and the Head of the Sector. Based on my intervention, the Commander agreed to send armed security to accompany the tankers and the water problem was solved.

The national staff, particularly the Nuba who had taken refuge in the compound, were afraid that they would be detained once they stepped out of the compound. They requested a safe passage through a UN flight to Wau. Mark Rutgers and I met with Ahmed Haroun and asked the same for the national staff who had sought refuge in the UNMIS compound. He promised to authorize their evacuation by the UN flight subject to receiving their names. We agreed to his demand since the flight manifest would have had their names anyway and he would have access to it. We thought if they travelled with a senior UN official, it would provide additional security to them. On 22 June, the UNMIS Deputy Special Representative of the Secretary-General (DSRSG/RC/HC) Georg Charpentier made a visit to Kadugli to meet with the governor and to assess the humanitarian situation. Mark Rutgers and I informed him about the evacuation of the national staff in his plane. He reluctantly agreed since he was not sure about the implications of such a move. During his meeting with Ahmed Haroun, we submitted the names of the national staff who would be taking the flight along with the DSRSG. Ahamed Haroun told us to proceed with the evacuation plan. Unfortunately, DSRSG did not seek from the governor any written or oral commitment regarding their safety. At Kadugli airport, NISS verified the names of 21 national staff leaving for Wau as part of the evacuation plan. While the national staff were boarding, the NISS forces arrived in several pickup trucks and forcibly removed six national staff and arrested them. The arrest was made in the presence of DSRSG, and we watched it in disbelief. On 27 June, another UNMIS national staff was arrested in Kadugli town.[56] Ahmed

---

[56] Office of the High Commissioner for Human Rights (2011). *A preliminary report on human rights violations*. During Armed in Southern Kordofan.

Haroun demonstrated again his notorious Darfur past by arresting the national staff. He sent NISS staff to intimidate IDPs living near the UNMIS perimeter fence saying that they should leave the camp on their own volition. On 20 June, SAF informed UNMIS that IDPs had 48 h to leave the site. We tried to contact Ahmed Haroun and failed. SAF brought buses and removed IDPs from the site, and consequently, UNMIS organized road convoys to evacuate all non-essential international and national staff to Khartoum. By the end of June, UNMIS in South Kordofan and in other sectors was preparing for the closure of the mission on 8 July. It was neither possible to monitor nor play any role in the ongoing conflict. The war in South Kordofan and the Blue Nile state continued, and the civilians had no access to humanitarian assistance.

Darfur[57]

Darfur is situated in the west part of Sudan. The 2003 conflict in Darfur caused major a humanitarian crisis and attracted global attention. Journalists narrated the conflict as one between Khartoum-supported 'Arab' tribes against the 'African' tribes. However, the conflict cannot be captured with this simple narrative. The 1984 famine that killed more than 90,000 Darfurians was an indication of Khartoum's total neglect of Darfur. According to Gerard Prunier, an expert on Darfur, 'since 1985 Darfur had been a time-bomb waiting for a fuse'.[58]

In the 1990s, the continuing marginalization and availability of arms in abundance due to the Libya-Chad war had made Darfur a volatile place. It did not attract Khartoum's attention since it was more concerned with finding a settlement for the war in the South. Bashir assumed power in a coup in 1989 and consolidated his control in 1999. In 2000, peace talks for ending the North–South conflict had begun. While the North-South talks were progressing and there was optimism about ending one of the longest wars in Africa, Darfur

---

[57] The author as Director of the UNMIS Human Rights Division established four human rights offices in Darfur and traveled widely in the region meeting with the IDPs, local leaders, rebel commanders and authorities.

[58] Prunier, G. (2005). *Darfur: The ambiguous genocide*. Hurts & Company.

exploded. The Darfurian rebellion assumed new character with the youth leading it and sidelining traditional tribal authorities.[59]

In April 2003, the Sudan Liberation Movement (SLM/A) and Justice and Equality Movement (JEM) launched coordinated attacks in which they blew up planes in El Fasher and killed several government soldiers. In May and June, the government lost several hundred soldiers and Bashir responded by declaring a state of emergency in Darfur. The Sudanese government decided to pursue military solution and end the rebellion swiftly. Its strategy was to arm the existing Janjaweed militias, and its aim was to attack the civilians to deprive the rebels of their support. The strategy was crude and Alex de Wall called it 'counter-insurgency on the cheap'.[60] The combination of aerial attacks along with brutal violence by the Sudanese army and the Janjaweed militia led to an enormous humanitarian crisis.

In September 2004, the Security Council established an International Commission of Inquiry on Darfur. The Commission established that the Government of Sudan and the Janjaweed are responsible for serious violations of international human rights and humanitarian law amounting to crimes under international law. In particular, the Commission found that government forces and militias conducted indiscriminate attacks, including killing of civilians, torture, enforced disappearances, destruction of villages, rape and other forms of sexual violence, pillaging and forced displacement, throughout Darfur. These acts were conducted on a widespread and systematic basis and, therefore, may amount to crimes against humanity. The Commission concluded that the atrocities committed in Darfur do not legally constitute 'genocide' and recognized them as crimes against humanity. The Commission recommended the Security Council to refer the situation to the International Criminal Court (ICC).[61]

[59] International Crisis Group. (2004). *Darfur raising—Sudan's new crisis* (ICG Africa Report, No. 76). https://www.crisisgroup.org/africa/horn-africa/sudan/darfur-rising-sudans-new-crisis

[60] As quoted by Prunier, G. (2005). *Darfur: The ambiguous genocide.*

[61] United Nations. (2000). *Report of the international commission of inquiry on East Timor.* https://reliefweb.int/report/indonesia/report-international-commission-inquiry-east-timor

In March 2005, the ICC opened an investigation on the alleged genocide, war crimes and crimes against humanity committed in Darfur.[62] The ICC, in 2007, indicted seven persons including President Bashir for genocide, crimes against humanity and war crimes.

UNITED NATIONS AND AFRICAN UNION PEACEKEEPING OPERATIONS IN DARFUR

In July 2004, the Security Council authorized UNMIS to extend its operations to Darfur. Meanwhile, the AU launched the Abuja talks to mediate between the Darfurian rebels and the Sudanese government. The AU deployed a small number of military advisers and protection troops in Darfur to monitor the humanitarian ceasefire agreed upon by the parties. In May 2006, the parties signed the Darfur Peace Agreement (DPA) in Abuja.

The Sudanese government opposed the setting up of a UN peace-keeping operation exclusively for Darfur. In July 2007, the UN collaborated with the AU to set up the United Nations–African Union Mission in Darfur (UNAMID). UNAMID was mandated to protect civilians, assist in delivery of humanitarian assistance and mediate between the Government of Sudan and those groups that have not signed the peace agreement based on the Doha Document for Peace in Darfur (DDPD).[63]

The conflict in Darfur till March 2020 had contributed to 480,000 deaths and displacement of 2.8 million people.[64] From the beginning, UNAMID was faced with a situation where there was no peace to monitor or enforce. Darfur included many layers of conflict with numerous armed groups that neither the government nor the rebels who signed DPA could control. Alex de Wall in 2007 commented that

[62] International Criminal Court. (2005, March). *Darfur, Sudan. Situation referred to the ICC by the United Nations Security Council*. https://www.icc-cpi.int/darfur

[63] United Nations. (2011). *Background: United Nations mission in Sudan*. https://unmis.unmissions.org/background-0

[64] World Without Genocide. (2017). Darfur genocide. Mitchell Hamline School of Law. http://worldwithoutgenocide.org/genocides-and-conflicts/darfur-genocide

international peacekeeping could impose its will was naive, impractical and dangerous.[65] In 2011, based on negotiations held in Qatar, an agreement called DDPD was adopted. In March 2020, the UN and the AU discussed proposals for closure of the mission and establishing a UN political mission.[66]

On 31 December 2020, UNAMID ended its operations. The most notable success of the mission was its ending of large-scale violence and killings. UNAMID is also credited with ensuring stability at times fragile but helped in the delivery of humanitarian aid. However, Alex de Wall considers that the peacemaking process was based on flawed premises. He considered it to be that of finding a 'square solution to the round problem'. The peacekeeping process did not take into account the history of marginalization and misgovernment.[67] UNAMID remained a holding operation despite spending several billions of dollars for running the mission.

Sudan Postscript

After the secession of South Sudan and the wars in three areas and in Darfur, many commentators offered gloomy predictions for Sudan's future. CPA helped in the separation of the North and the South but did not contribute to the expected democratic transformation. Bashir looked invincible with his politics of patronage and intimidation. Beginning at the end of 2018, what began as a protest against price rise and austerity measures, including cut in bread and fuel subsidies, evolved into a demand for removal of Bashir. On 6 April 2019, protesters gathered outside the military headquarters in Khartoum and refused to disperse. The Sudanese Professionals Association led the campaign with people from all walks of life joining it. Women joined

[65] De Waal, A. (2007). Darfur and the failure of the responsibility to protect. *International Affairs, 83*(6), 1039–1054. http://guillaumenicaise.com/wp-content/uploads/2013/10/Darfur-and-the-failure-of-the-R2p.pdf

[66] *Bangkok Post.* (2020, 17 March). UN report calls for political mission in Darfur. https://www.bangkokpost.com/world/1880560/un-report-calls-for-political-mission-in-darfur

[67] De Waal, A. (2014). *Violence and peacemaking in the political marketplace.* https://reliefweb.int/sites/reliefweb.int/files/resources/Accord25_ViolenceAndPeacemaking.pdf

the protest in large numbers. People from the Nile valley who had all along supported Bashir and his party deserted him as well.[68]

The growing protest and demand for the ousting of Bashir led to a coup on 11 April 2009. Bashir was removed by the Sudanese army led by Ahmed Awad Inb Auf. The army announced an emergency and imposed curfew. Despite the curfew, crowds continued to protest. The Sudanese Professionals Association did not recognize the Transitional Military Council and demanded that the power be handed over to a civilian government. On 24 April, three members of the Transitional Military Council resigned, and on 27 April, a transitional council consisting of civilians and military was established. Bashir and several leading members of his government and the party were arrested. On 21 August 2019, economist Abdalla Hamdok became the Prime Minister of Sudan. At last, the Sudanese had determined their political future on their own.

The challenges before the civilian government are many. These include fixing the economy and dealing with the impoverishment of the people, facilitating a peace process to engage with the conflicts in Darfur, South Kordofan and Blue Nile and establishment of an accountable and unified security system.[69] In June 2020, the Security Council authorized the deployment of a political mission, the United Nations Integrated Transition Assistance Mission in Sudan (UNITMAS). It is mandated to assist the country in its transition towards democratic governance, provide support for peace negotiations and bolster efforts to maintain accountable rule of law and security institutions.[70] In August 2020, the Sudanese government and the Sudan Revolutionary Front (SRF), an alliance of rebels from Darfur, South Kordofan and Blue Nile signed an agreement on security arrangements providing

---

[68] *BBC News.* (2019). *Sudan Coup: Why Omar al-Bashir was overthrown.* https://www.bbc.com/news/world-africa-47852496

[69] De Waal, A. (2019, 2 August). *Sudan's political marketplace and the prospects for democracy.* The London School of Economics and Political Science. https://blogs.lse.ac.uk/africaatlse/2019/08/02/sudan-political-marketplace-democracy/

[70] United Nations. (2020, 4 June). *Security council establishes integrated transition assistance mission in Sudan, Unanimously adopting resolution 2525 (2020).* Meeting Coverages and Press Releases, Security Council, SC/14202. https://www.un.org/press/en/2020/sc14202.doc.htm

for potential end to conflict in these areas. The Sudanese government is also engaged with Abdelaziz al-Hilu representing the Nuba to end the conflict in this region.[71]

CÔTE D'IVOIRE: MINUCI AND UNOCI—PEACEKEEPING WHEN THERE WAS NO PEACE TO KEEP

Côte d'Ivoire became independent in 1960. The country's first President Félix Houphouët-Boigny ran a one-party regime and banned all political parties. He maintained close links with France and aligned with the Western camp during the Cold War. In 1990, he lifted the ban on political parties and won the first multiparty elections held in the same year. Houphouët-Boigny died in 1993, after which Henri Konan Bédié became the president. He was re-elected in 1995 in an election that was boycotted by the opposition parties. In 1999, Alassane Quattara, a Muslim joined the fray for 2000 presidential election. In December 1999, General Robert Guéï displaced Bédié in a coup and proclaimed himself the president. However, after a popular uprising, he fled the country. Laurent Gbagbo became the next president, and it lead to a conflict between his Christian supporters from the South and Alassane Quattara's Muslim supporters from the North. The latent ethnic tension erupted during the 2000 elections and continued to impact the country. The 2000 violence soon evolved into a civil war between Muslims and Christians, splitting the country into two factions. In 2001, an agreement to deescalate the situation was reached, after which Quattara's RDR party joined the government. In 2002, soldiers concerned about demobilization mutinied. The mutiny grew into a rebellion, with rebels from the Patriotic Movement taking control of the north. The emergence of two armed groups, Ivorian Popular Movement of the Great West (MPIGO) and Movement for Justice and Peace (MJP), complicated the situation further.[72]

---

[71] Dahir, A. L. (2020). Sudan signs peace deal with rebel alliance. *The New York Times*. https://www.nytimes.com/2020/08/31/world/africa/sudan-peace-agreement-darfur.html

[72] Aljazeera Media Network. (2011). *Timeline: Ivory coast*. News Agencies. https://www.aljazeera.com/news/africa/2010/12/2010121971745317811.html; *BBC News* (2019). *Ivory coast profile—Timeline*. https://www.bbc.com/news/world-africa-13287585

In December 2002, the Economic Community of West African States (ECOWAS) deployed its ECOWAS Peace Force to stabilize the situation. However, due to the lack of human and material resources, the ECOWAS Force failed to bring order in the country. France, which had militarily intervened in 2002 (Operation Licorne) to evacuate its citizens, remained in the country as an interposition force between the rebels and the government forces. France began playing a direct political role and, in 2003, initiated a talk among the Ivorian political parties and rebel groups, resulting in a peace agreement. The agreement led to the formation of a new government with the consensus candidate Seydou Diarra as the prime minister. France was keen to involve the UN and the agreement included a role for the UN in its implementation. France also managed to obtain the Security Council's authorization for deployment of a peacekeeping operation despite opposition from other members of the Council. In May 2003, the Security Council authorized the establishment of the United Nations Mission in Côte d'Ivoire (MINUCI) to monitor the implementation of the agreement.

In 2004, based on the Secretary-General's recommendation, the Security Council ended MINUCI's mandate and established a multi-dimensional United Nations Operation in Côte d'Ivoire (UNOCI). Its objective was to facilitate the implementation of the agreement made by the Ivorian parties and monitor the military situation along with the security of the Liberian refugees. The mission also included political, legal, civil affairs; human rights; and election and media staff. In November 2004, the situation deteriorated with the Ivorian armed forces launching air strikes against the rebels. Consequently, the rebel forces went on a rampage in Abidjan leading to the evacuation of foreigners from the city. The UNOCI troops were directly involved in quelling the unrest. In 2005, the Security Council authorized an increase in UNOCI's troop strength, and on April 2005, under the auspices of South Africa, a new agreement was signed which called on the UN to play a role in the planned general elections. The UN assumed a major role in conducting the elections which also included the certification of its outcome. The UN appointed a high representative to coordinate the elections to ensure that UNOCI was not involved in the electoral process. President Laurent Gbagbo, under various pretexts, delayed the elections. In March 2007, the Ivorian parties signed another agreement (8th deal) in Ouagadougou, Burkina Faso (Ouagadougou Political Agreement [OPA] agreement), which was based on direct talks between Gbagbo and the rebels. However, Gbagbo sidelined both the UN and the Ivorian opposition political parties. The UN continued its operation without any say in the implementation of OPA. It was also concerned about the continued postponement of the election.

In August 2010, the Gbagbo government announced that the elections would be held on 31 October. The stakes were high for both Gbagbo and the opposition. Gbagbo was confident of winning the election, but he lost it in the second round. On 2 December 2010, the Ivorian Electoral Commission declared the opposition candidate Alassane Quattara as the winner and the UN Security Council endorsed the result. However, the president of the country's Constitutional Council set aside the results and announced Gbagbo as the winner. Both Gbagbo and Quattara took oath in different places and organized their respective administrations. Despite pressure from regional and international communities, Gbagbo refused to relent. The impasse led to violence between the supporters of Gbagbo and Quattara, resulting in 3,000 deaths and 200,000 thousand fleeing the country and 300,000 internally displaced. UNOCI was caught in the middle and Gbagbo accused it of supporting the rebels. He asked UNOCI to leave the country, and on 10 December, the non-essential staff were evacuated to Gambia. The Security Council was divided with some members supporting the outcome of the election while others accusing the Security Council of interfering in the internal affairs of the country.

The security situation further deteriorated when the UNOCI head-quarters and its forces were targeted by pro-Gbagbo forces. Quattara's forces resumed fighting and reached the outskirts of Abidjan. On 30 March 2011, the Security Council authorized UNOCI 'to use all necessary measures' to prevent the use of heavy weapons against the civilian population. The UN also sought French assistance to target Gbagbo forces and their heavy weapons. On 11 April, Gbagbo was captured and taken to The Hague and put under the custody of the ICC.[73]

UNOCI is an example of the UN intervening in a situation at the time when the situation itself was shifting and there was no peace to keep. It also demonstrated the difficulties of operating with tenuous consent and even hostility from the host government. UNOCI is also a case study of UN peacekeeping operations and the use of force without which it would not have succeeded. The active involvement by the French undermined the multilateral efforts and the role of African regional actors. As Jean-Marie Guéhenno put it, the Security Council members considered it as a problem for France to fix it since it owned Côte d'Ivoire.[74] UNOCI's robust intervention in support of one party against another raised questions regarding its impartiality. The fact that Gbagbo refused to step down after losing in an election endorsed by the UN justified UNOCI's action in removing him from power. However, this step also raised questions about the UN's role in regime change while being engaged in civilian protection.[75]

In 2012, President Quattara established the Commission for Dialogue, Truth and Reconciliation (CDVR) to identify the root causes of the conflict, its patterns and types of violations and strategies to fulfil victim rights. The government's focus was on criminal justice, and it established a Special Investigation and Examination Unit (CSEI). CSEI was criticized for its actions against the opposition and condoning the president's supporters. The government also established the National Committee for Reconciliation and Victim's Compensation (CONARIV) and the Ministry of Solidarity, Social Cohesion and

[73] Novosseloff, A. (2018). *The many lives of a peacekeeping mission: The UN operation in Côte d'Ivoire.* International Peace Institute. https://www.ipinst.org/wp-content/uploads/2018/06/1806_Many-Lives-of-a-Peacekeeping-Mission.pdf

[74] Guéhenno, J.-M. (2018). *The fog peace. Taken from Alexandra Novosseloff 'The many lives of a peacekeeping mission: The UN operation in Côte d'Ivoire'.* Center on International Cooperation.

[75] Bellamy, A. J., & Williams, P. D. (2011). The new politics of protection? Côte d'Ivoire, Libya and the responsibility to protect. *International Affairs, 87*(4), 825–850. https://doi.org/10.1111/j.1468-2346.2011.01006.x

Victim's Compensation (MSCSIV).[76] In 2015, the Security Council extended UNOCI's mandate with an intention to downsize and eventually end it. UNOCI ended its operation in 2017.[77]

In 2019, the International Center for Transitional Justice (ICTJ) was critical of the Ivorian authorities stating that they ignored the rights of victims and expected them to forgive while neglecting to address human rights violations and the causes of these violations.[78]

LIBERIA: UNOMIL, UNOL AND UNMIL—PEACEKEEPING HELPS IN TRANSITION TO DEMOCRACY BUT A LONG HAUL

Liberia, Africa's first independent country, had no long tradition of a constitutional government. Since the 1980s, Liberia entered into a phase of further political instability and conflict. In 1980, Samuel K Doe assumed power in a coup. In 1984, he restored multiparty elections and was elected president in a rigged election. The instability continued with a failed coup in 1985. In 1989, Charles Taylor's National Patriotic Front of Liberia (NPLF) invaded from Côte d'Ivoire to oust Doe. The ECOWAS deployed a Nigerian-led peacekeeping force. In 1990, a splinter NPLF group captured Doe and killed him. Charles Taylor rejected the ECOWAS-established interim government and set up a rival government. His forces attacked the ECOWAS peacekeepers, leading to the failure of ceasefire agreements.

In 1993, the parties signed a peace deal and the United Nations Observer Mission in Liberia (UNOMIL) was deployed to monitor the

[76] International Center for Transitional Justice. (2010). *Background: Confronting ethnic division, addressing impunity.* https://www.ictj.org/our-work/regions-and-countries/c%C3%B4te-divoire

[77] United Nations Security Council. (2003, 26 March). *Report of the Secretary-General on Côte d'Ivoire (S/2003/374).* https://reliefweb.int/report/côte-divoire/report-secretary-general-côte-divoire-s2003374

[78] Suma, M. (2019, 1 January). *Côte d'Ivoire's continued struggle for justice and reconciliation.* International Center for Transitional Justice. https://www.ictj.org/news/cote-d'ivoire's-continued-struggle-justice-and-reconciliation

implementation of the agreement. In 1997, Taylor was elected in a UN-assisted election. The civil war had killed about 150,000 people, mostly civilians, and had created 850,000 refugees. In 1997, the Security Council ended UNOMIL and set up the United Nations Peace-Building Support Office in Liberia (UNOL) to promote reconciliation and respect for human rights.[79]

In 2003, heavy fighting took place in the capital Monrovia between the government forces and the rebel group—Liberians United for Reconciliation and Deomcracy (LURD) based in Guinea. In August 2003, the UN authorized the deployment of a multinational stabilization force to defend the capital city and engage with the combatants. Taylor resigned and fled to Nigeria. The government and the rebels agreed on a peace deal. In October 2003, the Security Council authorized the deployment of a multi-dimensional United Nations Mission in Libya (UNMIL) with 15,000 peacekeepers and a large number of civilian staff.[80]

The civil war during 1989–2003 resulted in the deaths of more than 250,000 people. It displaced more than one million people and destroyed the country's infrastructure. Conflicts related to the sexual abuse of women and girls were widespread. The police, the army and the institutions of law had collapsed. UNMIL demobilized more than 100,000 combatants and contributed to the stabilization of the country. Besides peace enforcement, it moved into facilitating the conduct of elections, building the army, the police, the judiciary and human rights institutions and reconstruction and peacebuilding. UNMIL organized three elections. In 2005, Ellen Johnson Sirleaf, the first female president in Africa, was elected. In 2007, a successful democratic transition occurred with the election of George Weah as the president.[81]

[79] United Nations. (2003). *Liberia-UNOMIL background.* https://peacekeeping.un.org/sites/default/files/past/unomilS.htm

[80] United Nations. (2003). *Background: United Nations mission in Liberia.* https://unmil.unmissions.org/background

[81] Forti, D., & Connolly, L. (2018). *The mission is gone, but the UN is staying: Liberia's peacekeeping transition.* International Peace Institute. https://www.ipinst.org/wp-content/uploads/2018/12/1812_Liberias-Peacekeeping_-Transition.pdf

However, independent observers have noted that the gains cannot be sustained without continued international engagement and without addressing economic issues such as poverty and inequality.[82]

CENTRAL AFRICAN REPUBLIC: MINURCA, BONUCA AND MINUSCA—A DAUNTING TASK

The Central African Republic became independent in 1960. Till 1993, military rulers assumed power through coup d'etat. In 1993, multiparty elections were held for the first time and Ange-Félix Patassé became the country's president. His government inherited a bankrupt nation and was unable to pay the salaries of government employees and the army. The military attempted three coups in 1996, and there was widespread looting and violence in the capital. Patassé sought help of regional governments to mediate with the rebel forces. In 1997, with the authorization of the UN Security Council, a peacekeeping operation called MISAB consisting of regional forces was established. In 1998, the UN established the United Nations Mission in the Central African Republic (MINURCA). In 2000, after holding two peaceful elections, the Security Council decided to end MINURCA and replace it with the United Nations Peacebuilding Support Office in the Central African Republic (BONUCA).[83]

In 2013, the country was faced with another more intense and violent sectarian conflict. A loose alliance of Muslim groups called Seleka rebelled against President Bozizé who had assumed power in 2003 in a coup. The Seleka committed atrocities when they captured the capital Bangui in March 2013. A Christian militia called Anti-balaka opposed the Saleka and targeted Muslim civilians. The country was in effect divided into Christian and Muslim segments and was in a disarray. Officials fled the country, hospitals and schools did not function and

---

[82] United Nations Mission in Liberia. (2018). *The story of UNMIL*. https://reliefweb.int/report/liberia/story-unmil

[83] United Nations. (2014). *United Nations multidimensional integrated stabilization mission in the Central African Republic*. https://minusca.unmissions.org/en/about

the infrastructure was destroyed. Half the population of the country needed emergency assistance.[84]

In December 2013, the Security Council established the International Commission of Inquiry on the Central African Republic. The Commission in its report concluded that all parties committed human rights violations. It did not conclude there was genocide but observed that ethnic cleansing of the Muslim population by the Anti-balaka constituted a crime against humanity.[85]

In April 2014, the UN Security Council established the United Nations Multidimensional Integrated Stabilization Mission in the Central African Republic (MINUSCA). The mission's mandate included the protection of civilians, support to the political process, creating conditions for delivery of humanitarian assistance, return of internally displaced and refugees, protection of human rights and promotion of national dialogue.

The country continued to be in a flux even after the peaceful 2016 elections. In 2018, a conflict erupted among the armed groups and UN peacekeepers were also attacked. In February 2019, the government and 14 armed groups made a political agreement including the integration of the fighters into the army.

The UN Secretary-General, while recommending the deployment of MINUSCA, warned that responding to the crisis would be a daunting task and would require time and resources. He also stated that the problems facing the country exceeded the capacities of a United Nations peacekeeping operation and should be part of a long-term engagement of the international community.[86]

[84] United States Holocaust Memorial Museum. (2017). *Background: Political and ethnic violence in Central African Republic*. https://www.ushmm.org/genocide-prevention/countries/central-african-republic/case-study/background/political-and-ethnic-violence

[85] United Nations Security Council. (2014). *The International Commission of Inquiry on the Central African Republic* (Final report). https://reliefweb.int/report/central-african-republic/international-commission-inquiry-central-african-republic-final

[86] United Nations. (2014). *United Nations multidimensional integrated stabilization mission in the Central African Republic*. https://minusca.unmissions.org/en/about

MALI: MINUSMA—UN'S HOLDING OPERATION WHILE NOTHING CHANGES

Mali a former French colony became independent in 1960 but remained a one-party state till 1992 when the first multiparty elections were held. Mali faced a series of crises resulting from fragile state, ineffective governance, corruption and conflict arising from feeling of neglect by communities particularly in the North. Post-Libyan revolution and the availability of arms exacerbated the existing conflicts. In January 2012, a Tuareg movement known as the Mouvement national pour la libération de l'Azawad (MNLA), along with Islamic armed groups, including Ansar Dine, also known as Al-Qaeda in the Islamic Maghreb (AQIM), and the Mouvement pour l'unicité et le Jihad en Afrique de l'Ouest (MUJAO), in addition to deserters from the Malian armed forces, initiated a series of attacks against government forces in the north of the country. In March 2012, a military junta, the Comité national pour le redressement de la démocratie et la restauration de l'État, led by Captain Amadou Sanogo, took power, suspended the Constitution and dissolved the government institutions. In the north, MNLA used the instability following the coup to overrun government forces in the regions of Kidal, Gao and Timbuktu and proclaim an Independent State of Azawad. Immediately, after the coup, the ECOWAS initiated talks with the junta that led to the establishment of a transitional government, headed by a prime minister with executive powers. On 17 April, Cheick Modibo Diarra was appointed interim prime minister. On 20 August, the prime minister announced the formation of a GoNU.[87]

In January 2013, the Security Council authorized the deployment of the United Nations Multidimensional Integrated Stabilization Mission in Mali (MINUSMA). MINUSMA was tasked to support the political process and carry out security-related stabilization tasks, protecting civilians, human rights monitoring, the creation of conditions for the provision of humanitarian assistance and the return of displaced persons, the extension of state authority and the preparation of free, inclusive and peaceful elections.[88]

[87] *BBC News*. (2020). *Mali profile: Timeline*. https://www.bbc.com/news/world-africa-13881978

[88] United Nations. (2013). *United Nations multidimensional integrated stabilization mission in Mali*. https://minusma.unmissions.org/en/history

Meanwhile, in early January 2013, elements of Ansar Dine and the Movement for Unity and Jihad in West Africa, with the support of Al-Qaeda in the Islamic Maghreb, advanced southwards. They clashed with the Malian army north of the town of Konna, some 680 km from Bamako, forcing the soldiers to withdraw. Terrorist and other armed elements also advanced in the west, taking control of the town of Diabaly on 14 January. Malian transitional authorities requested the assistance of France to defend Mali's sovereignty and restore its territorial integrity. In response, military operations against terrorists and associated elements were initiated on 11 January under 'Operation Serval', led by France, in support of the Malian defence and security forces.[89] By the end of January, state control was restored in most major northern towns, such as Diabaly, Douentza, Gao, Konna and Timbuktu. In July–August, Ibrahim Boubacar Keïta was elected as the president. France formally handed over responsibility for security in the north to the MINUSMA forces. Jihadist violence continued to plague the north and east of the country. More than 100 peacekeepers have died since the UN mission's deployment in Mali in 2013, making it one of the deadliest places to serve for the UN. In August 2020, President Keïta was overthrown in a military coup after months of protests demanding his resignation.

After the August 2020 coup, International Crisis Group expert Jean-Hervé Jezequel commented that the situation has returned to what was in 2012, after eight years of effort, investment and international presence.[90] However, despite the complexity and the impossible challenge, most observers considered that without the presence of MINUSMA, the situation would become even more dire.[91]

[89] United Nations. (2013). *United Nations multidimensional integrated stabilization mission in Mali.*

[90] Jezequel, J.-H. (2020). *Crisis group role.* International Crisis Group. https://www.crisisgroup.org/who-we-are/people/jean-herve-jezequel

[91] Aljazeera Media Network. (2020). *Challenges ahead as UN set to extend 'most dangerous' mission.* https://www.aljazeera.com/news/2020/6/26/challenges-ahead-as-un-set-to-extend-most-dangerous-mission

Operations Deployed in Conflicts Due to Transition to Democracy from Authoritarian Rule

5

The increase in the deployment of peacekeeping operations in the 1990s reflected another phenomenon of conflicts erupting in countries that transited to multiparty democracy from one-party rule, military dictatorship and regimes that remained in power through sham elections. Transition to democracy was difficult and even led to violent conflicts due to weak or decaying state institutions, narrow power base of the ruling class that benefitted from authoritarian regimes and human rights violations committed to retain power.

Operation	Year	Purpose
HAITI UNMIH	1993–1996	To assist in modernizing the armed forces of Haiti and establishing a new police force
UNSMIH	1996–1997	Assistance to the Haitian authorities in the professionalization of the Haitian National Police (HNP) and assistance to the Haitian authorities in maintaining a secure and stable environment
UNTMIH	August–November 1997	To assist the Government of Haiti by supporting and contributing to the professionalization of the HNP

Operation	Year	Purpose
MIPONUH	1997–2000	To assist the Government of Haiti in the professionalization of the HNP
MINUSTAH	2004–2017	To restore a secure and stable environment, promote the political process, strengthen Haiti's government institutions and rule-of-law structures and promote and protect human rights
MINJUSTH	2017–2019	To further develop the HNP; strengthen rule of law institutions, including the justice systems and prisons; and promote and protect human rights
UN Observer Mission in Sierra Leone (UNOMSIL)	1998–1999	Monitor the military and security situation in the country, report on violations of international humanitarian law and human rights in Sierra Leone and reform and restructuring of the Sierra Leone police force
UN Mission in Sierra Leone (UNMASIL)	1999–2005	To assist the government and the parties in carrying out provisions of the Lomé Peace Agreement
United Nations Integrated Office in Sierra Leone (UNIOSIL) 2005–2008	2005–2008	Building the capacity of state institutions to develop and implement a strategy for addressing the root causes of the conflict and accelerate progress towards the Millennium Development Goals; developing a national plan of action for human rights and establishing a national human rights commission; enhancing good governance, transparency and accountability; and building the capacity of the National Electoral Commission to conduct free, fair and credible elections in 2007
United Nations Integrated Peacebuilding Office in Sierra Leone (UNIPSIL)	2008–2014	To provide support to the government of Sierra Leone in identifying and resolving tensions and threats of potential conflict, monitoring and promoting human rights and consolidating governance reforms

Operation	Year	Purpose
UN Organization Mission in Democratic Republic of the Congo (MONUC)	1999–2010	To monitor the implementation of the Ceasefire Agreement and investigate violations of the ceasefire; to facilitate humanitarian assistance and human rights monitoring, with particular attention to vulnerable groups including women, children and demobilized child soldiers. Later in a series of resolutions, the Council expanded the mandate of MONUC to the supervision of the implementation of the Ceasefire Agreement and assigned multiple related additional tasks
UN Organization Stabilization Mission in the Democratic Republic of the Congo (MONUSCO)	2010–present	To use all necessary means to carry out its mandate relating, among other things, to the protection of civilians, humanitarian personnel and human rights defenders under imminent threat of physical violence and to support the Government of the DRC in its stabilization and peace consolidation efforts
United Nations Support Mission in Libya (UNSMIL)	2010–present	To support the country's new transitional authorities in their post-conflict efforts; exercise mediation and good offices in support of the Libyan political agreement's implementation; the consolidation of governance, security and economic arrangements of the Government of National Accord and subsequent phases of the Libyan transition process

Source: The author.

DEMOCRATIC REPUBLIC OF THE CONGO: MONUC AND MONUSCO—PERSISTENT CRISIS AND DOUBTS ABOUT PEACEKEEPING AS A SOLUTION

Congo witnessed instability immediately after the Independence in 1960, and in response, the UN established its first complex mission in the country. Subsequently, it was impacted by the Cold War, engulfed by the transition from an authoritarian rule and consumed by the conflicts in the region. The country's elite and external vested interests exploited Congo's ethnic and other conflicts to plunder its vast minerals and other resources.

In 1999, the UN deployed the United Nations Organization Mission in the Democratic Republic of the Congo (MONUC). In 2010, in responding to the evolving situation, the Security Council renamed MONUC as the United Nations Organization Stabilization Mission in the Democratic Republic of the Congo (MONUSCO) which is still in operation.[1]

Last 60 Years: Political and Other Developments

Post Independence, the initial crisis lasted between 1960 and 1964 when the UN was involved. Before the country could settle down after the initial crisis, in 1965, Army Chief Joseph Mobutu seized power in a coup, ending the democratic experiment. He was in power till 1998, running a totalitarian regime.[2]

Mobutu followed the example set by the Belgian colonizers in exploiting the country's vast natural resources for personal gain. Mobutu's corruption was legendary with bank accounts in Switzerland and villas, ranches, palaces and yachts throughout Europe.[3] Mobutu also used his vast ill-gotten wealth to manipulate the politics of his country by co-opting his opponents through bribery.[4] His regime was infamous for human rights abuse. He left behind a country only in name without any development despite the country's rich resources.[5]

The global changes including the end of the Cold War impacted the country. In 1990, Mobutu ended the single-party rule and began the

---

[1] United Nations. (2010). *Background: United Nations Organization stabilization mission in the DR CONGO*. https://peacekeeping.un.org/mission/past/monuc/background.shtml

[2] In 1971, he renamed the country Zaire; Katanga became Shaba and the Congo River became the Zaire River. The original names were restored in 1997.

[3] Berkeley, B. (1993, August). Zaire: An African horror story. *The Atlantic*. https://www.theatlantic.com/magazine/archive/1993/08/zaire-an-african-horror-story/305496/

[4] Blackburn, P. (1984). Zaire's Mobutu rules through balance of respect ad repression. *The Christian Science Monitor*. https://www.csmonitor.com/1984/1203/120344.html; *The Irish Times*. (1997, 9 September). *Mobutu leaves legacy of chaos and corruption*. https://www.irishtimes.com/news/mobutu-leaves-legacy-of-chaos-and-corruption-1.104463

[5] Refer to footnote 3.

transition to democracy. As in other countries, this transition was also not easy. In 1991, underpaid troops went on large-scale looting and destruction in the capital Kinshasa and other places. The opposition government sworn in October 1991 lasted only six days. In 1992, in Katanga province, ethnic conflict erupted with the Katangans attacking Kasaiens and forcing nearly 70,000 out of their homes. In 1993, a similar conflict took place in Kolwezi.[6]

Rwandan Genocide and the Overthrow of Mobutu

Hutu militias and their supporters, after committing genocide against the Tutsis, fled to the neighbouring Congo to escape from the Tutsi-led RPF. The Hutu militias mounted terror attacks against Rwanda. In 1996, Rwanda and Uganda joined with Kabila's Alliance of Democratic Forces for the Liberation of Congo-Zaire (AFDL) to remove Mobutu from power. In what is known as the First Congo War, AFDL and Hutu militias committed human rights violations that included massacre of civilians. In May 1997, Laurent Kabila captured Kinshasa and Mobutu was overthrown. In 1998, Kabila's efforts to remove foreign forces from Congo resulted in a war with Rwanda. The region erupted in conflict with 9 African countries and 25 armed groups involved in the war. The Second Congo War was one of the deadliest wars in Africa. It caused 5.4 million deaths due to disease and starvation and displaced about 2 million people.[7]

Post-Mobutu Political Developments

In January 2001, Laurent Kabila was shot dead by his bodyguard and his son Joseph Kabila succeeded him.[8] In July 2002, Congo signed

---

[6] Human Rights Watch. (1994). *Human rights developments*. https://www.hrw.org/reports/1994/WR94/Africa-10.htm

[7] Soderlund, W. C., Briggs, E. D., Najem, T. P., & Roberts, B. C. (2013). *Africa's deadliest conflict: Media coverage of the humanitarian disaster in the Congo and the United Nations Response, 1997–2008*. Wilfrid Laurier University Press. http://muse.jhu.edu/books/9781554588787

[8] *BBC News*. (2019). *Democratic Republic of Congo profile: Timeline*. https://www.bbc.com/news/world-africa-13286306

peace deals with Rwanda and Uganda. In December 2002, the Congo government signed an agreement that included their participation in the interim government. Between 2003 and 2006, progress was made in setting up an interim government, finalizing a new constitution and election of Joseph Kabila as the President in the first democratic elections held after more than 40 years. In 2011, Kabila was elected again as the President. In 2016, Kabila signed an agreement with the opposition parties to postpone the elections to 2018 and established a new cabinet with participation of opposition members. In the 2018 elections, opposition candidate Félix Tshisekedi won against the ruling party candidate Ramazani Shadary.[9]

Continuing Conflict in the East

Despite the changes at the national level, conflicts continued particularly in the province of North Kivu in the eastern part of Congo. The conflict that broke out in Kivu in 1993 continues till now. RPF's victory and ending of the Rwandan genocide led to the mass exodus of Hutus to Congo and Tanzania. More than a million refugees reached North and South Kivu, the impact of which still lasts in the region.[10] The Hutu refugees lived in armed camps controlled by those responsible for the genocide in Rwanda. The humanitarian community, with tacit understanding of some Western governments, sustained the armed groups in the refugee camps. While in Tanzania, the refugees were disarmed, Mobutu's corrupt and decaying state was ineffective. Mobutu's army committed atrocities against the local population and aggravated the conflict.[11]

The armed refugees and the conflict militarized and changed the character of local armed groups. Initially, they emerged to protect their local community's interests but soon morphed into militias associated

---

[9] Ibid.

[10] Mamdani, M. (2001). *When victims become killers: Colonialism, nativism and the genocide in Rwanda.* Fountain Publishers.

[11] Stearns, J. (2012). *North Kivu: The background to conflict in North Kivu province of Eastern Congo.* The Usalama Project, RIFT Valley Institute. https://www.refworld.org/pdfid/51d3d5f04.pdf

with national and regional business interests.[12] In 2019, there were at least 100 armed groups in Kivu. The Armed Forces of the Democratic Republic of the Congo (FARDC) fought against them, resulting in multiple displacements of local populations and violations of human rights and humanitarian laws.[13] Responding to the growing cycle of violence, the Security Council authorized an 'intervention brigade' in 2013.[14] While the UN force diminished the role of a few armed groups, it was still an unending task to tackle so many armed groups.

The conflict was also fuelled by the support provided to the armed groups by governments in the region. In some respects, the conflict in the east was a proxy war. Another reason for the conflict was the illegal exploitation of mineral resources with the active support of foreign and national entities. The local armed groups financed their operations through illegal mining activities and displaced civilians to gain control over resource-rich areas. Mineral resources available in the region were 'the engines of chaos'.[15] The political economy of war was based on control and exploitation of vast natural wealth of the country. The Congolese armed groups, along with some governments in the region, and globally, benefitted from the war as well. A Security Council–appointed panel in 2000 examined the link between the war in the east and Congo's natural resources. It concluded that between 2001 and 2003, mineral exploitation was funding the armed groups, the Congolese elite and military officers from Rwanda, Zimbabwe and Uganda.[16] In its 2009 report,

---

[12] Ibid.

[13] Geneva Academy. (2019, 5 February). *DRC: A mapping of non-international armed conflicts in Kivu, Kasai and Ituri*. http://www.rulac.org/news/democratic-republic-of-the-congo-a-mapping-of-non-international-armed-confl

[14] United Nations. (2013, 28 March). *Intervention brigade' authorized as Security Council grants mandate renewal for United Nations mission in Democratic Republic of Congo*. Meetings Coverage and Press Releases.

[15] Katunga, J. (2007). *Minerals, forests, and violent conflict in the Democratic Republic of the Congo* (Report from Africa: Population, Health, Environment, and Conflict, ECSP Report, Issue 2). https://www.wilsoncenter.org/publication/minerals-forests-and-violent-conflict-the-democratic-republic-the-congo; Lyall, G. (2017). *Rebellion and conflict minerals in North Kivu*. Conflicts Trends 2017/1. ACCORD. https://www.accord.org.za/conflict-trends/rebellion-conflict-minerals-north-kivu/

[16] Human Rights Watch. (2006, 1 August). *Democratic Republic of Congo: On the brink*. Finest Finance. https://www.hrw.org/news/2006/08/01/democratic-republic-congo-brink

the panel expressed concern that exploitation of natural resources by armed groups is contributing to prolongation of the conflict.[17]

MONUC and MONUSCO

In 1999, the parties signed a ceasefire agreement, and in 2000, the Security Council authorized the deployment of MONUC. In the last 20 years, the UN peace operations in Congo has responded to the evolving situation by adjusting its mandate, its troop strength and other resources. Initially, the Security Council set up MONUC to monitor the ceasefire agreement. Subsequently, it modified its mandate to assume other tasks. In 2010, MONUC was changed to MONUSCO with the additional mandate to assist in the stabilization of the country, protection of civilians, humanitarian personnel and human rights defenders and peace consolidation. Responding to the cycles of violence and their impact on the civilians, the Security Council in 2013 authorized deployment of an 'intervention brigade' to strengthen peacekeeping, to reduce the threats posed by armed groups and create conditions for carrying out stabilization activities.[18] Even before the deployment of the 'intervention brigade', the mission, since 2004, had operated under Chapter VII of the UN Charter and had one of the most robust mandates.[19] In 2008, the Security Council mandated that the protection of civilians was the mission's priority.[20]

A report assessing the effectiveness of the peace operation in Congo divided the UN's presence into four phases. The initial phase was engaging with the immediate crisis and expanding the deployment. The second phase was concerned with assisting the interim government and holding

---

[17] United Nations. (2019, 18 December). *Expert group brief's security council's Democratic Republic of Congo sanctions committee on midterm report.* Meetings Coverage and Press Releases, SC/14058. https://www.un.org/press/en/2019/sc14058.doc.htm

[18] United Nations. (2010). *Background: United Nations organization stabilization mission in the DR CONGO.* https://monusco.unmissions.org/en/background

[19] United Nations. (2013, 28 March). *Intervention brigade' authorized as Security Council grants mandate renewal for United Nations mission in Democratic Republic of Congo.* Meetings Coverage and Press Releases.

[20] United Nations. (2008). *MONUSCO: United Nations organization stabilization mission in the Democratic Republic of the Congo.* http://www.unmonusco.org/www.un.org/en/peacekeeping/missions/monusco/mandate.html

elections in 2006. The third phase was to assist in the stabilization process. The fourth phase was regarding the deployment of the 'intervention brigade' and the conduct of 2019 elections.[21] The final phase was supporting the newly elected president and planning for the mission's exit.[22]

The same report concluded that while the mission made a real difference in protection of the civilians, in some instances, it failed to respond adequately. The UN force defeated or diminished the threat of some major armed groups, but its goal of forcefully disarming the groups in the east 'will continue to be futile exercise if the larger political issues are not addressed'.[23] The mission was not successful in security sector reforms since the government was not interested in bringing about effective reforms. The government resisted the mission's efforts since real reforms would challenge the vested interests' power over the security sector. Intervention by states in the region by supporting illegal armed groups further dented the mission's efforts. The Security Council's permanent five members also did not demonstrate their full support and left the mission to fend for itself. The mission faced the challenge of continuity in leadership. It made a major contribution in strengthening civil society and appreciation for democracy.[24]

MONUC and MONUSCO faced numerous challenges and a fair share of criticism on their response to the protection of civilians. The mission had to respond to the Kisangani massacre in 2002, the Ituri crisis in 2003, the Bukavu offensive in 2004 and the Goma crisis and Kiwanja massacre in 2008. The mission faced criticism in September 2010, when MONUC peacekeepers while stationed less than 30 km away failed to protect civilians when systematic rapes took place in 13 villages in North Kivu.[25]

---

[21] United Nations. (2013, 28 March). *Intervention brigade' authorized as Security Council grants mandate renewal for United Nations mission in Democratic Republic of Congo*. Meetings Coverage and Press Releases.

[22] Novosseloff, A., Abdenur, A. E., Mandrup, I., & Pangburn, A. (2019). *Assessing the effectiveness of the United Nations Mission in the DRC/MONUC—MONUSCO*. Norwegian Institute of International Affairs.

[23] Ibid.

[24] Ibid.

[25] Human Rights Watch. (2006, 1 August). *Democratic Republic of Congo: On the brink*. Finest Finance. https://www.hrw.org/news/2006/08/01/democratic-republic-congo-brink

The Rift Valley Institute in 2013 observed that UN Security Council's military solutions and stronger protection mandate is not a solution. They give the impression of the international community doing something, but they remain a temporary solution. International community or the Congolese parties cannot fight their way out of the Congo's persistent crises.[26]

Writing at the end of 2009, calling it the 'MONUSCO Dilemma', the International Crisis Group observed that after 20 years, the Security Council members are concerned that MONUSCO has cost too much for what it has achieved.[27]

HAITI: UNMIH, UNSMIH, UNTMIH, MIPONUH, MINUSTAH AND MINJUSTH—ONE STEP FORWARD AND TWO STEPS BACKWARD

Haiti has the distinction of being the first republic of people of African descent and the second oldest nation in the Americas. In 1956, Francois 'Papa Doc' Duvalier captured power in a coup. In 1957, he was elected president in a free election. He used his network of executioners called the 'Tonton Makouts' to intimidate his opponents to remain in power.[28] He was infamous for his cruelty and ran one of the most repressive regimes in the region. When Duvalier died in 1971, his son Jean-Claude Duvalier 'Baby Doc' assumed power. He continued in his father's footsteps and the rule of father and the son was known as a 'rule by thieves'.[29]

---

[26] Paddon, E. (2013, 18 April). *The perils of peacekeeping without politics: MONUC and MONUSCO in the DRC* (Briefing Paper). Rift Valley Institute.

[27] International Crisis Group. (2019, 4 December). *A new approach for the UN to stabilize the DR Congo* (Briefing No. 148). Multilateral Diplomacy. https://www.crisisgroup.org/africa/central-africa/democratic-republic-congo/b148-new-approach-un-stabilise-dr-congo

[28] Watkins, T., Valley, S., & Alley, T. (1995). *Political and economic history of Haiti.* https://www.sjsu.edu/faculty/watkins/haiti.htm

[29] *BBC News*. (2019c). *Haiti profile—Timeline*. https://www.bbc.com/news/world-latin-america-19548814; Watkins, T., Valley, S., & Alley, T. (1995). *Political and economic history of Haiti.* https://www.sjsu.edu/faculty/watkins/haiti.htm

In 1986, Haitians mounted a massive protest against Baby Doc's corrupt rule and he fled the country. Between 1986 and 1990, Haiti was ruled by short-lived military governments. In 1990, in an election conducted with the UN's assistance, the National Front for Change and Democracy's Jean-Bertrand Aristide was elected as the president. His government was overthrown by a military coup in 1991. The UN and the Organization of American States (OAS) condemned the coup and, in 1993, set up a joint International Civilian Mission in Haiti (MICIVIH). The mission was mandated to monitor and investigate human rights violations.[30]

In July 1993, the UN facilitated an agreement with the coup leaders that included Aristide's return to Haiti in October. Based on the agreement, the Security Council established the United Nations Mission in Haiti (UNMIH) to modernize Haitian army and set up a new police force. The military government did not comply with the agreement and forced UNMIH, MICIVIH and other international agencies to leave the country. In July 1994, the Security Council authorized the deployment of a US-led 20,000 strong multinational force to re-establish democratic rule. In October 1994, the military regime stepped down and Aristide returned. In 1995, UNMIH took over from the multinational force and continued the stabilization process including assisting in the conduct of election that elected Aristide again as the president.[31]

Starting in 1995 and till 2008, the UN deployed (excluding MICIVIH and UNMIH) five peacekeeping operations. The first was the United Nations Support Mission in Haiti (UNSMIH), from July 1996 to July 1997, and its mandate was to provide assistance to the Haitian authorities in the professionalization of the Haitian National Police (HNP) and to assist the Haitian authorities in maintaining a secure and stable environment. The second was the United Nations Transition Mission in Haiti (UNTMIH), from July 1997 to November 1997, to assist the Government of Haiti by supporting and contributing to the professionalization of the HNP. The third was the United

---

[30] United Nations. (2015). *Haiti background: Summary*. https://peacekeeping.un.org/en/mission/past/unmihbackgr1.html.

[31] Ibid.

Nations Civilian Police Mission in Haiti (MIPONUH), from December 1997 to March 2000, to continue assisting the Government of Haiti in the professionalization of the HNP. The fourth was the United Nations Stabilisation Mission in Haiti (MINUSTAH), from 2004 to 2017, and it aimed at restoring a secure and stable environment, promoting the political process, strengthening the Haitian government institutions and rule of law structures as well as promoting and protecting human rights. The fifth was the United Nations Mission for Justice Support in Haiti (MINJUSTH), from October 2017 to March 2018, that aimed to further develop HNP and strengthen the rule of law institutions, including the justice systems and prisons, and to promote and protect human rights.

United Nations Stabilisation Mission in Haiti

MINUSTAH, which ran from 2004 to 2017, was the largest and the longest mission deployed in Haiti. The mission cost more than US$7 billion.[32]

In January–February 2004, President Aristide was forced into exile the second time due to massive protests against his government. The country was in a crisis. The Haitian National Police Force disintegrated, and the country was under the grip of armed thugs. MINUSTAH's first priority was restoring order and creating conditions for the initiation of the political process.[33]

By 2007, MINUSTAH had contributed to stabilizing the situation. The election was conducted and the reformed HNP showed positive signs including removal of more than 1,000 rogue officers from the force. The Secretary-General, in his 2009 report to the Security Council, noted that significant advancement was made in the areas of political dialogue and elections, extension of state authority, ensuring

---

[32] Danticat, E. (2017, 19 October). A new chapter for the disastrous United Nations mission in Haiti? *The New Yorker.* https://www.newyorker.com/news/news-desk/a-new-chapter-for-the-disastrous-united-nations-mission-in-haiti

[33] Maguire, R. (2009, November). *USI peace briefing: What role for the United Nations in Haiti?* United States Institute of Peace. https://www.usip.org/sites/default/files/haiti_united_nations_pb_0.pdf

of stability and rule of law and human rights. He also noted that not much progress was made in social and economic development.[34]

The 2010 Earthquake

In January 2010, Haiti was hit by an earthquake causing death and devastation. Nearly three million people were affected by the quake, and the death toll ranged between 100,000 and 160,000. The quake also caused extensive damage to residences and commercial buildings. The UNICEF issued a report after one year and estimated that more than one million people remain displaced under unsustainable living conditions.[35]

Immediately after the earthquake, Haiti faced another major health crisis with an outbreak of cholera. Till June 2011, Haiti's health ministry had recorded 555,300 cases and 7,260 deaths. The cholera source was attributed to the UN's Nepalese peacekeepers camp.[36] The cholera outbreak and the slow pace of relief and reconstruction after the quake contributed to reinforcing Haitians' negative view of MINUSTAH. However, MINUSTAH, during its presence, significantly diminished political violence and dominance of organized armed gangs. It facilitated peaceful elections and created conditions for the democratic process, which was historical.[37]

Haiti's transition from many years of authoritarian rule (one-man rule) to democratic structure was compounded by extreme inequality, poverty and the absence of credible state institutions. MINUSTAH's major challenge was about sustaining the gains made in the political

---

[34] United Nations. (2009, 1 September). *Report of the secretary general on the United Nations stabilization mission in Haiti.* United Nations Security Council, S/2009/439. https://www.securitycouncilreport.org/un-documents/document/haiti-s-2009-439.php

[35] United Nations Children's Fund. (2011, 11 January). *Children in Haiti: One year after—The long road from relief to recovery.* http://www.unicefusa.org/assets/pdf/Children-in-Haiti-One-Year-After.pdf

[36] International Crisis Group. (2012, 22 August). *Towards a post-MINUSTAH Haiti: Making an effective transition* (Report No. 44). https://www.crisisgroup.org/latin-america-caribbean/haiti/towards-post-minustah-haiti-making-effective-transition

[37] Ibid.

and security sectors by contributing to improvements in the social and economic conditions of the people. After the end of MINUSTAH's presence, the challenge still continues.[38]

SIERRA LEONE: UNAMSIL, UNIOSIL AND UNIPSIL—A SUCCESS STORY AFTER INTERVENTION BY ITS FORMER COLONIAL POWER

Sierra Leone became independent in 1961 and was governed by elected governments. In 1967, Siaka Stevens' government was overthrown in a military coup. He returned to power in 1968 following another coup, declared Sierra Leone a republic and appointed himself as its Executive President. The country was a one-party state, and Stevens' All People's Congress remained the only legal political party. Stevens and his cronies benefitted enormously from the diamond trade, and corruption was chronic. In 1985, Stevens nominated the head of the army Joseph Momoh as his successor. The country faced economic and social crisis. The 1980s saw the fall in commodity prices, and Sierra Leone's economy took a hit. The corruption and cronyism meant that the revenue from the sale of diamonds did not reach the state coffers, and black marketers associated with the government profited from it. The Bretton Woods Institutions' conditions that led to liberalization of the economy resulted in devaluation of its currency and hyperinflation. The government reduced its funding on health and education, among others, impacting the living conditions of the middle class and the poor. The two parties that dominated Sierra Leon's politics since independence did not have ideological or policy differences, but their differences were based on patronage networks. Sierra Leone People's Party (SLPP) supported the Mendes of the south and the All People's Congress (APC) party supported the Temnes of the north. These divisions became more acute as economic and social conflicts erupted in the country.[39]

[38] Ibid.

[39] Kandeh, J. D. (1992, April). Politicization of ethnic identities in Sierra Leone. *African Studies Review, 35*(1), 81–99. https://www.cambridge.org/core/journals/african-studies-review/article/politicization-of-ethnic-identities-in-sierra-leone/9C608170100D-0F3B576C8495128AAEB0

In 1991, the Revolutionary United Front (RUF), led by Foday Sankoh and based in Liberia, started a rebellion and captured towns bordering Liberia. In 1992, Valentine Strasser in a military coup toppled Momoh's government. In January 1996, Julius Maada Bio removed Strasser in a coup. The UN, OAU and the ECOWAS mediated with the military rulers to restore civilian rule in the country. In February 1996, parliamentary and presidential elections were held, and Alhaji Ahmad Tejan Kabbah won the election. RUF boycotted the elections. In November, Kabbah and RUF signed an agreement to end the hostilities. In May 1997, in a third coup, Johnny Koroma removed Kabbah and became the head of the state. Koroma joined hands with Foday Sankoh. In February 1998, the Nigeria-led ECOMOG forces defeated the rebels, and in March, Kabbah returned to Freetown. In January 1999, RUF seized parts of Freetown, and the ECOMOG troops after bitter fighting pushed them out.[40]

Revolutionary United Front's Atrocities

During the 1998 and January 1999 offensives, the RUF forces committed unimaginable atrocities against civilians. RUF was notorious for its practice of hacking the limbs of children and adults. Rebels systematically killed and raped civilians. It abducted young women and girls and sexually abused them. This was a war in which the civilians were targets not collateral victims.[41]

UNOMSIL and UNAMASIL

In March 1998, after Kabbah reclaimed his power, the Security Council deployed the United Nations Observer Mission in Sierra

---

[40] Gascoigne, B. (2005). *History of Sierra Leone: Slavery and freedom: 17th–19th century*. http://www.historyworld.net/wrldhis/plaintexthistories.asp?historyid=ad45

[41] Aline, L. (2008, 5 March). *Sierra Leone: List of extremely violent events perpetrated during the war, 1991–2002*. Mass Violence and Resistance (Online). https://www.sciencespo.fr/mass-violence-war-massacre-resistance/en/document/sierra-leone-list-extremely-violent-events-perpetrated-during-war-1991-2002; Human Rights Watch. (1999). *Shocking war crimes in Sierra Leone: New testimonies on mutilation, rape of civilians*. https://www.hrw.org/news/1999/06/24/shocking-war-crimes-sierra-leone

Leone (UNOMSIL). The mission was deployed with 70 military observers. UNOMSIL's office was evacuated when the RUF forces attacked Freetown in December 1998, and in January 1999, UNOMSIL personnel too were evacuated from the country.

In July 1999, Kabbah and Sankoh entered into an agreement in Lomé, Togo. The controversial agreement provided for power-sharing between Sankoh and the elected Kabbah government. Sankoh was offered the post of vice-president and control over the ministry dealing with diamond trade. The deal offered amnesty to rebel forces. The United Nations signed the deal as a witness with an explicit reservation that the United Nations does not accept immunity for war crimes and crimes against humanity.[42]

Human rights advocates opposed the blanket amnesty given to the rebels who had committed brutal crimes. Such an amnesty was also generally not permitted under international law. However, at the national level, it was accepted as an inevitable factor for ending the war.[43]

After the Lomé agreement was signed, in August 1999, the Security Council authorized UNMOSIL's expansion with additional 140 military observers. It also authorized the presence of civil, political, civil affairs, human rights and child protection officers. In September 1999, the Security Council authorized a larger mission, the United Nations Mission in Sierra Leone (UNAMSIL), with 6,000 peacekeepers including 260 military observers.

Despite the agreement, Sankoh did not disarm his forces. In April 2000, the rebels attacked the UN and kidnapped 300 members of the UN force. Britain militarily intervened, and the rebels were driven out. Sankoh was arrested. The situation remained tense with the RUF rebels, and Koroma's forces engaged in violent attacks against

---

[42] United Nations. (1999,12 July). *Peace agreement between the government of Sierra Leone and the revolutionary United Front of Sierra Leone.* S/1999/777. https://peacemaker.un.org/sierraleone-lome-agreement99

[43] Hayner, P. (2007). *Report: Negotiating peace in Sierra Leone: Confronting the justice challenge.* Centre for Humanitarian Dialogue. https://www.files.ethz.ch/isn/55192/SierraLeoneReportrevise_1207.pdf

the government. They controlled 60 per cent of the country and the diamond mines.[44]

The Security Council increased UNAMSIL's forces, and in 2002, there were 17,500 peacekeepers. In January 2002, President Kabbah signed a peace treaty with the rebels and the war officially ended. In the elections held in May 2002, Kabbah won with a massive 70 per cent vote.

Despite the false start with breakdown of the accord including the kidnapping of its forces, UNAMSIL managed to become a success story. UNAMSIL's major achievement was the disarmament of rebel forces in less than a year. It assisted the government in organizing presidential and parliamentary elections, four months after the combatants were disarmed. The mission facilitated the reintegration of ex-combatants and assisted in resettling of returnees and internally displaced persons. It played an important role in reviving the civil administration and in establishing the government's effective authority throughout the country. The mission assisted the government in setting up the Special Court for Sierra Leone to try those responsible for war crimes and the Truth and Reconciliation Commission to bring about reconciliation. Sierra Leone was the first country where for the first time national and international judges jointly conducted the trials on war crimes. The Special Court was the first to indict a sitting president, Charles Taylor.[45]

The Truth and Reconciliation Commission functioned from 2002 to 2004. An insider view of the Commission was that the Commission was able to achieve justice for victims despite limited human and other resources.[46]

---

[44] Gascoigne, B. (2005). *History of Sierra Leone: Slavery and freedom: 17th–19th century.* http://www.historyworld.net/wrldhis/plaintexthistories.asp?historyid=ad45

[45] International Center for Transitional Justice. (2012). *Exploring the legacy of the special court for Sierra Leone.* https://www.ictj.org/sites/default/files/subsites/scsl-legacy/about-project/

[46] Mahony, C., & Sooka, Y. (2015). The truth about the truth: Insider reflections on the Sierra Leonean truth and reconciliation commission. In K. Ainley, R. Friedman, & C. Mahony (Eds.), *Evaluating transitional justice* (pp. 35–54). Palgrave Macmillan.

A UN report attributed UNAMSIL's success to political will and commitment of the parties.[47] The rebels had opposed the mission, and the British forces had intervened to create conditions for the mission to function. The report also stated that the support and pressure from the international community contributed to its success. However, Mahoney and Sooka noted that the UN responded to the war-weary Sierra Leones and did not address issues such as role of external players, the economic crisis aggravated by the Bretton Woods Institutions' interventions and the internal divisions based on regional and ethnic identities.[48]

LIBYA[49]: UNSMIL—INITIAL OPTIMISM, FALSE SENSE OF EUPHORIA AND DESCENT INTO CHAOS

In 1951, Libya achieved independence under King Idris al-Sanussi. In 1969, Col. Mohamed Qadhafi deposed King Idris in a military coup. Qadhafi ruled the next 42 years under a system of government called 'state of the masses'.[50] The 2010 demand for democratization that happened in the region called the 'Arab Spring' impacted Libya too. In February 2011, in the city of Benghazi, relatives of more than 1,200 prisoners, massacred in Abu Salim prison in 1996 by Qadhafi, planned a protest. The Qadhafi regime responded by arresting their lawyer and it ignited the Libyan revolution. Qadhafi deployed massive military forces to suppress the protests that emerged in Benghazi and other cities. In March 2011, the UN Security Council authorized a no-fly zone and 'all necessary measures' to protect civilians, giving rise to NATO airstrikes. In September, the National Transitional Council (NTC) was admitted as a member of the UN General Assembly

---

[47] United Nations. (2003). *Today's peacekeepers: UNAMSIL: The story behind the success in Sierra Leone.* International Day of United Nations Peacekeepers, 29 May 2003, Press Kit Fact Sheet 10. https://www.un.org/en/events/peacekeepersday/2003/docs/sierraleone.htm

[48] Britain was fully involved at various stages of the conflict to safeguard its interest in the diamond trade.

[49] The author was the director of UNSMIL Human Rights Division between October 2011 and November 2012.

[50] *BBC News.* (2011). *Libya profile: Timeline.* https://www.bbc.com/news/world-africa-13755445

recognizing it as the legitimate government of Libya. On 20 October 2011, Qadhafi was captured and killed. NTC announced the liberation of Libya from Qadhafi's forces.[51]

United Nations Support Mission in Libya

In September 2011, the Security Council established the United Nations Support Mission in Libya (UNSMIL). Unlike most UN peace-keeping operations, the Libyan mission benefitted from early planning process. While the war was ongoing, the UN Secretary-General appointed Ian Martin in late April 2011 as the Special Adviser to coordinate the planning process. The Secretary-General also appointed Abdul llah al-Khatib as his Special Envoy to mediate a peaceful transition. Ian Martin and the Special Envoy engaged with NTC and international actors on the political process. NTC consistently identified three priority areas for UN assistance in the post-conflict period. The first was assistance in organizing democratic elections; the second was advice on reforming the security forces including the police, integration of revolutionary fighters and taking control of Qadhafi's weapons; the third was concerning transitional justice, protection of human rights and setting up the rule of law institutions.[52]

Ian Martin proposed to the Security Council five principles that should guide the UN's post-conflict engagement in Libya. The first was national ownership; the second was speedy response to political developments; the third was effective coordination of international assistance so that the mission was not overburdened with numerous assessment visits; the fourth was acknowledging Libya's unique situation of material wealth and the absence of credible institutions; and lastly, in the words of Ian Martin, 'humility—not the most obvious characteristics of external agencies—but it is hard to dispute that the international community's record in post-conflict transitions displays at least as many mistakes as successes'.[53]

---

[51] Ibid.

[52] Martin, I. (2015). The United Nations role in the first year of the transition. In P. Cole & B. McQuinn (Eds.), *The Libyan revolution and its aftermath*. C. Hurst & Co.

[53] Ibid.

The Libyans' general aversion to international community and their wish to avoid domination by external actors led to NTC and others firmly rejecting 'boots on the ground',[54] which meant no deployment of armed or unarmed UN troops. UNSMIL was a political mission without peacekeepers on the ground.

July 2012 General Elections

The Libyan opposition was organized neither inside nor outside the country. There was no structure or leaders waiting to guide the transitional process. Qadhafi had ruthlessly put down all opposition inside and outside the country. NTC was an ad hoc arrangement whose members were not popular nationally and lacked a following that cut across regional or local identities. Lacking long-term legitimacy, NTC was keen to end the transitional process and handover the country to an elected government.[55] In August 2011, NTC's Constitutional Declaration proposed setting up an election commission within 90 days of the Declaration of Liberation and conducted an election for a 200-member General National Congress (GNC) within 240 days of the Declaration. It meant that elections had to be held in July 2012.

UNSMIL faced numerous challenges in helping to ensure that the elections were held in July as stipulated in the Declaration. NTC appointed an Electoral Committee (EC) only in November 2011. The drafting of electoral laws began only after the appointment of EC. EC and NTC had to make several contentious decisions about the type of electoral system (proportional or majoritarian), representation of regions in GNC, the role of political parties, delimitation of constituencies and special measures to promote the representation of women.[56]

On January 2012, NTC established a High National Election Commission (HNEC) that passed electoral laws. Since the country had no recent experience in conducting elections, HNEC had to

[54] Ibid.

[55] Vandewalle, D. (2015). Libya's uncertain revolution. In P. Cole & B. McQuinn (Eds.), *The Libyan revolution and its aftermath*. C. Hurst & Co.

[56] Martin, I. (2015). The United Nations role in the first year of the transition. In P. Cole & B. McQuinn (Eds.), *The Libyan revolution and its aftermath*. C. Hurst & Co.

do everything anew. Despite the challenges, with the assistance of UNSMIL, HNEC was confident to announce the election date as 7 July 2012. In Benghazi, Ajdabiya and Tuburq, some groups attempted to sabotage the elections by storming the election commission's offices and setting fire to ballot papers, and a helicopter transporting election materials was shot at killing an election commission worker.[57] Despite such incidents, the election was conducted without any major crisis. In numerous places, Libyans openly demonstrated their happiness in voting in an election, a first-time experience for most of them. The conduct of the election and the assumption of power by the elected GNC was remarkable and provided optimism for a smooth transition.[58]

Descent into Conflict and Chaos

The optimism generated by the elections did not last long. The government under the GNC faced many challenges. In September 2012, Islamist militants attacked the US Consulate in Benghazi, causing the deaths of Ambassador Christopher Stevens and three others. GNC, at the end of its two years' term, refused to disband, and in the elections held in 2014, a new parliament was elected. The unelected former members of GNC declared themselves as National Salvation Government and opposed the newly elected House of Representatives (HoR).[59] Amidst this turmoil, General Khalifa Haftar's forces based in the east, under the banner of Libyan National Army, attacked Islamist militant groups and captured large territories including oil fields.[60]

In 2014, Tobruk-based HoR and the Tripoli-based GNC engaged in armed conflict and the UN staff and other international actors were evacuated from Libya. In January 2016, the UN brokered a deal that

---

[57] Ibid., p. 127.

[58] Vandewalle, D. (2015). Libya's uncertain revolution. In P. Cole & B. McQuinn (Eds.), *The Libyan revolution and its aftermath*. C. Hurst & Co.

[59] In 2016, GNC announced its dissolution and set up the High Council of State.

[60] Haftar was a former Libyan Army Officer who lived in exile in the United States and was active during the 2011 revolution that deposed Qadhafi.

established the GoNU which was recognized by the international community. Despite international recognition, the GoNU is not yet able to assert its authority. The country continues to be divided across political, ideological, regional and tribal identities.

Libya's Transition to Democracy and Its Challenges

UNSMIL's leadership in the first year was sensitive and keen to ensure that the transition was Libyan led and Libyan owned. When the elections were held in July 2012, the Libyan civil society, UNSMIL staff and the international community were optimistic that Libya would succeed in its transition to democracy. However, the last eight years demonstrate that it was weighed down by the past (Qadhafi legacy) and the intervention by external actors in the transition process.

The Libyan revolution was part of the Arab Spring. However, unlike in Tunisia and Egypt, the revolution in Libya overhauled the state symbols and the modes of governance.[61] The collapse of the state in Libya was not unexpected, since Qadhafi did not build viable state institutions.[62] Qadhafi used oil wealth to pursue politics of patronage without any governance policy, and the population was dependent on government handouts.[63] The patronage politics undermined the sense of solidarity and cooperation and generated an exaggerated sense of entitlement. Post revolution, when the state collapsed, it became free for all. Through his patronage and terror, Qadhafi had ensured that the opposition was dysfunctional and kept under control within regional, tribal and ethnic groups. The latent tensions and demands of various groups that were suppressed by Qadhafi became dominant during and after the revolution. The assertion of identity and demands from western, southern and eastern regions complicated the transition process.[64]

---

[61] Cole, P., & McQuinn, B. (Eds.). (2015). *The Libyan Revolution and its aftermath.* C. Hurst & Co.

[62] Vandewalle, D. (2015). Libya's uncertain revolution. In P. Cole & B. McQuinn (Eds.), *The Libyan revolution and its aftermath.* C. Hurst & Co.

[63] Ibid.

[64] Ibid.

Qadhafi had also suppressed the Islamic groups. Post revolution, they emerged as victims under Qadhafi's rule, contested NTC's idea of Libya and feared the secularists within NTC. The Islamists controlled many of the armed groups that participated in the overthrow of Qadhafi and used those armed groups to pursue their agendas; for example, the armed groups, in May 2013, occupied several government buildings to pressure GNC for the adoption of 'political isolation' law.[65] They pushed for the adoption of this stringent law to oust Qadhafi-era officers. It brought under its purview not only national level officials but whole range of actors at various levels of the society. GNC, in May 2013, adopted the law with serious consequences for Libya's transitional process. The UN criticized the law as being expansive, vague and which could violate the civil and political rights of citizens.[66] Libyan Islamists saw the law as a means to consolidate their influence against the secularists. They wanted to avoid the fate of their brethren in Tunisia and Egypt where they were not able to consolidate their power despite electoral gains. The adoption of the law accelerated the tensions between those supporting and opposing the Islamists. The availability of arms ensured that the political conflict descended into a military-style confrontation.[67]

The post-Qadhafi Libya was confronted with regional, tribal and ideological divisions, and international actors exacerbated the situation with their meddling. Qatar and the UAE were openly involved in the conflict, with Qatar extending support to the Islamists and the UAE opposing it. France worked behind the scenes supporting one or another group. Khalifa Haftar's emergence and his attack against the Islamists further complicated the scene. Egypt and the UAE supported Khalifa Haftar's forces.[68] Turkey was fully involved in supporting the forces fighting against Haftar. Libyan war also witnessed large-scale use of mercenaries by external actors to support their Libyan parties.

[65] Wierda, M. (2015). Confronting Qadhafi's legacy: Transitional justice in Libya. In C. Peter & B. McQuinn (Eds.), *The Libyan revolution and its aftermath*. C. Hurst & Co.

[66] Ibid.

[67] Meiloud, A. (2015). *Foreign actors and the Libyan civil war*. Middle East Eye. https://www.middleeasteye.net/big-story/foreign-actors-and-libyan-civil-war

[68] Ibid.

What began as an internal conflict with international backers is on the verge of becoming a 'full-fledged proxy war'.[69]

In euphoria of the revolution, NTC underestimated the pulls and pressures of tribes, regional groups and Islamist movements in building the post-Qadhafi Libya. The 2012 election to a large extent created a false sense of optimism ignoring the fact that it takes years to rebuild national institutions in a fractured society.[70]

Briefing the Security Council on 19 May 2020, Stephanie Williams, UNSMIL's Acting Special Representative of the Secretary-General, alerted that due to conflict and economic distress, more than a million people were dependent on humanitarian assistance. Williams stated that foreign intervention has undermined the Libyan voices and called on the Security Council to apply consistent and credible pressure on regional and international actors meddling in Libya.[71]

[69] International Crisis Group. (2020, 29 January). *Honouring commitments to end Libya's Civil War*. Commentary/Middle East & North Africa. https://www.crisisgroup.org/middle-east-north-africa/north-africa/libya/honouring-commitments-end-libyas-civil-war

[70] Vandewalle, D. (2015). Libya's uncertain revolution. In P. Cole & B. McQuinn (Eds.), *The Libyan revolution and its aftermath*. C. Hurst & Co.

[71] United Nations. (2020). *Acting SRSG Stephanie Williams briefing to the security council—19 May 2020*. https://unsmil.unmissions.org/sites/default/files/acting_srsg_briefing_to_the_security_council_-_19_may_2020.pdf

Operations Deployed Post US-led Interventions

6

In both Afghanistan and Iraq, the UN deployed peacekeeping operations after the US-led interventions which are unique in the history of UN. The UN member states have intervened in many countries before and during peacekeeping operations to support the UN in its peace enforcement efforts. In the case of Iraq, the United States and its allies made unilateral intervention, and the UN peacekeeping operation was a postscript. In both these countries, the UN had previously set up observation missions. In May 1988, the UN set up Good Offices Mission in Afghanistan and Pakistan. In August 1988, the United Nations Iran–Iraq Military Observer Group was set up. These two missions were a 'simple interposition'[1] between the parties, and a full-fledged operation was set up after the United States intervened in both these countries.

Operation	Year	Purpose
United Nations Assistance Mission for Iraq (UNAMI)	2003– present	The UN Security Council did not authorize the March 2003 invasion and occupation of Iraq by the US-led coalition. Two months later, despite doubts about the legality of the war, the Security Council Resolution 1483 authorized the UN Assistance Mission in Iraq (UNAMI). In August 2003, a massive bombing at the UN headquarters killed 15 UN staff including its Special Representative Sérgio Vieira de Mello. The UN withdrew its staff and redeployed the mission in February 2004 and expanded its role in 2007.

[1] Hatto, R. (2013). From peacekeeping to peacebuilding: The evolution of the role of the United Nations in peace operations. *International Review of the Red Cross, 95*(891/892), 495–515. https://www.icrc.org/en/doc/assets/files/review/2013/irrc-891-892-hatto.pdf

Operation	Year	Purpose
		UNAMI's mandate is to advise and assist the government and people of Iraq. This includes advancing inclusive political dialogue and national reconciliation, assisting in the electoral process and in the planning for a national census, facilitating regional dialogue between Iraq and its neighbours and promoting the protection of human rights, judicial and legal reforms.[a]
United Nations Assistance Mission in Afghanistan (UNAMA)	2002–present	The 9/11 attack against the United States by the Al-Qaeda terrorists led to the US-led coalition's military action against the Taliban regime that had harboured Al-Qaeda in Afghanistan. After displacing the Taliban from power, they sponsored an Afghan peace conference in December 2001 that led to the establishment of an interim administration prior to convening a National Assembly (Loya Jirga) in June 2002.

In March 2002, the Security Council authorized the establishment of the United Nations Assistance Mission in Afghanistan (UNAMA). Its responsibilities include national reconciliation, human rights monitoring, rule of law, women's rights and humanitarian affairs and reconstruction efforts[b] |

Source: The author.

Note: [a]United Nations. (2003). *United Nations assistance mission for Iraq.* http://www.uniraq.com/index.php?option=com_k2&view=item&layout=item&id=943&lang=en

[b]Chesterman, S. (2002). *Tiptoeing through Afghanistan: The future of UN State-building.* International Peace Academy. United Nations Plaza. https://www.ipinst.org/2002/09/tiptoeing-through-afghanistan-the-future-of-un-statebuilding-simon-chesterman

AFGHANISTAN UNAMA: AFTER 18 YEARS OF UN PEACEKEEPING OPERATION—BACK TO SQUARE ONE

Afghanistan's modern history consists of numerous conflicts perpetrated by internal and external actors. The 1979 Soviet Union invasion of Afghanistan started the turmoil which is still gripping the country. The US-led support to Mujahideen groups against the Soviet occupation unleashed a war that led to the displacement of half the population of the country. In 1986, Najibullah became the head of a Soviet-backed regime. In 1988, the Soviet Union began pulling out its troops and completed the process in 1989. In 1992, Najibullah was toppled and a dreadful civil war ensued. In 1996, Taliban seized power and introduced a harsh Islamic system including banning women from work, prohibiting cultural programmes and entertainments and meting out severe Islamic punishments like stoning to death and amputations. The Mujahideen who fought against the Soviets morphed into people with various extreme Islamic tendencies and made Afghanistan their home. The Al-Qaeda, headed by Osama bin Laden from his base in Afghanistan, waged war against the United States and the Western countries. In 1999, the United States bombed Bin Laden's bases in Afghanistan and the UN imposed sanctions against the Taliban government. After the Al-Qaeda's 11 September 2001 attacks, the United States invaded Afghanistan and toppled Taliban. In December 2001, in UN-sponsored talks held in Bonn, Germany, Afghan groups minus the Taliban signed an agreement on modalities of governance of the country.[2]

United Nations Assistance Mission in Afghanistan

During the US-led invasion of Afghanistan, there were discussions at the UN Secretariat about the UN's role in the post-conflict period. Some within the UN considered that the UN would be made to bear the consequences of US intervention. Others considered it as an opportunity similar to Kosovo and East Timor to run a multidimensional mission to rebuild Afghanistan.[3]

In March 2002, the UN Security Council authorized the deployment of the United Nations Assistance Mission in Afghanistan (UNAMA). The US-led International Security Assistance Force (ISAF) continued

---

[2] *BBC News.* (2019). *Afghanistan profile: Timeline.* https://www.bbc.com/news/world-south-asia-12024253

[3] Chesterman, S. (2002). *Tiptoeing through Afghanistan: The future of UN State-building.* International Peace Academy. United Nations Plaza. https://www.ipinst.org/2002/09/tiptoeing-through-afghanistan-the-future-of-un-statebuilding-simon-chesterman

to be engaged in fighting the Taliban and other groups inimical to the Afghan government. UNAMA, therefore, did not include peacekeepers and was restricted to providing support to the Afghan government in the areas of national reconciliation, human rights (monitoring, reporting, investigating violations and recommending corrective action), rule of law (supporting the Judicial Commission established by the Bonn Agreement), the role of women (supporting women's rights and participation in society) and humanitarian affairs (coordinating UN relief, recovery and reconstruction efforts within the UN system and with the Afghan authorities).[4]

Under its first SRSG Lakhdar Brahimi, UNAMA pursued the principle that it should first and foremost strengthen Afghan capacity, both official and non-governmental. The Bonn Agreement had also provided a limited role to the UN in the post-conflict period.

After 18 Years

In 2020, the UN Secretary-General in his report to the Security Council stated that the security situation remained volatile.[5] It has been the case in the last 18 years. UNAMA began systematically documenting civilian casualties in 2009. Since then, it has documented more than 100,000 casualties with more than 35,000 killed and 65,000 injured.[6]

UNAMA, despite functioning in a dangerous security environment, pursued its mandated tasks. Along with others, it has contributed to the return of more than 2 million refugees. Children, particularly girls, began attending schools. After several decades of suppression, the civil society emerged with women finding their voices. The Afghan

---

[4] The Henry L. Stimson Center. (2002, June). *Rebuilding Afghanistan: The United Nations Assistance Mission in Afghanistan (UNAMA)*. Peace Operations Backgrounder. https://www.stimson.org/wp-content/files/file-attachments/UNAMAbackgrounder_1.pdf

[5] United Nations Assistance Mission in Afghanistan, & United Nations Human Rights Office of the High Commissioner. (2020, February). *Afghanistan: Protection of civilians in armed conflict 2019*. https://unama.unmissions.org/sites/default/files/executive_summary_-_afghanistan_protection_of_civilians_annual_report_2019_english.pdf

[6] Ibid.

people's pursuit to peace faced the challenges of violence by powerful regional warlords, resurgent Taliban and their violent activities, criminal activities related to drugs and the interference of international and regional actors.[7]

On 29 February 2020, the US government and the Taliban signed an agreement in Doha on the withdrawal of foreign troops and the Taliban guaranteed on preventing the terrorists using Afghanistan as a safe haven. It was followed by intra-Afghan talks to arrive at a settlement between the Taliban and the Afghan government. The civil society, particularly women's groups, fear that they would lose the historic gains they have made since 2002. Women have improved access to health care, and maternal mortality has halved from the Taliban period. More than 100,000 women attend university, and 3.5 million girls are enrolled in schools. The number of elected women in the parliament has increased, and 27 per cent of women hold civil service jobs.[8] UNAMA facilitated dialogue with more than 1,000 women regarding their vision for peace. In January 2020, a joint declaration by 100 women stressed that the gains of the past 18 years should be preserved, past atrocities should be addressed and the peace process should be victim centred.[9] There is a general feeling inside and outside Afghanistan that a peace deal between the Taliban and the Afghan government would jeopardize women's rights.[10]

In his report to the Security Council, the Secretary-General reiterated the importance of an inclusive Afghan-led process with meaningful participation of women, young people and minorities.[11] Ensuring such

[7] Zia-Zarifi, S. (2004). *Losing the peace in Afghanistan.* https://www.hrw.org/legacy/wr2k4/download/5.pdf

[8] International Crisis Group. (2020). *What will peace talks bode for Afghan Women?* https://www.crisisgroup.org/asia/south-asia/afghanistan/what-will-peace-talks-bode-afghan-women

[9] Rutting, T. (2019, 15 April). *Women and Afghan peace talks: 'Peace consensus' gathering left Afghan women without reassurance.* Report War and Peace, Afghanistan Analysts Network. https://www.afghanistan-analysts.org/en/reports/war-and-peace/women-and-afghan-peace-talks-peace-consensus-gathering-left-afghan-women-unassured/

[10] Ibid.

[11] Ibid.

a meaningful peace process would be a major challenge, particularly the absence of trust between the Taliban and the Afghan government and the lack of preparations on both sides to negotiate on the basis of a vision for the country.[12]

In 2002, the United States had intervened to topple the Taliban. In 2020, it has reached an agreement with the same Taliban so that it could withdraw from Afghanistan. It is possible that the UN will have to begin all over again.

IRAQ: UNAMI—LEGITIMIZING AN ILLEGAL WAR

In 2003, the United States and the United Kingdom invaded Iraq on the pretext of dismantling Saddam Hussein's so-called weapons of mass destruction. The Security Council did not authorize the invasion of Iraq. The late Kofi Annan, who was the UN Secretary-General during the Iraq War, said that the invasion was not sanctioned by the UN Security Council and was illegal.[13]

The United States and the UK, despite the Security Council's refusal to endorse the invasion, wanted the UN to be involved after the fall of Saddam Hussein. They wanted the UN's assistance to provide legitimacy after the post-invasion chaos in Iraq and the widespread criticism on it. There were two opinions about the UN's involvement in a situation created by an illegal war. Some believed that the UN could be a bridge between the United States, the UK and the Iraqi people and contribute to the withdrawal of foreign forces. On the other hand, some thought that the UN's involvement would discredit the organization and that it should not be identified with an illegal war and occupation.[14]

---

[12] International Crisis Group. (2020c, 30 March). *Are the Taliban serious about peace negotiations?* (Briefing Note). https://www.crisisgroup.org/asia/south-asia/afghanistan/are-taliban-serious-about-peace-negotiations

[13] MacAskill, E., & Borger, J. (2004, 16 September). Iraq war was illegal and breached UN charter, says Annan. *The Guardian*. https://www.theguardian.com/world/2004/sep/16/iraq.iraq

[14] Global Policy Forum. (2007). *UN role in Iraq*. https://archive.globalpolicy.org/security/issues/iraq/unindex.htm

Under pressure from the United States, two months after the war, the Security Council adopted a resolution authorizing the United Nations Assistance Mission for Iraq (UNAMI). Kofi Annan appointed Sérgio Vieira de Mello as his Special Representative to head UNAMI. On 19 August, a devastating bomb that targeted the UN headquarters in Baghdad killed 15 UN staff including de Mello. More than 100 people were wounded. The UN pulled out of Iraq after the incident.[15]

In February 2004, again under US pressure, UNAMI returned to Iraq to assist in the establishment of an interim government. The UN Staff Council opposed the UN staff's deployment in Iraq. Despite the Staff Council's protest, the Secretary-General Ban Ki-moon supported an increased UN role in the country.[16] In 2007, the Security Council expanded UNAMI's role to include

> provision of advice, support and assistance to the Government and the people of Iraq on advancing inclusive political dialogue and national and community-level reconciliation; and on assistance to the electoral process; as well as facilitating regional dialogue and cooperation between Iraq and its neighbours; promoting accountability and the protection of human rights and judicial and legal reform; promoting gender equality; and promoting coordination and facilitating, in coordination with the Government of Iraq delivery in the humanitarian and development areas.[17]

In January 2005, elections were held for a Transitional Assembly. In December 2005, the Iraqis elected a parliament and a government. Starting in 2005, the Sunni sectarian violence intensified. In 2011, the US troops withdrew from Iraq. In 2013, sectarian conflict intensified again.[18] Between 2014 and 2017, the Islamic State of Iraq and the Levant (ISIL) overran Iraqi forces and captured large parts of the country. UNAMI described the consequences of ISIL's capture

---

[15] Ibid.

[16] Ibid.

[17] United Nations. (2003). *United Nations assistance mission for Iraq.* http://www.uniraq.com/index.php?option=com_k2&view=item&layout=item&id=943&lang=en

[18] *BBC News.* (2018). *Iraq profile: Timeline.* https://www.bbc.com/news/world-middle-east-14546763

of territory in 2014 as contributing to systematic and egregious violations including killing of ethnic and religious minorities and rape of women. ISIL also attacked infrastructure including hospitals and schools.[19]

At the end of 2017, Iraqi forces, with the assistance of the United States, Iran and other countries, defeated ISIL. UNAMI recorded more than 85,000 casualties between 2014 and 2017.[20] In 2019, widespread protests erupted in Bagdad and other cities against corruption and mismanagement. The protesters called for institutional reforms to end the chronic corruption. Unlike previous protests, this time, it was extensive and sustained itself for a longer period. The government responded with force, killing more than 450 people.[21]

In 2017, the Security Council requested the Secretary-General to conduct an independent assessment of UNAMI. Two independent consultants conducted the assessment and submitted the report in November 2017. The report noted that Iraqis appreciate the work of UNAMI. However, UNAMI lacked robust strategy and operational effectiveness.[22] The assessment report provided some practical suggestions for improving the structure and strategic planning. However, UNAMI's challenges are not restricted to its internal strategic planning process or the structure. UNAMI continues to be burdened with the US-led invasion and the chaotic administration that followed it. Iraq is confronted with internal and external fault lines. Internally, the issues are sectarian conflict, marginalization of the Sunni population, chronic corruption and lack of basic services.

---

[19] UNAMI/OHCHR. (2014). *Report on the protection of civilians in the non international armed conflict in Iraq: 5 June to 5 July 2014.* https://www.ohchr.org/Documents/Countries/IQ/UNAMI_OHCHR_POC%20Report_FINAL_18July2014A.pdf

[20] Ibid.

[21] ICG-International Crisis Group. (2020). *Rescuing Iraq from the Iran-U.S. crossfire* (Document #2022398). European Country of Origin Information Network. https://www.ecoi.net/en/document/2022398.html

[22] United Nations. (2017, 20 November). *Letter dated 15 November 2017 from the Secretary-General addressed to the President of the Security Council.* Security Council, S/2017/966. http://www.securitycouncilreport.org/atf/cf/%7B65BFCF9B-6D27-4E9C-8CD3-CF6E4FF96FF9%7D/s_2017_966.pdf

Externally, Iraq has to contend with Iran-US tensions, conflicts in Syria and Yemen, tension between Iran and its Gulf neighbours, Israel and its role in the region, Kurdish question and Turkey. As observed by an International Crisis Group report, 'for reasons of geography and history, Iraq finds itself squarely in the path of the gathering storm'.[23]

---

[23] International Crisis Group. (2019, 29 August). *Iraq: Evading the gathering storm* (Crisis Group Middle East Briefing No. 70). https://www.crisisgroup.org/mirldle-east-north-africa/gulf-and-arabian-peninsula/iraq/070-iraq-evading-gathering-sto.m

Second Phase in the Evolution of Peacekeeping Operations Doctrine*

1992–2015

Since the end of the Cold War, peacemaking, peacekeeping and post-conflict peacebuilding in civil wars have become the operational face of the UN in maintaining international peace and security.[1] After the end of the Cold War, in 1991, the international community responded collectively against Iraq's aggression against Kuwait. Apartheid, which had been a blot on the community of nations, also met its demise. It was an optimistic period with major Western powers and others, reiterating their support for collective security.

The Security Council in its summit held on 31 January 1992 asked the newly appointed Secretary-General, Boutros Boutros-Ghali, to submit a document proposing ideas for strengthening the UN's peacekeeping, preventive diplomacy, peacemaking and peacebuilding capacities.[2]

---

* The UN does not use the term 'doctrine'. Due to lack of consensus on institutionalizing peace operations, states have left it to the Security Council and the General Assembly's Special Committee on Peacekeeping to make ad hoc pronouncements on various elements of peace operations.

[1] United Nations. (2004, 2 December). *A more secure world: Our shared responsibility*. Report of the High-level Panel on Threats, Challenges and Change, A/59/565. https://www.un.org/en/ga/search/view_doc.asp?symbol=A/59/565

[2] United Nations. (1992). *The responsibility of the Security Council in the maintenance of international peace and security*. https://www.un.org/en/sc/repertoire/89-92/Chapter%208/GENERAL%20ISSUES/Item%2028_SC%20respons%20in%20maint%20IPS.pdf

In June 1992, the Secretary-General published 'An Agenda for Peace'.[3] He recalled that since the creation of the UN in 1945, over 100 major conflicts around the world have left some 20 million people dead. The UN was rendered powerless to deal with many of these crises because of the vetoes—279 of them—cast in the Security Council, which demonstrated the divisions of that period.[4] The Secretary-General identified the UN's aims in the areas of peace and security as prevention through diplomacy, peacemaking aimed at resolving issues that contributed to the conflict, peacekeeping to preserve peace and assist in the implementation of agreements, and peacebuilding by rebuilding the institutions and the infrastructure.[5]

'An Agenda for Peace'[6] departed from Hammarskjöld's traditional concept regarding consent of the parties prior to the deployment of a mission and defined peacekeeping as 'the deployment of a United Nations presence in the field, hitherto with the consent of all the parties concerned'.[7] By using the term 'hitherto',[8] it implied that peacekeeping operations could be deployed without the consent of the host state. The document challenged the traditional peacekeeping practice of the use of force only for self-defence and proposed that UN should have the option of military action to ensure its credibility and as guarantor of international security.[9] The Secretary-General went further and recommended that the Security Council consider the utilization of peace enforcement units in clearly defined circumstances and with their terms of reference specified in advance.[10] He

---

[3] United Nations. (1992, 17 June). *An agenda for peace: Preventive diplomacy, peacemaking and peace-keeping* (Report of the Secretary-General pursuant to the statement adopted by the Summit Meeting of the Security Council on 31 January 1992, A/47/277–S/24111). https://www.un.org/ruleoflaw/files/A_47_277.pdf

[4] Ibid.

[5] Ibid., para 15.

[6] Ibid.

[7] Ibid., para 20.

[8] Ibid.

[9] Ibid, para 43.

[10] Ibid., para 44.

proposed peace enforcement to assist peacekeeping forces when they lack capacity to restore or maintain ceasefire. The Secretary-General introduced the concept of preventive deployment to alleviate suffering and to limit or control violence. He reminded the Security Council of the non-establishment of the Military Staff Committee stipulated under the Charter [Article 43 and 47(2)]. He recommended that its establishment should be a part of the use of coercive powers under Chapter VII and not as a part of planning or conduct of peacekeeping operations.[11]

The Secretary-General's 'An Agenda for Peace'[12] document foresaw the growing demand for deploying multidimensional missions. He identified tasks of peacekeeping operations as disarming warring parties and restoration of order, custody and possible destruction of weapons, repatriating refugees, support for security personnel, monitoring elections, protection of human rights and strengthening governmental institutions.[13]

After nearly four decades, the UN in 1992 created the Department of Peacekeeping Operations (DPKO) as one of the four assigned departments that would report directly to the Secretary-General. The number of Military Advisers (MILAD) in DPKO was increased. In addition, the Secretary-General established a Policy and Analysis Cell and a Situation Centre to monitor information from the missions around the clock every day.[14]

The 1990s saw the deployment of several missions, and some of them were multidimensional.[15] UNTAC was the first large multidimensional

---

[11] Ibid., paras 42 and 43.

[12] Ibid.

[13] Ibid., para 55.

[14] Findlay, T. (2002). *The use of force in UN peace operations*. Stockholm International Peace Research Institute (SIPRI). Oxford University Press. https://www.sipri.org/sites/default/files/files/books/SIPRI02Findlay.pdf

[15] Countries where major missions were deployed in the 1990s: Angola, Cambodia, East Timor, El Salvador, Western Sahara, Somalia, Eritrea, Mozambique, Liberia, Haiti, Rwanda, Former Yugoslavia, Guatemala, Central African Republic, Kosovo, Sierra Leone and Congo.

mission in the post-Cold War era. The decade ended with the deployment of UNTAET, another large multidimensional mission. Both these missions were successful despite the complexities involved and the challenges they faced in implementing their respective mandates. El Salvador, Guatemala, Namibia and Mozambique were other success stories. However, the decade is also remembered for the following failed missions: UNPROFOR in former Yugoslavia, UNAMIR and UNOSOM I and UNOSOM II.

In 1991, the collapse of the Somalian state and the violence unleashed by warlords led to an unprecedented humanitarian disaster in which an estimated 300,000 Somalis died and about two million fled the country with similar numbers internally displaced. In 1992, the UN intervened to ensure humanitarian assistance. After the deployment of the UN forces, the militias targeted the UN, killed the peacekeepers and looted humanitarian supplies. The Security Council authorized the deployment of UNITAF to use force to deter the warlords and their forces. Despite UNITAF's presence, violence continued and Somali armed groups killed and injured several US troops. By 1995, the US and the UN withdrew from Somalia.

The collapse of former Yugoslavia in 1990 resulted in a war between different components of the former state. The Serbs waged war against both Croatia and Bosnia and Herzegovina that had proclaimed independence after the collapse of Yugoslavia. In February 1992, the Security Council authorized the deployment of UNPROFOR. Initially, it was set up to deal with the Croatian and Serbian conflict. The Security Council extended its operational mandate to cover Croatia, Bosnia and Herzegovina, Macedonia and Montenegro and Serbia. In April 1993, Serbian forces captured large parts of eastern Bosnia and created a humanitarian crisis. The Security Council responded by declaring Srebrenica in Bosnia as a 'safe area' and free from any armed attack.[16] UNPROFOR came to be associated with the July 1995 Serb massacre of Bosniaks in Srebrenica 'safe area' under the protection of the UN Dutch forces.[17]

---

[16] United Nations. (1999).

[17] Ibid.

In Rwanda, in the mid-1960s, more than 300,000 minority Tutsis fled to countries in the neighbouring region to escape the Hutu-dominated Rwandan government. In 1990, the Tutsi RPF invaded Rwanda, and in 1993, in Arusha, Tanzania, both parties signed a peace deal. In October 1993, the Security Council authorized the deployment of UNAMIR to assist in the implementation of the peace deal. The mission had a limited mandate and did not include recovery of arms as proposed by the Secretary-General. In April 1994, RPF launched a major offensive. The extremist Hutu elements embarked on a systematic massacre of Tutsis and moderate Hutus in Rwanda leading to genocide.

> Approximately 800,000 people were killed during the 1994 genocide in Rwanda. The systematic slaughter of men, women and children which took place over the course of about 100 days between April and July of 1994 will forever be remembered as one of the most abhorrent events of the twentieth century.[18]

Post-Cold War, the UN peacekeeping operations' mandates referred to humanitarian considerations as the basis for their deployment. The UN's interventions in Somalia, former Yugoslavia and Rwanda came under the ambit of humanitarian interventions.[19] The Security Council in its resolutions 770 (1992) for the former Yugoslavia and 794 (1992) for Somalia authorized the UN forces to use 'all measures necessary' to deliver humanitarian aid to the people.[20] All three missions, in various ways, faced the problematic issue of the use of force other than for self-defence.

---

[18] Carlsson, I., Sung-Joo, H., & Kupolati, R. M. (1999). *Report of the independent inquiry into the actions of the United Nations during the 1994 genocide in Rwanda.* United Nations.

[19] Roberts, A. (2000). Humanitarian issues and agencies as triggers for international military action. *International Review of the Red Cross, 82*(839), 673–698. https://www.cambridge.org/core/journals/international-review-of-the-red-cross/article/abs/humanitarian-issues-and-agencies-as-triggers-for-international-military-action/C7D1B849CDA3DDFCFB7DC34EA978380C

[20] Findlay, T. (2002). *The use of force in UN peace operations.* Stockholm International Peace Research Institute (SIPRI). Oxford University Press. https://www.sipri.org/sites/default/files/files/books/SIPRI02Findlay.pdf

In Srebrenica, a few hundred lightly armed UN forces protected 'safe areas' with the threat of NATO airstrikes as a ploy.[21] The concept of 'safe areas' was vague.[22] In fact, the UNPROFOR Force Commander opposed the concept of establishing safe areas other than by agreement between the belligerents. Protecting the safe areas, in his view, was a job for a combat-capable, peace enforcement operation.[23] In Rwanda, UNAMIR lacked resources, military capacity and coordination. It failed to play a proactive and assertive role in dealing with the emerging situation.[24] In Somalia, violence became more complex and intense once the Security Council decided to enforce Chapter VII's provisions and deploy international force.[25]

Subsequent to their failure, the mandates of UNOSOM I and UNOSOM II, UNAMIR and UNPROFOR came under scrutiny and were considered responsible for the failure of these missions. Commenting on the failure of UNPROFOR, Secretary-General Kofi Annan opined that 'UNPROFOR mandate [became] rhetorically more robust than the Force itself'.[26]

The Secretary-General in his report on the fall of Srebrenica noted that peacekeeping operations must not be used as a substitute for the lack of political consensus in responding to military conflicts. Peacekeepers must not be allowed to use their peacekeeping tools to implement ill-defined mandate of the international community against belligerents.[27]

---

[21] United Nations. (1999).

[22] Ibid.

[23] United Nations. (1999, 15 November). *Report of the Secretary-General pursuant to general assembly resolution 53/35: The fall of Srebrenica*. A/54/549. https://www.refworld.org/docid/3ae6afb34.html

[24] Carlsson, I., Sung-Joo, H., & Kupolati, R. M. (1999). *Report of the independent inquiry into the actions of the United Nations during the 1994 genocide in Rwanda.* United Nations.

[25] Duică, A.-F. (2016). *The role of the United Nations security council in the evolution of peacekeeping* (Case Studies: Congo and Somalia). University of Bucharest. https://www.academia.edu/31629054/The_role_of_the_United_Nations_Security_Council_in_the_evolution_of_peacekeeping_Case_Studies_The_Congo_and_Somalia

[26] Ibid.

[27] United Nations. (1999, 15 November). *Report of the Secretary-General pursuant to general assembly resolution 53/35: The fall of Srebrenica*. A/54/549. https://www.refworld.org/docid/3ae6afb34.html

The experience in the first five years of the 1990s, particularly after the debacles faced by some peacekeeping operations, led the Secretary-General in 1995 to issue a Supplement to his 1992 'An Agenda for Peace'.[28] Unlike the 1992 document, the Secretary-General in the 1995 upgrade reiterated the importance of the three principles of peacekeeping operations: 'the consent of the parties, impartiality and the non-use of force except in self-defence'. He also stated that the missions succeeded when these principles were respected.[29]

After the sobering experience of peacekeeping operations in the early 1990s, the Secretary-General acknowledged the challenges involved in dealing with increasing intrastate conflicts and engaging with militias with little discipline or chain of command. The UN had to deal with collapsed states and the ensuing chaos and violence against civilians. Another qualitative change was the role of the UN forces to protect humanitarian operations impeded by armed groups. The changing situation led to the authorization of the use of force other than for self-defence but for humanitarian purposes, restricted to local levels, and not to bring an end to war. The Secretary-General expressed concern that the UN's stature and credibility might be affected when the use of force is assigned to the Member States. He also referred to the potential danger of Member States manipulating enforcement role and claiming legitimacy for the use of force in a manner not envisaged by the Security Council.

He acknowledged the difference between peacekeeping and peace enforcement and stressed that force is not a solution for ensuring settlements. He alerted the dangers of blurring the difference between peacekeeping and peace enforcement. The Secretary-General reminded the Member States that solving international problems requires patient diplomacy and time and to avoid the temptation to use military power to speed them up.[30]

---

[28] United Nations Secretary General. (1995, 25 January). *Supplement to an agenda for peace: Position paper of the Secretary-General on the occasion of the 50th anniversary of the United Nations* (United Nations Secretary-General Reports (1994–1995), A/50/60-S/1995/1). United Nations. https://digitallibrary.un.org/record/168325?ln=en

[29] Ibid.

[30] Ibid.

In the next decade, the UN faced the major challenge of tackling intrastate conflicts, protection of civilians and the problematic use of force other than for self-defence.

2000: BRAHIMI REPORT

Peacekeeping in the 1990s was remembered for the failures despite some major successes. Between 1995 and 1999, the UN deployed a few small missions and the UN peacekeeping operations seemed to have reached a crisis point.[31] On 7 March 2000, Secretary-General Kofi Annan established a high-level panel to undertake an in-depth study of the UN peacekeeping operations. The panel headed by Lakhdar Brahimi submitted its report on 21 August 2000.[32] On 13 November 2000, the Security Council welcomed the 'Brahimi Report' and based on the report adopted a resolution containing recommendation and decisions on peacekeeping operations.[33]

The Brahimi Report focused on politics, strategy, operational and organizational aspects of peacekeeping operations. Reflecting on missions deployed in the 1990s, the report observed that the UN operations were not 'deployed in post-conflict situations but tried to create them', making it difficult to accomplish their goals.[34] The panel summarized its proposals.

The panel while reiterating the three principles of peacekeeping operations—consent, impartiality and use of force only in self-defence—identified the challenges in upholding them in the context of 'intra-State/transnational conflicts'.[35] The panel noted that consent

---

[31] Durch, W. J., Holt, V. K., Earle, C. R., & Shanahan, M. K. (2003). *The Brahimi report and the future of UN peace operations.* The Henry L. Stimson Center. https://www.stimson.org/wp-content/files/file-attachments/BR-CompleteVersion-Dec03_1.pdf

[32] United Nations. (2000, 21 August). *Report of the panel on United Nations peace operations.* A/55/305-S/2000/809. United Nations. https://undocs.org/A/55/305

[33] United Nations. (2000, 21 August). *Report of the panel on United Nations peace operations* (Brahimi Report). United Nations. https://www.un.org/en/events/pastevents/brahimi_report.shtml

[34] Ibid.

[35] Ibid.

may be manipulated, impartiality should not mean equal treatment of parties when one of them violates the norms and the continued equal treatment of all parties 'may amount to complicity with evil'[36]; as for the use of force, the panel said that the UN military units must defend themselves, mandate and other mission's components.[37] One of the most quoted statement from the report is

> The Secretariat must tell the Security Council what it needs to know, not what it wants to hear, when recommending force and other resource levels for a new mission, and it must set those levels according to realistic scenarios that take into account likely challenges to implementation.[38]

The panel recommended that planning should be done for new missions through Integrated Mission Task Forces (IMTFs) so that staff from throughout the UN system could contribute to the planning process. The panel stressed strengthening the functioning of civilian police with support from criminal justice system and training in human rights. It called for reinforcing OHCHR to support human rights components of peacekeeping operations. In addition, it called for combining the rule of law teams with police, judicial, legal and human rights experts. However, Member States did not approve the panel's proposals for increasing OHCHR staff to strengthen its capacity.[39]

The panel reaffirmed the principal activities of peacekeeping operations as conflict prevention and peacemaking, peacekeeping and peacebuilding.[40] It noted that post-Cold War characteristics of conflicts

---

[36] Ibid.

[37] Ibid.

[38] United Nations. (2000, 21 August). *Report of the panel on United Nations peace operations* (Brahimi Report). United Nations. https://www.un.org/en/events/pastevents/brahimi_report.shtml

[39] Durch, W. J., Holt, V. K., Earle, C. R., & Shanahan, M. K. (2003). *The Brahimi report and the future of UN peace operations*. The Henry L. Stimson Center. https://www.stimson.org/wp-content/files/file-attachments/BR-CompleteVersion-Dec03_1.pdf

[40] United Nations. (2000, 21 August). *Report of the panel on United Nations peace operations* (Brahimi Report). United Nations. https://www.un.org/en/events/pastevents/brahimi_report.shtml

include their transnational character and involvement of actors such as arms vendors, buyers of illicit commodity exports, regional powers and neighbouring states that host refugees.[41]

Among the changes that the panel supports are a doctrinal shift in the use of civilian police and related rule of law elements in peacekeeping operations for upholding the rule of law and respect for human rights and helping communities coming out of a conflict to achieve national reconciliation. It proposed using the UN's budget as opposed to voluntary contribution to implement disarmament, demobilization and reintegration programmes. It recommended that heads of UN peacekeeping operations have flexibility to fund 'quick impact projects' to assist communities. It proposed that the support to governance institutions should integrate provision of electoral assistance.[42]

The panel considered the protection of civilians as a duty of peacekeepers under the UN Charter. It justified the use of force, since often local parties include both aggressors and victims. It noted that 'genocide in Rwanda went as far as it did in part because the international community failed to use or to reinforce the operation then on the ground'.[43] It reiterated the Security Council resolution 1,296 (2000) that targeting of civilians in armed conflict and the denial of humanitarian access to civilian populations during war would constitute threats to international peace and security and warrant Security Council action. The Brahimi Report was generally opposed by the developing countries on the fear that the UN might take on a more interventionist role and downplay economic and social development issues.[44]

Secretary-General Kofi Annan, in his report to the Security Council on the implementation of the Brahimi Panel Report, while recognizing the need for robust operations, assured the Member States that the use of force would apply only to those operations in which armed UN

[41] Ibid.

[42] Ibid.

[43] Ibid.

[44] Findlay, T. (1995). *Cambodia: The legacy and lessons and UNTAC* (Stockholm International Peace Research Institute [SIPRI], Research Report No. 9). Oxford University Press. https://www.sipri.org/sites/default/files/files/RR/SIPRIRR09.pdf

peacekeepers have been deployed with the consent of the parties concerned. He clarified that the principles that govern the use of force will not be fundamentally changed. He assured that recommendations of the report do not mean that UN would turn into 'a war-fighting machine'.[45]

2003: HIGH-LEVEL PANEL ON THREATS, CHALLENGES AND CHANGE

In 2003, the UN Secretary-General Kofi Annan established a High-level Panel on Threats, Challenges and Change. The panel submitted its report in December 2004.[46] The panel proposed that the UN, to be effective, should resolve long-standing disputes such as Palestine, Kashmir and the Korean Peninsula that fester and feed into new contemporary threats. The panel reiterated the role of the Security Council in dealing with every kind of threats faced by the states. A common understanding when the use of force is both legal and legitimate is essential for the maintenance of global peace and security. The panel acknowledged that force may be necessary for the prevention and removal of threats to peace. It noted that the use of force to individual cases has posed difficulties in arriving at a consensus. On Article 51 of the UN Charter that provides for inherent right of individual or collective self-defence, the panel was of the view that the Security Council–authorized collective action is preferable to states acting on their own. 'Allowing one to so act is to allow all'.[47]

The panel endorsed the Security Council authorizing military intervention as a last resort in the event of genocide and other large-scale killing, ethnic cleansing or serious violations of international humanitarian law which governments are unable or unwilling to prevent.[48] It identified the

---

[45] United Nations Secretary General. (2000, 20 October). *Report of the Secretary-General on the implement of the report of the panel on United Nations peace operations.* A/55/502. United Nations. https://digitallibrary.un.org/record/426824?ln=en

[46] United Nations. (2004, 2 December). *A more secure world: Our shared responsibility* (Report of the High-level Panel on Threats, Challenges and Change, A/59/565). United Nations. https://www.un.org/en/ga/search/view_doc.asp?symbol=A/59/565

[47] Ibid., para 191.

[48] Ibid., para 203.

following guidelines while resorting to the use of force: seriousness of threat, proper purpose, last resort, proportional means and balance of consequences.

The panel observed that peace enforcement is done by multinational forces, while the UN peacekeepers are deployed in situations where parties to the conflict consent to its deployment. The panel considered such a categorization confusing which has led to attributing peacekeeping operations as consent-based 'Chapter VI' missions and enforcement missions as coercion-based 'Chapter VII' operations.[49] The report considered that 'the robust use of force is integral to the mission from the outset'.[50] It reiterated the Brahimi Report recommendation that peacekeeping operations under Chapter VI, operating without enforcement powers, have the right to use force in self-defence which extends to the 'defence of the mission'.[51]

2008–2009: THE UN'S INTERNAL GUIDANCE DOCUMENTS

The UN Department of Peacekeeping Operations (DPKO) and the Department of Field Support (DFS) produced two internal documents: The 'United Nations Peacekeeping Operations' Principles and Guidelines'[52] and a non-paper called 'A New Partnership Agenda: Charting a New Horizon for UN Peacekeeping'.[53] UNDPKO and DFS produced them to provide guidance to peacekeeping personnel.[54]

[49] Ibid., paras 210 and 211.

[50] United Nations. (2004, 2 December). *A more secure world: Our shared responsibility* (Report of the High-level Panel on Threats, Challenges and Change, A/59/565, para 213). United Nations. https://www.un.org/en/ga/search/view_doc.asp?symbol=A/59/565

[51] Ibid.

[52] United Nations. (2008). *United Nations peacekeeping operations: Principles and guidelines.* Department of Peacekeeping Operations and Department of Field Support. https://peacekeeping.un.org/sites/default/files/capstone_eng_0.pdf

[53] United Nations. (2009). *A new partnership agenda: Charting a new horizon for UN peacekeeping.* Department of Peacekeeping Operations and Department of Field Support. https://peacekeeping.un.org/sites/default/files/newhorizon_0.pdf

[54] United Nations. (2008). *United Nations peacekeeping operations: Principles and guidelines.* Department of Peacekeeping Operations and Department of Field Support.

2008: THE UNITED NATIONS PEACEKEEPING OPERATIONS' PRINCIPLES AND GUIDELINES (CAPSTONE DOCTRINE)

The 2008, Capstone Doctrine reiterated that UN peacekeeping operations are complex and multidimensional and that the tasks have expanded to respond to the changing nature of the conflict. It identified peacekeeping as one of the range of activities undertaken by the UN and other actors to maintain international peace and security. The document defined other actions related to peacekeeping such as conflict prevention, peacemaking, peace enforcement and peacebuilding.

Conflict prevention involves the application of structural or diplomatic measures to keep intra-state or inter-state tensions and disputes from escalating into violent conflict. Ideally, it should build on structured early warning, information gathering and a careful analysis of the factors driving the conflict. Conflict prevention activities may include the use of the Secretary- General's 'good offices', preventive deployment or confidence-building measures.

Peacemaking generally includes measures to address conflicts in progress and usually involves diplomatic action to bring hostile parties to a negotiated agreement. The United Nations Secretary-General, upon the request of the Security Council or the General Assembly or at his/her own initiative, may exercise his or her 'good offices' to facilitate the resolution of the conflict. Peacemakers may also be envoys, governments, groups of states, regional organizations or the United Nations. Peacemaking efforts may also be under-taken by unofficial and non-governmental groups, or by a prominent personality working independently.

Peacekeeping is a technique designed to preserve the peace, however fragile, where fighting has been halted, and to assist in implementing agreements achieved by the peacemakers. Over the years, peacekeeping has evolved from a primarily military model

https://peacekeeping.un.org/sites/default/files/capstone_eng_0.pdf; United Nations. (2009). *A new partnership agenda: Charting a new horizon for UN peacekeeping.* Department of Peacekeeping Operations and Department of Field Support. https:// peacekeeping.un.org/sites/default/files/newhorizon_0.pdf

of observing cease-fires and the separation of forces after inter-state wars, to incorporate a complex model of many elements – military, police and civilian – working together to help lay the foundations for sustainable peace.

Peace enforcement involves the application, with the authorization of the Security Council, of a range of coercive measures, including the use of military force. Such actions are authorized to restore international peace and security in situations where the Security Council has determined the existence of a threat to the peace, breach of the peace or act of aggression. The Security Council may utilize, where appropriate, regional organizations and agencies for enforcement action under its authority.

Peacebuilding involves a range of measures targeted to reduce the risk of lapsing or relapsing into conflict by strengthening national capacities at all levels for conflict management, and to lay the foundation for sustainable peace and development. Peacebuilding is a complex, long-term process of creating the necessary conditions for sustainable peace. It works by addressing the deep-rooted, structural causes of violent conflict in a comprehensive manner. Peacebuilding measures address core issues that effect the functioning of society and the State, and seek to enhance the capacity of the State to effectively and legitimately carry out its core functions.[55]

Capstone Doctrine acknowledged that prevention, peacemaking, peacekeeping, peace enforcement and peacebuilding do not happen in a linear or sequential manner. The document for the first time elaborated on the question of the use of force while maintaining that the three basic principles (consent of parties, impartiality and use of force only for self-defence) of peacekeeping remain valid. However, it acknowledged that upholding them is a major challenge in the contemporary period.

As for consent, the document clarified that parties may create obstacles by imposing restrictions despite the initial consent given by

[55] United Nations. (2008). *United Nations peacekeeping operations: Principles and guidelines*. Department of Peacekeeping Operations and Department of Field Support. https://peacekeeping.un.org/sites/default/files/capstone_eng_0.pdf

them. Consent would be tenuous particularly at local levels controlled by armed groups without command structure or other groups (spoilers) intent on subverting the peacekeeping operations. The document acknowledged that in such situations, as a last resort, the use of force may be required to manage the situation. Regarding impartiality, the document clarified that it should not be confused with neutrality or inactivity. The document stated that impartiality does not mean condoning of actions that undermine the mandate. Thus, it reaffirmed Brahimi Panel's famous statement that equal treatment of parties when one of them violates the norms 'may amount to complicity with evil'.[56]

The document stated that the 1950s' concept of the use of force (only for self-defence) has evolved to include self-defence and protection of the mandate at the tactical level. The document noted that often peacekeeping operations are deployed in situations where militias, criminal gangs and other spoilers undermine the peace process. In such situations, if the Security Council authorizes a 'robust' mandate, peacekeeping operations, as a last resort, could 'use all necessary means' (force) at the tactical level. Among others, it is to deter disruption of political process, protect civilians under imminent threat of physical attack and/or assist authorities to maintain law and order. It clarified that robust peacekeeping entails the Security Council's authorization and consent of the host nation, whereas peace enforcement does not require consent of the parties and may involve the use of force at the strategic international level with the Security Council's authorization. The document alerted that force must be used only as a last resort to deter spoilers who undermine the peace process or harm the civilians and not to militarily defeat them. Peacekeeping operations while using force should strive for early de-escalation of violence and return to non-violent approach. Use of force by UN peacekeeping operations has political implications and may give rise to unintended consequences. Decision to resort to the use of force should take into consideration the mission's capability, humanitarian impact, safety and security of personnel and its impact on the consent for the mission.

[56] United Nations. (2000, 21 August). *Report of the panel on United Nations peace operations* (Brahimi Report). United Nations. https://www.un.org/en/events/pastevents/brahimi_report.shtml

2009: DPKO AND DFS A NON-PAPER— 'A NEW PARTNERSHIP AGENDA: CHARTING A NEW HORIZON FOR UN PEACEKEEPING'[57]

In 2009, DPKO and DFS issued a non-paper document called 'A New Partnership Agenda: Charting a New Horizon for UN Peacekeeping'. It reaffirmed the conclusions and recommendations of the 2008 Capstone document. It reiterated that peacekeeping is part of a political solution and it is one among many international peace and security tools.[58]

The DPKO/DFS non-paper defined 'robust approach'[59] as 'a political and operational strategy to signal the intention of a UN mission to implement its mandate and to deter threats to an existing peace process in the face of resistance from spoilers'.[60] It reiterated that the robust approach is tactical in nature, limited in time and space. It involves significant operational support. Ultimately, success of a robust approach would depend on the Security Council's commitment and the willingness of troop and police–contributing countries to implement it. The non-paper noted the lack of shared understanding among Member States on robust peacekeeping and its serious implications for missions operating in unstable conflict situations.[61]

After the Brahimi Report, the concept of stabilization missions emerged. They are mandated to stabilize a country or assist the government in its efforts to bring stability to the country. Its deployment is not based on a peace agreement, and the peacekeepers support the state against spoilers. Stabilization missions operate in

---

[57] United Nations. (2009). *A new partnership agenda: Charting a new horizon for UN peacekeeping.* Department of Peacekeeping Operations and Department of Field Support. https://peacekeeping.un.org/sites/default/files/newhorizon_0.pdf

[58] Ibid.

[59] Ibid.

[60] Ibid.

[61] United Nations. (2009). *A new partnership agenda: Charting a new horizon for UN peacekeeping.* Department of Peacekeeping Operations and Department of Field Support. https://peacekeeping.un.org/sites/default/files/newhorizon_0.pdf

active conflict zones or what the report called where there is 'no peace to keep'.[62]

The Capstone Doctrine and the non-paper clarified the distinction between robust peacekeeping and peace enforcement. Peace enforcement is the domain of Security Council–authorized multinational operations with or without the consent of the host government. Robust peacekeeping is done by peacekeeping operations with the authorization and consent of the host government; it is tactical in nature and limited in time and space.

By mid-2000, peacekeeping operations often had three characteristics: focus on protection of civilians, robust peacekeeping and stabilization missions. In effect, the use of force that went beyond self-defence became routine in most UN peacekeeping operations.[63]

2014: THE HIGH-LEVEL INDEPENDENT PANEL ON UN PEACE OPERATIONS

The UN Secretary-General Ban Ki-moon, in October 2014, appointed HIPPO to review peacekeeping operations and make recommendations. The panel's exhaustive and comprehensive report stressed that politics matters, and that peacekeeping is only a tool. It emphasized partnership at all levels and reaffirmed the centrality of the community, including religious, youth and women's groups, and global business community. The report acknowledged the progress made in the previous decade and highlighted 'significant chronic challenges', such as scarce resources for prevention and mediation work, slow engagement with emerging crises, mandates and missions not tailored to the context or political strategy but produced on the basis

[62] Karlsrud, J. (2015). The UN at war: Examining the consequences of peace-enforcement mandates for the UN peacekeeping operations in the CAR, the DRC and Mali. *Third World Quarterly, 36*(1), 40–54. https://www.tandfonline.com/doi/full/10.1080/01436597.2015.976016

[63] Bellamy, A. J., & Hunt, C. T. (2015). Twenty-first century UN peace operations: Protection, force and the changing security environment. *International Affairs, 91*(6), 1277–1298. https://doi.org/10.1111/1468-2346.12456

of templates and technical and military approaches given priority as opposed to political efforts.[64]

The panel reaffirmed the core principles of UN peacekeeping but called for progressive interpretation and flexibility to cope with the new challenges. It called for four essential shifts: first, primacy to politics with a reminder that lasting peace is not achieved through military means; second, the UN should use the full spectrum of peacekeeping operations to respond to situations with sequenced and prioritized mandates; third, foster a more inclusive peace and security partnership including the UN system acting in an integrated manner and fourth, the UN Secretariat must become more field-focused and peacekeeping operations more people-centred.

The panel stressed upon conflict prevention and embracing a 'culture of prevention' by the organization and its Member States.[65] The UN must make increased investment in its prevention and mediation capacity and should forge partnership with the civil society, namely religious, youth and women's groups as well as the global business community. Protection of civilians remained the core obligation, and the UN personnel must use all available tools to protect civilians under imminent threat. To ensure effective protection of civilians, improvements must be made in planning, collection of timely information and communication, leadership and training.

The panel proposed a number of ways to integrate women in the areas of peace, security and human rights throughout the mission and the mandate tasks. It called for accountability at the senior mission leadership level for integrating gender and human rights in missions. On sexual exploitation and abuse committed by peacekeepers and the civilian staff, the panel strongly condemned such practices. It proposed that immunity does not apply to civilian staff; the Secretary-General must report on actions taken on credible allegations, and the UN

---

[64] United Nations. (2015, 17 June). *Report of the High-level Independent Panel on Peace Operations on uniting our strengths for peace.* A/70/95-S/2015/446. United Nations. https://www.un.org/en/ga/search/view_doc.asp?symbol=S/2015/446

[65] Ibid.

should ensure that individual victims of abuse and exploitation were compensated for the harm they had suffered.

The panel sought further clarity on the use of force and the role of UN peacekeeping operations in managing conflicts. The panel acknowledged that the Security Council in the last decade had deployed 'stabilization missions' to support the extension or restoration of state authority. It opined that the UN needed to clarify the term 'stabilization'.[66] The panel acknowledged the challenges faced by peacekeeping operations in situations of ongoing conflict and claimed that they were often not suited to operate in such environments. In situations where a parallel force was engaged in offensive combat operations, the UN should maintain a clear distinction in roles and division of labour. Such operations should be exceptional, time-limited and undertaken with full awareness of the risks and responsibilities for the UN mission as a whole.

The panel did not legitimize or endorse the targeted offensive operations undertaken in Somalia in 1993 and in the Democratic Republic of the Congo in 2013. It said that it was the prerogative of the Security Council to authorize such missions. Such mandates were different from the tactical use of force to protect civilians and UN personnel. It demonstrated a shift on the use of force from tactical purposes to degrade, neutralize or defeat an opponent which should be authorized with extreme caution. UN operations mandated to undertake enforcement tasks should be an exceptional measure and limited in time. Such interventions run the risk of making the UN forces and the mission become party to the conflict. The UN should pay attention to humanitarian and other consequences of its enforcement actions. The panel categorically stated 'UN troops should not undertake military counter-terrorism operations'.[67] The panel reminded that peacekeeping operations were one among many tools and repeatedly stressed the importance of politics in dealing with the crisis and conflicts. It reiterated the need for a more systematic

[66] Ibid.

[67] Ibid.

approach and not respond to each crisis by assembling a 'hasty and ad hoc response'.[68]

2016: SANTOS CRUZ REPORT

Two years after the HIPPO report, the UN appointed a panel led by Lieutenant General (Retired) Carlos Alberto dos Santos Cruz to examine the security of peacekeeping personnel. The panel's report (known as dos Santos Cruz report) stated that the peacekeeping environment had changed and involved armed groups, terrorists, organized crime, street gangs, criminal and political exploitation and other threats. The report made a bold assertion that the UN Troop/Police contributing countries (T/PCCs) were still 'gripped by a Chapter VI'[69] syndrome. If the UN and T/PCCs did not change their mindset, took risks and showed a willingness to face these new challenges, they would be consciously sending troops into harm's way. It identified the lack of leadership as a major factor for not adapting to the changed situation, and that the UN was most often attacked due to its inaction. On the use of force, the report emphasized the need for the UN to be strong and not fear to use force. It stated that hostile forces did not understand a language other than force. The report called for an updated interpretation of the basic principles of peacekeeping, and that troops should not view them as restricting their use of force. Contrary to other UN reports, it proposed that the principles should provide for troops to use overwhelming force in areas featuring high-intensity conflicts. It stated 'the United Nations need to win, or troops, police and civilian personnel will die'.[70] The dos Santos Cruz report concerned itself with the safety and security of peacekeeping personnel and proposed the use of overwhelming force to defend themselves, thus, opening again

---

[68] Ibid.

[69] Armed Forces Division. (2020, 29 May). *United Nations Peacekeepers Journal*, 6(6), Bangladesh. https://www.afd.gov.bd/sites/default/files/journal/UN%20Day%20Journal%202020-converted.pdf

[70] United Nations. (2017, 19 December). *Improving security of United Nations peace-keepers: We need to change the way we are doing business*. https://peacekeeping.un.org/sites/default/files/improving_security_of_united_nations_peacekeepers_report.pdf

a debate about the use of force in the context of self-defence but with consequences for peacekeeping doctrine as well.

The Santos Cruz report attracted much criticism particularly from humanitarian actors; for example, Mona Ali Khalil, a former Senior Legal Officer with the UN Office of the Legal Counsel, stated that peacekeeping operations' military components may become party to the conflict and become legitimate military targets. A peacekeeping mission's military, by engaging in offensive military actions, may pose a danger to the civilians they are meant to protect in the first place. By becoming party to the conflict, a peace operation would restrict its ability to carry out its broader mandate to facilitate peace talks and those related to political, humanitarian and human rights tasks.[71]

---

[71] Khalil, M. A. (2018). *The world needs robust peacekeeping not aggressive peacekeeping*. International Committee of the Red Cross. https://reliefweb.int/report/world/world-needs-robust-peacekeeping-not-aggressive-peacekeeping

Use of Force

An Unresolved Issue of
UN Peacekeeping Operations

UN PEACEKEEPING OPERATIONS AND THE USE OF FORCE

> The use of force issue is the most vexing of all the challenges that face UN peace operations, since it has the greatest potential to derail or destroy a mission entirely.[1]

The UN was established on the edifice of sovereignty of states, and it was affirmed in Article 2(4) of the Charter. States that were fighting for independence and those that had attained freedom pinned their hopes on the idea of self-determination. They considered sovereignty as paramount. Initially, dealing with interstate conflicts, the UN pursued an approach that respected the concept of sovereignty and self-determination. Hammarskjöld's 'holy trinity' of principles—consent of the member state party to the conflict, impartiality and the non-use of force except in self-defence—reflected the balancing act to reconcile sovereignty and intervention. In interstate conflicts, upholding Hammarskjöld's 'holy trinity' of principles was not a challenge when peacekeepers were deployed for observing ceasefires and implementing peace agreements.[2]

The UN's intervention in Congo in 1962 set the precedent for deploying peacekeepers in an intrastate conflict. Belgium, by supporting the

[1] Findlay, T. (2002). *The use of force in UN peace operations*. Stockholm International Peace Research Institute (SIPRI). Oxford University Press. https://www.sipri.org/sites/default/files/files/books/SIPRI02Findlay.pdf

[2] Rhoads, E. P., & Laurence, M. (2019). Peace operations, principles, and doctrine. In R. Oliver & V. Gëzim (Eds.), *The Palgrave Encyclopedia of peace and conflict studies*. Palgrave Macmillan.

secessionist in the resource-rich Katanga region, had threatened the sovereignty of Congo and its self-determination. The UN intervention in Congo was controversial, but in fact, it ensured Congo's territorial integrity. It also set the precedent for intervention in intrastate conflicts.[3]

The UN's intervention in intrastate conflicts increased after the end of the Cold War. UN operations faced many challenges in dealing with intrastate conflicts. They had to engage with non-state actors without clear command structures; respond to conflicts with cross-border implications; and manage conflicts of transnational character with involvement of neighbouring countries, arms dealers and companies interested in commodities from the conflict zones. In some conflict zones, combatants are motivated by economic reasons and not necessarily on ideology, identity or past grievances. As noted by the Brahimi Panel Report, 'United Nations operations thus did not *deploy into* post-conflict situations but tried *to create* them'.[4]

The challenges faced by UN operations in such conflict situations included the use of force to stabilize a situation, ensure humanitarian assistance and protect civilians.

In 1992, the Secretary-General Boutros Boutros-Ghali, in his 'An Agenda for Peace', proposed that when peaceful means of settlement fail, the use of force by the peacekeeping operation becomes essential to restore the organization's credibility.[5] He also recommended establishment of peace enforcement units with capacity to ensure the implementations of the Security Council's decisions.[6]

However, the use of force remained a sensitive subject among the UN Member States. It led to confusion regarding the use of force,

[3] Lewis, P. (1992). *A short history of United Nations peacekeeping.* https://www.historynet.com/short-history-united-nations-peacekeeping.htm

[4] United Nations. (2000, 21 August). *Report of the panel on United Nations peace operations.* A/55/305-S/2000/809. United Nations. https://undocs.org/A/55/305

[5] United Nations. (1992).

[6] United Nations. (1992, 17 June). *An agenda for peace: Preventive diplomacy, peace-making and peace-keeping* (Report of the Secretary-General pursuant to the statement adopted by the Summit Meeting of the Security Council on 31 January 1992, A/47/277–S/24111). https://www.un.org/ruleoflaw/files/A_47_277.pdf

doctrinally and in practice. According to a scholar, UN was entering into a no man's land without any guiding principles contributing to strategic failure.[7]

The Brahimi Panel reasserted the importance of UN operations using force (as and when required) to ensure their credibility. It proposed that the UN forces must be capable of defending themselves, other mission components and the mission's mandate. The Brahimi Report for the first time explicitly propounded the doctrine that a UN force that witnesses violence against civilians should be presumed to be authorized to stop it. It affirmed the concept of 'robust force posture' along with political support as conditions for success of complex missions.[8] The Brahimi Panel, thus, expanded the use of force from strictly individual defence to a defence of the mandate. Its ideas on the use of force coincided with the emergence of concern about protection of civilians (POC) in armed conflict. Subsequently, several initiatives and discourses happened on the idea of POC including the UN's acceptance of responsibility to protect.[9]

USE OF FORCE: ILLUSTRATIVE EXAMPLES FROM UN PEACEKEEPING OPERATIONS

Angola was an example of the UN pursuing a traditional approach to peacekeeping (force limited to self-defence) despite parties to the agreement undermining the peace process. The UN deployed its mission in 1991 based on an agreement signed between the Angolan government and the rebel movement UNITA. The UN withdrew in

[7] Ruggie, J. G. (1993, November/December). Wandering in the void: Charting the UN's new strategic role. *Foreign Affairs, 72*(5), 26–31. https://www.jstor.org/stable/20045810?origin=crossref&seq=1

[8] United Nations. (2000, 21 August). *Report of the panel on United Nations peace operations.* A/55/305-S/2000/809. United Nations. https://undocs.org/A/55/305

[9] See the 2001 International Commission on Intervention and State Sovereignty (ICISS); the 2004 High-level Panel on Threats, Challenges and Change; the 2005 UN World Summit; the UN's internal documents on peace operations and use of force; and Security Council resolutions and Secretary-General's reports (January 2009 report on Implementing the Responsibility to Protect and the May 2009 resolution on Protection of civilians).

1997 due to continued fighting between the parties which resulted in the collapse of the peace process.

In Somalia, in April 1992, the UN deployed a traditional peacekeeping force for assisting in humanitarian deliveries. In a situation of a failed state and based on agreement with two warlords, deployment of a peacekeeping operation meant that the UN treated the warlords and other factions as sovereign entities. The mission was flawed from the beginning. With no end to violence including attacks against peacekeepers, the UN sought the assistance of a multinational force.[10] In December 1992, the UN deployed a multinational force (UNITAF) to assist in the delivery of humanitarian assistance. It was the first time that the UN had authorized a non-UN military mission for humanitarian purposes. Despite the use of force by well-equipped multinational troops led by the United States, chaos continued, and the US forces incurred many casualties. In June 1993, the Security Council responded by adopting resolution 837. The resolution for the first time since the Korean War authorized military operations against a Somalian entity, thus, moving away from the principle of upholding impartiality during peacekeeping. In 1994, the multinational force and the UN decided to withdraw. In Somalia,

> [the] UN force was drawn into sustained armed conflict with one of the parties to a civil war, abandoning its impartiality and irretrievably damaging consent to its presence. An estimated 800 largely urban guerrillas were able to frustrate and severely harass 28000 UN troops and outwit highly capable US support units. The mission cost the lives of 136 UN and associated soldiers and thousands of Somali lives, both combatants and civilians.[11]

In former Yugoslavia (UNPROFOR), the Security Council authorized the establishment of 'safe areas' to protect the Bosnian population from hostile Serb attacks.[12] It also authorized use of force by the UN troops to protect the Bosnians in safe areas and, if necessary, through

---

[10] Findlay, T. (2002). *The use of force in UN peace operations*. Stockholm International Peace Research Institute (SIPRI). Oxford University Press. https://www.sipri.org/sites/default/files/files/books/SIPRI02Findlay.pdf

[11] Ibid.

[12] UN Security Council Resolution (16 April 1993), S/Res/819 (1993), https://digital-library.un.org/record/164939?ln=en.

the application of NATO air power. Despite authorization for the use of force, UN forces were not able to prevent the massacre of Bosnians in the Srebrenica safe area.

In Rwanda, genocide occurred because the UN operation (UNAMIR) mandate was limited and was not equipped to deal with the extremely volatile situation. The UNPROFOR and UNAMIR failures demonstrated the confusion regarding the use of force due to the lack of political will by the Security Council members.

The Security Council established UNAMIR on 5 October 1993. The mission was authorized under Chapter VI of the Charter. The Security Council did not authorize the elements recommended by the Secretary-General, including a proposal that UNAMIR assist in the recovery of arms to prevent escalation of violence. By the end of 1993, the situation deteriorated, with Hutu militia targeting Tutsi civilians and Hutu moderate elements. On 11 January 1994, UNAMIR Force Commander Brigadier General Roméo A. Dallaire sent a cable to Major General Baril, Military Adviser to the Secretary-General. In the cable, Dallaire shared the information from a Hutu informant[13] that Interahamwe were registering all Tutsi in Kigali and planning to exterminate them and planning also to kill the Belgian UN troops. Dallaire recommended providing protection to the informant and said that he intended to take action to raid the extremists' arms cache. He ended the cable with a call for action: 'Peux ce que veux. Allons-y' ('when there's a will, there's a way').[14]

Kofi Annan, Under Secretary-General for peacekeeping operations, responded (signed off by Assistant Secretary-General for DPKO, Iqbal Riza) to Booh-Booh, the SRSG, requesting his further assessment regarding the cable sent by Dallaire. The cable also stated 'No reconnaissance or other action, including response to request for protection, should be taken by UNAMIR until clear guidance is received from Headquarters'.[15]

---

[13] A top-level trainer in the cadre of Interahamwe, the largest and most deadly Hutu militia who were recruited from the youth wing of the President's party, Mouvement Revolutionnaire National pour le Developpement (MRND).

[14] Carlsson, I., Sung-Joo, H., & Kupolati, R. M. (1999). *Report of the independent inquiry into the actions of the United Nations during the 1994 genocide in Rwanda*. United Nations.

[15] Ibid.

In his response, Booh-Booh emphasized the urgency of the situation since the informant only had 24–48 h before he had to distribute the arms and requested guidance on how to handle the situation, including the request for protection for the informant. The final paragraph of the telegram, para 7, stated that Dallaire was

> prepared to pursue the operation in accordance with military doctrine with reconnaissance, rehearsal and implementation using overwhelming force. Should at any time during reconnaissance, planning or preparation, any sign of a possible contravening or possibility of an undue risky scenario present itself, the operation will be called off.[16]

Kofi Annan, in another cable, instructed UNAMIR SRSG and the Force Commander to appraise the Rwandan president of activities of the Interahamwe militia. SRSG and Force Commander were also instructed to meet the Ambassadors of Belgium, France and the United States in Kigali and request them to meet with the Rwandan president and raise their concerns. The cable stated that actions proposed by Dallaire, in their view, clearly went beyond the mandate entrusted to UNAMIR and ended with a clear-cut statement that 'the overriding consideration is the need to avoid entering into a course of action that might lead to the use of force and unanticipated repercussions'.[17]

According to the report of the Independent Inquiry into the Actions of the UN during the 1994 Genocide in Rwanda,

> The decisions taken with respect to the scope of the initial mandate of UNAMIR were an underlying factor in the failure of the mission to prevent or stop the genocide in Rwanda. The planning process failed to take into account remaining serious tensions which had not been solved in the agreements between the parties. The United Nations mission was predicated on the success of the peace process. There was no fall-back, no contingency planning for the eventuality that the peace process did not succeed.[18]

The Denmark-initiated Joint Evaluation Report in 1994 on UNAMIR stated that with the lack of experience in protecting civilians, the UN

---

[16] Ibid.

[17] Ibid.

[18] Ibid.

framed its response using the conventional Chapter VI versus Chapter VII dichotomy. It did not provide the Security Council other options to deal with genocidal violence.[19]

In Cote d'Ivoire (UNOCI), a peacekeeping operation was deployed in a situation where the parties were not interested in pursuing peace.[20] Cote d'Ivoire's 10-year conflict ended with 1 week of war against rebels by the UN and French forces. The Security Council authorized UNOCI to take all necessary measures to protect the civilians and provided a robust mandate to UNOCI forces. UNOCI's robust mandate and the assistance of French forces that were on the ground made it possible to end the conflict within a short time. UNOCI's use of force was tactically limited to the capital Abidjan to desist rebels' use of heavy weapons against civilians.

Liberia witnessed internal strife from 1989 to 2003 with a short period of tenuous halt in conflict between 1997 and 2000. Starting in 1990, ECOWAS intervened by deploying a peacekeeping force. In 2003, the deployment of a multinational stabilization operation with the authorization to use force contributed to ending the conflict.

In Sierra Leone, in April 2000, the RUF rebels attacked UNMOSIL and kidnapped 500 members of the UN force. The RUF fighters threatened to capture the capital Freetown with serious consequences for the civilian population. In May 2000, the British deployed their forces initially to evacuate foreigners from the city but joined hands with the UN forces to defeat the RUF rebels. The Security Council did not authorize the deployment of British forces. In Sierra Leone, the support provided by a well-equipped national military helped the UN to stabilize the situation.

Similarly, Haiti witnessed repeated breakdown of agreements and eruption of conflicts. In 1994, the UN-authorized 20,000 strong multinational force stabilized the situation, contributing to the UN's continued involvement in the country.

---

[19] Findlay, T. (2002). *The use of force in UN peace operations*. Stockholm International Peace Research Institute (SIPRI). Oxford University Press. https://www.sipri.org/sites/default/files/files/books/SIPRI02Findlay.pdf

[20] Novosseloff, A. (2018). *The many lives of a peacekeeping mission: The UN operation in Côte d'Ivoire*. International Peace Institute. https://www.ipinst.org/wp-content/uploads/2018/06/1806_Many-Lives-of-a-Peacekeeping-Mission.pdf

Since 2004, MONUC has operated under Chapter VII with a robust mandate. In 2010, MONUC was changed to MONUSCO, reflecting the mission's additional stabilization mandate. In 2008, the Security Council mandated that POC was the mission's highest priority. In 2013, the Security Council made a major shift by authorizing an 'intervention brigade' to neutralize armed groups in Goma to protect civilians and stabilize the situation.[21] The intervention brigade was established under the direct command of the MONUSCO Force Commander which was contrary to the UN's normal practice of out-sourcing enforcement tasks to non-UN multinational forces. In many ways, MONUC and MONUSCO reflected the UN's increasing shift towards mandating the use of force for POC.

In South Sudan, the Security Council in 2011 deployed UNMISS with the mandate to assist in long-term state-building and economic development. The mission, under Chapter VII, was authorized to use all necessary means (use of force) to deter violence and protect civilians under imminent threat of physical violence. In 2013, when a civil war broke out in the country, the Security Council increased the number of troops and modified the mandate to prioritize POC and suspended capacity-building activities. UNMISS established POC sites adjacent to its bases to provide shelter to people fleeing the conflict. This was the first time that the UN had opened its gates to offer shelter to civilians and continued to do so for several months.

In Central African Republic, in April 2014, the UN deployed a multidimensional mission (MINUSCA) that subsumed the previous UN peacekeeping operation in the country. The Security Council mandated MINUSCA's utmost priority as POC. Under Chapter VII, MINUSCA was authorized to pursue a proactive and robust approach. In the context of weak state security forces, the Security Council authorized MINUSCA (on an exceptional basis) to maintain basic law and order and fight impunity.

In July 2013, the Security Council deployed a stabilization mission (MINUSMA) in Mali. It also authorized French troops (over 1,000) that

---

[21] United Nations. (2013, 28 March). *Intervention brigade' authorized as Security Council grants mandate renewal for United Nations mission in Democratic Republic of Congo.* Meetings Coverage and Press Releases.

were previously engaged in neutralizing armed militias in the country to support MINUSMA by using all necessary means (use of force). By authorizing the French troops to intervene on behalf of MINUSCA, the Security Council in effect created an intervention force outside the mission structure.

DEBATE ON UN'S USE OF FORCE IN ITS PEACEKEEPING OPERATIONS

The evolution of use of force in UN operations has raised both legal and practical issues on the ground. In Mali, authorizing the French forces to assist MINUSMA demonstrated the risk of French troops misusing the mandate to combat against the armed groups, which was different from the UN mission's aim to deter armed groups for the purposes of implementing the mandate. France deployed its troops in Mali to defeat the armed elements in the Sahelian north; the UN, by mandating them to assist MINUSMA, might have compromised the mission's impartiality and its security. The deployment of the Force Intervention Brigade (FIB) in the DRC to neutralize an armed group in collaboration with the DRC's armed forces risked undermining the mission's impartiality and the principle of using force only in self-defence. In Congo, peacekeepers' collaboration with government forces with terrible human rights record damaged its credibility. The UN applied 'due diligence' principle to verify the human rights record of government forces to avoid collaborating with those who had committed human rights violations[22]. However, the UN is often reluctant to severe ties with the government forces due to its dependence on logistics and its interest in reforming them through active collaboration. 'Due diligence has been implemented only patchily'.[23] The MONUSCO experiment in deploying FIB crossed the line over the tactical use of force for protection of the mandate.[24]

---

[22] Bellamy, A. J., & Hunt, C. T. (2015). Twenty-first century UN peace operations: Protection, force and the changing security environment. *International Affairs, 91*(6), 1277–1298. https://doi.org/10.1111/1468-2346.12456

[23] Ibid.

[24] Ibid.

When missions are deployed for stabilization purposes, the use of force becomes the main tool. It appears to be contrary to the use of force as a last resort to deal with unexpected circumstances that impact on implementation of the mandate. Stabilization missions go beyond peacekeeping and end up also facing the challenge of state-building and peace building.[25]

The UN could have abstained from organizing peacekeeping missions to avoid deploying in places where there was no peace to keep. However, the explosion of information technology and the cable television meant it was not possible for the Security Council to ignore the plight of civilians in armed conflicts. On the ground, however, nuanced use of force as defined in the 1960s was a challenge. It gave false hope that long-standing internal problems could be solved by the use of force by external actors. The purpose got confused, and peacekeeping operations were blamed when they failed. It raised expectations on the role of peacekeeping operations to protect civilians in complex intrastate conflict situations. As seen in South Sudan, increasingly, civilians gather around the UN mission sites seeking protection. Consequently, the UN peacekeeping operations got involved directly in humanitarian activities for which they were not equipped. The UN's protection sites often create concerns such as the mission's capacity to engage in law-and-order issues including disarming of armed elements within such protection sites. In South Sudan and in other situations, host governments perceived protection sites as locations that provided refuge to the opponents, and this increased the danger of armed attacks against the civilians at such sites.

Normally, attacks against peacekeepers are considered a war crime. However, when peacekeepers use force against specific armed groups, they assume the role of combatants and may become legitimate targets. Since the 1990s, an increased number of peacekeepers have been taken hostage, physically attacked and several killed in operations.

---

[25] Reynaert, J. (2011). *MONUC/MONUSCO and civilian protection in the Kivus*. Interns & Volunteers Series. https://monusco.unmissions.org/sites/default/files/monuc-monusco_and_civilian_protection_in_the_kivus_0.pdf

In providing combat role to peacekeepers, the door is opened for their engagement in normal law-and-order situations as part of their stabilization role as it happened in Haiti and Mali. In playing such a role, peacekeepers could get mired in local parochial divisions and lose their credibility with the local population. The regularization of peacekeepers' combat role may lead to their engagement in counterterrorism actions, which has happened in Mali.[26]

Two anecdotes from the past would demonstrate how much the UN has moved away from its original doctrine on the use of force (only for self-defence purposes). When the UN Under Secretary-General Brian Urquhart visited the United Nations Interim Force in Lebanon (UNIFIL), he found that UNIFIL troops considered the PLO and Haddad elements as enemies and were eager to use force against them. He told the troops that 'peacekeepers had no enemies, just a series of difficult and sometimes homicidal clients'.[27]

In Cambodia in 1992, Khmer Rouge forces stopped Yasushi Akashi, UNTAC's SRSG, and his force commander from proceeding beyond a roadblock. The roadblock consisted of a bamboo pole across the road which the mission leadership respected and returned without challenging the diktat. UNTAC's leadership was criticized for not using force to establish their freedom of movement. Akashi reportedly acknowledged that UNTAC had interpreted self-defence in a very strict manner and failed to confront Khmer Rouge's harassment of peacekeepers.[28]

Post-2000, the peacekeeping operation mandates include the use of force for purposes other than strictly for self-defence. However, despite its evolution in practice, the use of force is mired in controversy and conceptual confusion.[29]

---

[26] Bellamy, A. J., & Hunt, C. T. (2015). Twenty-first century UN peace operations: Protection, force and the changing security environment. *International Affairs, 91*(6), 1277–1298. https://doi.org/10.1111/1468-2346.12456

[27] Findlay, T. (2002). *The use of force in UN peace operations*. Stockholm International Peace Research Institute (SIPRI). Oxford University Press. https://www.sipri.org/sites/default/files/files/books/SIPRI02Findlay.pdf

[28] Ibid.

[29] Ibid.

The UN peacekeeping operations' confusion and failure on the use of force arise from unclear mandates provided by the Security Council. Adoption of weak or unclear mandates often resulted from the Security Council's internal political dynamics, its unwillingness to face the fact on the ground and its (intentional) assumptions on the potential good behaviour of the parties to the conflict. In effect, the Security Council's mandate reflects its intentions to avoid as much as possible robust interventions. As discussed previously, most often the peacekeeping operations are not sufficiently endowed with troops and resources. The Security Council's decisions are often based on its budgetary concerns and not on the mission's requirements. Voting among the Security Council members depends on their respective country's immediate concerns and interests and not necessarily on the doctrine, past precedents or nature of the conflict. According to Trevor Findlay, 'the Rwanda and Srebrenica episodes were, as has been seen, as much a result of the Security Council's pusillanimity, ineptness and wishful thinking as of UN peacekeepers' reluctance to use force'.[30]

The Security Council is yet to institutionalize an effective mechanism for rapid deployment of troops to conflict situations. To protect its own role and interests, it has been reluctant to delegate responsibilities or provide adequate resources to the UN Secretariat to manage peacekeeping operations. On the ground, some mission heads including force commanders have lacked understanding on the use of force and have not demonstrated leadership as well. As for peacekeepers, often they are confused about the use of force and are not trained on the nuances of their mission's mandate. Some contingents are deployed without adequate weaponry and resources.

In the evolution of the 'use of force' notion, the Security Council justified it for deterrence, to ensure right of freedom of movement, defence of the mission staff and resources, defence of mandate and POC[31]. Past experience of peacekeeping operations has demonstrated that the use of force for these purposes has not been consistent across various missions. As stipulated by Findlay, effective use of force would

[30] Ibid.

[31] Ibid.

require well-established doctrine, adequate resources, analytical information on trouble spots, rapid action force, effective civilian components and finally a clear mandate from the Security Council.[32]

CONCLUSION

After more than 50 years of the UN's involvement in peacekeeping operations, the landmark Brahimi Report asserted the fact that peacekeeping operations are about politics. The report highlighted that the UN Secretariat, constrained by politics within the Security Council, was communicating what the Council wanted to hear. In 2015, HIPPO stressed the importance of politics in ending conflicts. Through this statement, HIPPO put the onus on the Member States for the success of peacekeeping operations.

It is politics that determines the deployment of peacekeeping operations. Among others, Haiti, Sierra Leone, Mali and Central African Republic show that if permanent members of the Security Council are concerned about the situation, peace could be enforced even if parties to the conflict are not fully committed to it. On the other hand, lack of support from regional powers could prevent the UN's involvement even if a situation warrants such an intervention. The case of Sri Lanka is a classic example of a conflict that could have been prevented but resulted in the deaths of thousands of civilians.[33] Similarly, an investigative team appointed by the Secretary-General confirmed that killings of Hutu refugees in Eastern Congo by the Congolese and Rwandan armies constitute crimes against humanity.[34] Despite the report, the Security Council neither did authorize deployment of military personnel nor did

[32] Ibid.

[33] United Nations. (2011, 31 March). *Report of the Secretary-General's panel of experts on accountability in Sri Lanka.* https://www.securitycouncilreport.org/atf/cf/%7B65BFCF9B-6D27-4E9C-8CD3-CF6E4FF96FF9%7D/POC%20Rep%20on%20Account%20in%20Sri%20Lanka.pdf

[34] United Nations. (1998, 29 June). *Report of the Secretary-General's investigative team charged with investigating serious violations of human rights and international humanitarian law in the Democratic Republic of the Congo.* S/1998/581. https://documents-dds-ny.un.org/doc/UNDOC/GEN/N98/177/22/IMG/N9817722.pdf?OpenElement

it establish an international tribunal to deal with the crimes committed in Eastern Congo.

In 2018, the Secretary-General initiated the 'Action for Peacekeeping' (A4P) with the aim to commit the UN Member States on a 'Declaration of Shared Commitments on UN Peacekeeping Operations'.[35] The Declaration reflects the concerns of the Brahimi and HIPPO reports and affirms that Member States commit to pursue clear, focused, sequenced, prioritized and achievable mandates by the Security Council matched by appropriate resources; to seek measures to enable greater coherence between mandates and resources; and to support the implementation of Security Council resolutions through our bilateral and multilateral engagements. The A4P initiative tried to rebuild consensus on peacekeeping operations.

However, the path ahead depends on how the international community resolves the contemporary crisis arising from increasing nationalism, populism, total disregard for multilateralism by major powers and the impact of COVID-19 pandemic on livelihoods of people on a global scale. Responding to the HIPPO Report, a Security Council permanent member said 'Politics is what we do in the Security Council'.[36] It is possible that the UN Member States may continue with business as usual and, in the post-pandemic crisis, may even resort to further undermining of the UN and its role.

---

[35] United Nations. (2019). *Declaration of shared commitments on UN peacekeeping operations.* https://peacekeeping.un.org/sites/default/files/dpko-dfs-declaration-shared-commitments-unpeacekeeping-1812605e.pdf

[36] United Nations. (2019). *The politics of action for peacekeeping.* United Nations University, Centre for Policy Research. https://cpr.unu.edu/the-politics-of-action-for-peacekeeping.html

Integration of Thematic Areas in Peace Operations

INTRODUCTION

The evolution of peacekeeping operations, both its doctrine and practice, included integration of thematic areas such as human rights and the rule of law; women, peace and security; children and armed conflict; and the protection of civilians in armed conflict. Increasingly, UN peacekeeping operations were associated not just with peace but also other thematic areas such as human rights protection, protection of civilians, protection of children and the role of women in peacebuilding.

In the initial years, UN peacekeeping missions did not include civilian components. It was in 1992 that the Secretary-General Boutros Boutros-Ghali, in his 'Agenda for Peace', identified human rights as a crucial factor to four interrelated processes involved in peacekeeping operations—preventive diplomacy, peacemaking, peacekeeping and peacebuilding.[1] He acknowledged the role of non-military personnel in peacekeeping operations as civilian political officers, human rights monitors, electoral officials, refugee and humanitarian aid specialists and police.[2]

---

[1] United Nations. (1992, 17 June). *An agenda for peace: Preventive diplomacy, peacemaking and peace-keeping.* Report of the Secretary-General pursuant to the statement adopted by the Summit Meeting of the Security Council on 31 January 1992, A/47/277 -S/24111. https://www.un.org/ruleoflaw/files/A_47_277.pdf

[2] Ibid.

HUMAN RIGHTS

Increasingly, especially at the end of the Cold War, the international community considered human rights violations as a cause and not merely a consequence of conflicts. Beginning in the 1990s, peacekeeping operations began incorporating human rights in their mandates.

During the first four decades, the UN Human Rights Division and its successor Human Rights Centre were mainly involved in standard setting and in servicing the UN Commission on Human Rights, treaty bodies and other subsidiary bodies. Unlike UNHCR or UNICEF, Human Rights Division (HRD)/Centre did not deploy staff in the field and states were reluctant to authorize such deployment. The UN Human Rights Centre in Geneva was not involved in managing the human rights components of missions deployed in Cambodia (1992), EL Salvador (1991), Guatemala (1994), Angola (1995) and Haiti (1993). The UN Department of Political Affairs managed El Salvador, Guatemala and Haiti. DPKO managed Cambodia and Angola. However, the Human Rights Field Operation in Rwanda (HRFOR) was managed by the High Commissioner for Human Rights, even though UNAMIR was present in the country.

In 1994, the establishment of OHCHR and the appointment of Mr Jose Ayala Lasso as the first High Commissioner increased its involvement within the UN system on human rights concerns and establishment of human rights field offices.[3]

In 1997, the Secretary-General launched his 'Programme of Reform' and stated that human rights cut across each of the UN's four substantive pillars—peace and security, economic and social affairs, development cooperation and humanitarian affairs. The reform proposals included the integration of human rights into all UN activities.[4]

---

[3] The High Commissioner had to deal with the situation in Rwanda the day after he assumed office. He convened the Special Session of the Human Rights Commission, visited Rwanda and deployed human rights observers in the country. In 1992, there were no human rights field activities; by 1997, there were offices in 11 countries in all regions.

[4] United Nations. (1997). *Strengthening human rights in peace operations*. https://www.ohchr.org/EN/newyork/Stories/Pages/Strengtheninghumanrightsinpeaceoperations.aspx

The Brahimi Report for the first time called for the integration of human rights into peacekeeping operations. The Brahimi Report noted that 'the human rights component of a peace operation is indeed critical to effective peacebuilding'.[5] While the Brahimi Panel was preparing its report, in 1999, the OHCHR and DPKO signed a memorandum of understanding (MoU) to increase cooperation between the two and strengthen peacekeeping and human rights activities. By 2000, OHCHR made a policy decision to deploy human rights officers (HROs) in the field including enhancing its role in peacekeeping operations.[6]

OFFICE OF THE HIGH COMMISSIONER FOR HUMAN RIGHTS' INTERNAL DEVELOPMENTS

In 1998, Mary Robinson, the UN High Commissioner for Human Rights, appointed Ian Martin to review the role, functioning and support needs of the field operations of the Office of the High Commissioner. Among others, Ian Martin recommended enhancing OHCHR's capacity to coordinate field presences by appointing an additional senior staff member with human rights field experience to act as adviser to the High Commissioner.[7]

After Brahimi Report, OHCHR established a Peace Mission Support Unit (PMSU), and in 2014, it became a separate entity called the Peace Mission Support Section (PMSS). PMSS is OHCHR's dedicated, in-house capacity on backstopping human rights in UN peacekeeping operations and implementation of Security Council's mandates on human rights. It facilitates the political, strategic and operational integration of human rights in the UN peace and security agenda. It carries out strategic planning for new, transitioning and downsizing human rights components, including integrating human rights analysis into

---

[5] United Nations. (2000, 21 August). *Report of the panel on United Nations peace operations*. A/55/305-S/2000/809. United Nations. https://undocs.org/A/55/305

[6] United Nations. (2000). *OHCHR in the world: Making human rights a reality on the ground.* https://www.ohchr.org/EN/Countries/Pages/WorkInField.aspx

[7] Unpublished document—copy with the author.

the planning for peacekeeping operations. It supports the recruitment of human rights staff for the heads of human rights components. PMSS also facilitates the gathering of good practices and sharing of information among human rights components through the maintenance of a resource centre on the integration of human rights in peacekeeping operations and through the production and dissemination of monthly bulletins and induction packages.[8]

UN-WIDE POLICY DEVELOPMENT

The 1999 MoU became a UN-wide policy under the Secretary-General's 2005 'Policy on Integrated Human Rights Missions'.[9] The policy made all UN entities responsible for promotion and protection of human rights in their field operations. Commitment to human rights should be an important factor in the selection of heads/deputy of missions. It affirmed OHCHR as 'lead agency' in discharging human rights functions and in mainstreaming human rights across all mission activities. It clarified that public reporting by the mission and/or the High Commissioner should be routine. It reiterated that the chief of a human rights component should report to the head of the mission and the High Commissioner. The chief of the human rights component should represent the High Commissioner while being part of a peacekeeping operation. The UN Secretary-General's Policy was reaffirmed in DPKO/DFS Capstone Doctrine (2008) and their Principles and Guidelines (2009 non-paper). The documents stressed the importance of the integration of human rights in peacekeeping operations, and that it should be a part of the planning of peacekeeping operations.[10]

---

[8] Based on the information provided by OHCHR Peace Mission Support Section staff.

[9] United Nations. (2005). *Decisions of the Secretary-General policy committee meeting of 26 October 2005* (Decision No. 2005/24). Human Rights in Integrated Missions.

[10] United Nations. (2008). *United Nations peacekeeping operations: Principles and guidelines.* Department of Peacekeeping Operations and Department of Field Support. https://peacekeeping.un.org/sites/default/files/capstone_eng_0.pdf; United Nations. (2009). *A new partnership agenda: Charting a new horizon for UN peacekeeping.* Department of Peacekeeping Operations and Department of Field Support. https://peacekeeping.un.org/sites/default/files/newhorizon_0.pdf

In 2011, OHCHR and DPKO, DPA and DFS issued a joint policy note on 'Human Rights in UN Peace Operations and Political Missions'.[11] The policy called for integration of human rights in peacekeeping and political missions. In the absence of a specific reference to human rights, the norms should be an integral part of the normative framework guiding the missions. It called for early involvement of OHCHR in mission planning. It reaffirmed issuing of public reports as an essential function of human rights component and that it will be a routine. The note identified various functions of a human rights component such as advocacy, working with government, civil society and providing guidance and assistance to other components of a mission.[12]

In 2015, HIPPO further elaborated the integration of human rights in peacekeeping operations. The HIPPO report acknowledged the progress made in integrating human rights in peacekeeping operations, including in policy, training and staffing. It noted that human rights expertise is not always included in the assessment, planning and review of peacekeeping operations. The report recommended that the Secretariat should seek resources for the timely recruitment and deployment of human rights staff. It also recommended coherence and avoiding duplication of effort among human rights and protection functions.[13]

ROLE OF HUMAN RIGHTS COMPONENTS IN PEACEKEEPING OPERATIONS

OHCHR assists UN peacekeeping operations in their work related to human rights. A human rights component's activities are derived from the mission's mandate under the relevant Security Council resolutions.

---

[11] United Nations. (2011). *Human Rights in United Nations peace operations and political missions*. Office of the High Commissioner for Human Rights, United Nations.

[12] Ibid.

[13] United Nations. (2015, 16 June). *Uniting our strengths for peace-politics, partnership and people* (Report of the High-Level Independent Panel on United Nations Peace Operations). https://peaceoperationsreview.org/wp-content/uploads/2015/08/HIPPO_Report_1_June_2015.pdf

Human rights components deployed in peacekeeping operations among others conduct the following activities subject to the nature of the mandate:

1. Daily monitoring, investigating, documenting and reporting on the human rights situation.
2. Issuing public reports periodically on human rights situation and or on thematic issues.
3. Providing guidance and tools to the missions on upholding human rights standards in implementing the mission's mandate.[14]
4. Advocacy with the government officials on human rights concerns including providing training and expert advice.
5. Assisting in establishment or strengthening of judicial systems and national human rights institutions.
6. Assisting in the establishment and functioning of transitional justice mechanisms.

WOMEN AND PEACE AND SECURITY

In May 2000, the Windhoek Declaration and the Namibia Plan of Action were adopted at the 10th anniversary of UNTAG, Namibia. The Declaration called for the participation of women and men as equal partners and beneficiaries in all aspects of the peace process.[15]

In October 2000, the Security Council adopted resolution 1325 that for the first time addressed the issue of women and conflict and their contribution to sustainable peace.[16] The landmark resolution acknowledged the immense impact of violent conflict and war on women and

---

[14] United Nations. (2015). *Human rights due diligence policy on United Nations support to non-united nations security forces* (Guidance Note and Text of the Policy). https://unsdg.un.org/sites/default/files/Inter-Agency-HRDDP-Guidance-Note-2015.pdf

[15] United Nations General Assembly Security Council. (2000, 14 July). *Windhoek declaration on the tenth anniversary of the United Nations Transition Assistance Group*, A/55/138=S/2000/693. http://www.equalpowerlastingpeace.org/resource/windhoek-declaration-and-namibia-plan-of-action-2000/#:~:text=A%20follow%20up%20on%20the,peace%20operations%20and%20peace%20processes

[16] United States Institute of Peace. (2000). *What is UNSCR 1325? An explanation of the landmark resolution on women, peace and security*. https://www.usip.org/gender_peacebuilding/about_UNSCR_1325

girls. It stressed the role of women in all aspects of peace and security including in prevention and resolution of conflicts, peace negotiations, peacebuilding, peacekeeping, humanitarian response and in post-conflict reconstruction. The resolution proposed four basic pillars related to women and peace and security. First, participation of women in all institutions and processes related to peace and security issues. Second, protection of women and girls from sexual and gender-based violence (SGBV). Third, prevention of violence against women and establishing accountability of perpetrators and supporting local women's conflict resolution and peace initiatives. Fourth, relief and recovery that is implemented with gendered focus. The resolution stressed implementation at the national level, and since 2005, it has led to the development of National Action Plans (NAP). The Secretary-General made a commitment to increase women's leadership role across all levels at the UN.[17]

The adoption of resolution 1325 led to the establishment of Interagency Taskforce on Women, Peace and Security that brought together 20 UN entities to coordinate the UN's efforts to strengthen the role of women in peace and security issues.[18] The resolution has contributed to some incremental changes. However, HIPPO observed that resolution 1325 suffers from the lack of understanding of the potential of increasing both integrating gender perspective and participation of women in peace processes.[19]

The present UN Secretary-General António Guterres acknowledged the importance of resolution 1325 and promised to implement stronger policy on women, peace and security including emergency measures to ensure gender balance at all levels of peacekeeping operations.[20]

---

[17] Ibid.

[18] Ibid.

[19] United Nations. (2015, 17 June). *Report of the high-level independent panel on peace operations on uniting our strengths for peace: Politics, partnership and people*. A/70/95-S/2015/446. https://www.un.org/en/ga/search/view_doc.asp?symbol=S/2015/446

[20] United Nations. (2020, February). *Secretary-General stresses need for less talk, more action on women, peace, security, in remarks at Book Launch of 'She Stands for Peace'*. UN Secretary-General. https://reliefweb.int/report/world/secretary-general-stresses-need-less-talk-more-action-women-peace-security-remarks-book

SEXUAL AND GENDER-BASED VIOLENCE IN CONFLICT

Historically, recruiting women for forced labour, rape and sexual abuse was common in all wars. In the conflicts that broke out in the last four decades, increasingly, rape was used as a weapon of war by the combatants. In several cases, while the UN peacekeeping operations were present in the territory, women were raped and abused. In 2008, the UN Security Council adopted resolution 1820. The resolution considered sexual violence used as a tactic of war as impeding restoration of international peace and security. It expressed its readiness to take appropriate steps to address widespread or systematic sexual violence.[21]

In 2009, the Security Council adopted resolution 1888, authorizing the appointment of a Special Representative on sexual violence in armed conflict to strengthen the UN and governments' efforts to deal with the issue of sexual violence in armed conflicts. Resolutions 1820 and 1888 changed the way the international community viewed sexual violence in conflict and war. It is no more seen as an inevitable consequence of conflict but as a crime under international humanitarian law and human rights law.[22]

In 2010, the Secretary-General appointed the first Special Representative of the Secretary-General on Sexual Violence in Conflict (SRSG–SVC). The SRSG–SVC's Office has contributed to increased visibility and political commitment to deal with sexual violence in conflict, development of legislative framework, greater coordination with security and justice sectors and progress in bringing to justice perpetrators of sexual violence in conflict. The office established Monitoring, Analysis and Reporting Arrangements (MARA) on sexual violence including rape in situations of armed conflict and post-conflict situations.[23]

---

[21] United Nations. (2008, 19 June). *Resolution 1820 (2008). Adopted by the Security Council at its 5916th meeting, on 19 June 2008*. S/RES/1820 (2008). United Nations. https://undocs.org/en/S/RES/1820(2008)

[22] United Nations. (2009). *Office of the special representative of the Secretary-General on sexual violence in conflict (OSRGG-SVC)*. https://www.un.org/sexualviolenceinconflict/about-us/about-the-office/

[23] Ibid.

SEXUAL ABUSE BY UN PEACEKEEPERS

While the UN was working hard to deal with the issue of rape and sexual abuse committed by combatants in conflicts, it faced the problem of sexual abuse committed by its own forces. In 2004, peacekeepers in MONUC were accused of involvement in a pattern of sexual exploitation of Congolese women.[24]

In November 2004, the UNDPKO acknowledged that in Congo, it is investigating a total of 150 allegations of sexual exploitation and abuse which included rape and underage sex exploitation. The UN Secretary-General acknowledged that acts of grave misconduct have taken place and he is outraged by it.[25]

In 2005, based on a request made by the UN General Assembly's Special Committee on Peace Operations, the Secretary-General appointed Prince Zeid to prepare a report on sexual exploitation and abuse by UN peacekeeping personnel. In his report, Prince Zeid noted that the UN's investigations into sexual exploitation and abuse are ad hoc and inadequate to deal with the problem. He recommended unifying all rules against sexual abuse by peacekeeping personnel, strengthening the investigation process, establishing command responsibilities and, for peacekeepers who commit sexual abuse, and exploitation to be held individually accountable.[26]

Despite the UN's zero tolerance policy, the problem continued to haunt several UN peacekeeping operations. The problem persisted in Congo, Central African Republic and South Sudan. The UN stepped up its efforts by publishing the nationalities of the UN soldiers alleged

---

[24] Human Rights Watch. (2005). *MONUC: A case for peacekeeping reform*. https://www.hrw.org/news/2005/02/28/monuc-case-peacekeeping-reform

[25] United Nations. (2004). *Press briefing on sexual exploitation allegations related to UN mission in Democratic Republic of Congo*. Meeting Coverage and Press Releases. https://www.un.org/press/en/2004/lute041122.doc.htm

[26] United Nations. (2005). *A comprehensive strategy to eliminate future sexual exploitation and abuse in United Nations peacekeeping operations*. https://www.un.org/en/ga/search/view_doc.asp?symbol=A/59/710

to have committed sexual abuse and exploitation. It also set up a trust fund to provide support to victims of sexual abuse.[27]

The UN Secretary-General António Guterres, immediately after assuming office, announced his commitment to end sexual abuse and exploitation by the UN staff and peacekeepers. He pledged to 'put victim rights and dignity first'.[28] He appointed a human rights expert in his office tasked with advocating for victim's rights. He also proposed to appoint victim's rights advocates on the ground in Central African Republic, the Democratic Republic of the Congo, Haiti and South Sudan where peacekeepers were accused of sexual abuse of women.[29]

CHILDREN AND ARMED CONFLICT

In 1993, the UN General Assembly and the UN Committee on the Rights of the Child requested the Secretary-General to appoint an expert to study the impact of conflict on children including their participation in wars as child soldiers.[30]

The Secretary-General appointed Graça Machel, Mozambique's former Minister of Education, to conduct the study. Machel's landmark study took two years to complete and was submitted in 1996. In her global study, she documented deaths of two million children in armed conflicts in the previous decade, a period in which six million were seriously injured or permanently disabled and 250,000 child soldiers existed around the world.[31]

[27] Wheeler, S. (2020, 11 January). UN peacekeeping has a sexual abuse problem. *The Hill*. Human Rights Watch. https://www.hrw.org/news/2020/01/11/un-peacekeeping-has-sexual-abuse-problem

[28] Kumar, A. (2017, 10 March). *UN plan to stop peacekeeper abuse puts victims first: Focus on Victims a refreshing change.* Human Rights Watch. https://www.hrw.org/news/2017/03/10/un-plan-stop-peacekeeper-abuse-puts-victims-first

[29] Ibid.

[30] United Nations. (1993). *Graça Machal and the impact of armed conflict on children.* https://childrenandarmedconflict.un.org/about-us/mandate/the-machel-reports/

[31] Klot, J. (2012, October). *The impact of armed conflict on children.* Humanitarian Practice Network. https://odihpn.org/magazine/the-impact-of-armed-conflict-on-children/

The expert in her report recommended the appointment of a Special Representative of the Secretary-General on Children in Armed Conflict (SRSG–CAC) and to consider the protection of children as high priority 'on the international human rights, peace, security and development agendas'.[32]

In 1997, the UN appointed the first SRSG–CAC. In July 2005, the Security Council adopted resolution 1612 on the protection of children affected by armed conflict. Building on the previous resolutions, it strengthened the role of the SRSG–CAC. It established the UN-led Monitoring and Reporting Mechanism (MRM) and national level Task Forces on Children and Armed Conflict. The resolution 1612 stipulated that monitoring 'will be undertaken only in the context of and for the specific purpose of ensuring the protection of children affected by armed conflict'.[33] It also established the Security Council Working Group on the subject which was the first of its kind. The Working Group's powers include taking concrete actions for halting violations and for holding perpetrators accountable.

Under resolution 1612, the Secretary-General reports to the Security Council on six grave violations: killing and maiming of children, recruiting and using child soldiers, attacks against schools or hospitals, rape or other grave sexual violence against children, abduction of children and denial of humanitarian access to children. The monitoring and reporting is done through the SRSG–CAC office and National Task Forces. National Task Forces normally include the concerned government's representative, the UNICEF representative and (where available) the OHCHR representative. The Secretary-General's list includes both governments and armed groups that commit any of the above six grave violations. SRSG–CAC, in collaboration with the National Task Force, engages with the concerned government and if possible with the armed groups particularly concerning the use of

---

[32] Ibid.

[33] United Nations. (2005). *Resolution 1612 (2005). Adopted by the Security Council at its 5235th meeting, on 26 July 2005*. S/RES/1612 (2005). United Nations. https://www.securitycouncilreport.org/atf/cf/%7B65BFCF9B-6D27-4E9C-8CD3-CF6E4FF96FF9%7D/CAC%20SRES%201612.pdf

child soldiers. Based on the information submitted by SRSG–CAC, the Secretary-General delists a government or an armed group if it ends the recruitment and use of child soldiers and other grave violations against children.[34]

Normally, the delisting process includes monitoring by the National Task Force and signing of MoU between the government and SRSG–CAC. MoU is signed once the use of child soldiers (including release of all children from their ranks) is ended and commitments are made on stopping other violations.[35]

The UN resolution 1612 and the SRSG–CAC mandate covers conflicts in all countries. However, the role played by the SRSG–CAC is particularly valuable in conflict situations where the UN peacekeeping operations are deployed. SRSG–CAC plays a complementary role and assists the peacekeeping operation in engaging with an issue that is often complex and requires multiple advocacy efforts. Since 2001, increasingly, the UN peacekeeping operations mandates have included specific provisions on child protection and deployment of child protection adviser as a part of the civilian component of a mission.[36]

A study conducted in 2008 concluded that

> At the policy and process level, the MRM has played a significant part in promoting and progressing the Children and Armed Conflict agenda, both within the Security Council and the broader humanitarian and human rights communities. [...] The MRM can be said to have had a significant impact on the direction and profile of the issue of children and conflict

---

[34] Watch List on Children and Armed Conflict. (2009). *UN security council resolution 1612 and beyond: Strengthening protection for children in armed conflict.* https://reliefweb. int/sites/reliefweb.int/files/resources/B47350B9C3111673C12575C9006152B8-Watchlist-PolicyPaper-colour-LOWRES.pdf

[35] The author as the OHCHR representative facilitated the signing of MoU with the governments of Uganda and Sudan, respectively.

[36] Barnett, K., & Jefferys, A. (2008, September). *Full of promise: How the UN's monitoring and reporting mechanism can better protect children.* Commissioned and Published by the Humanitarian Practice Network at ODI (Network Paper, No. 62). Overseas Development Institute. https://odihpn.org/wp-content/uploads/2008/09/networkpaper062.pdf

within the peace and security agenda. [...] On the ground, the release of children by some parties to conflict where the MRM is applied is a notable positive apparent impact of the mechanism.[37]

PROTECTION OF CIVILIANS

In the 1990s, almost all UN peacekeeping operations were faced with the challenge of operating amidst extreme violence against civilians perpetrated by the combatants. Violence against civilians led to genocide in Rwanda and former Yugoslavia. In Congo, Darfur in Sudan, Sierra Leone, Liberia, Haiti and Somalia, combatants committed violence against civilians, rape and sexual abuse of women, recruited children as soldiers, displaced a vast number of people and denied civilians access to humanitarian aid.

The Security Council in 1999 adopted resolution 1265 which was the Council's first thematic resolution on the protection of civilians. The resolution noted that civilians accounted for the vast majority of casualties in armed conflicts. It expressed its willingness to respond to situations of armed conflict where civilians were being targeted and to consider how to ensure peacekeeping mandates address protection of civilians.[38]

As mandated by resolution 1265, the Secretary-General submitted a report on September 1999 on the protection of civilians in armed conflict. The Secretary-General noted that in many armed conflicts, civilian casualties and destruction of civilian infrastructure are the result of deliberate targeting of non-combatants. Forced displacement of civilians is another feature of armed conflicts. The report identified specific problems faced by women and children. Combatants restrict civilians' access to food and other assistance. Humanitarian workers and peacekeeping personnel are increasingly targeted. The Secretary-General recommended that the Security Council promote the protection of civilians by using peacekeeping or enforcement measures under the UN Charters VI, VII or VIII. The Secretary-General further

---

[37] Ibid.

[38] United Nations. (1999). *Adopted by the Security Council at its 4046th meeting on 17 September 1999.* http://unscr.com/en/resolutions/doc/1265

recommended deployment of preventive peacekeeping, investigation of disputes at an early stage, establishment of Security Council Working Groups on specific volatile situations and use of information and analysis provided by human rights experts and other reliable sources to take preventive action.[39]

In 2000, the Security Council adopted resolution 1296. With this resolution, the Security Council reaffirmed resolution 1265 and indicated in situations characterized by the threat of genocide, crimes against humanity and war crimes against the civilian population, it is willing to consider setting up temporary security zones and safe corridors for the protection of civilians and the delivery of humanitarian assistance.[40]

In April 2000, the Secretary-General submitted his second report on the protection of civilians in armed conflict. He noted the need for updating the political, legal instruments available for the protection of civilians in armed conflict, since they were developed when the UN was almost exclusively focused on the interaction of Member States. He recommended, among others, a provision of additional support for existing or future international tribunals to bring perpetrators to justice, to develop clear criteria and procedure for the identification and separation of armed elements in situations of massive population displacement and to continue investigating the linkages between illicit trade in natural resources and the conduct of war and take appropriate measures against corporate actors and individuals and entities involved in such acts.[41]

In 2009, UNDPKO and the UN Office for the Coordination of Humanitarian Affairs (OCHA) published the findings of a joint

[39] United Nations. (1999). *Report of the Secretary-General to the Security Council on the protection of civilians in armed conflict.* https://undocs.org/S/1999/957

[40] United Nations. (2000, 19 April). *Resolution 1296 (2000): Adopted by the security council at its 4130th meeting, on 19 April 2000* (para 15). Security Council, S/RES/1296 (2000). http://unscr.com/en/resolutions/doc/1296

[41] United Nations. (2001). *Report of the Secretary-General to the Security Council on the protection of civilians in armed conflict.* Protection of Civilians in Armed Conflict—SecGen Report, Security Council, S/2001/331. https://www.un.org/unispal/document/auto-insert-177959/

independent study on 'Protecting Civilians in the Context of UN Peacekeeping Operations'[42]. A major finding of the study was that missions often fail in their protection of civilians mandate due to failings in policy, planning and preparedness.[43] In 2015, DPKO/DFS issued a new policy on protection of civilians in its field operations. The guidelines proposed three layers of action: first, through engagement and dialogue, second, through provision of physical protection and third, through military tasks for creating a protective environment.[44]

In 2019, the UN issued the POC policy followed by a POC Handbook in 2020. The policy recognized different contexts in which protection of civilians happens and proposed flexible approach to changing situations.

The 2020 Handbook, based on best practices, proposed the following principles.

- Protecting civilians is the primary responsibility of governments.
- Peacekeepers with a mandate to protect civilians have the authority and responsibility to provide protection within their capabilities and areas of deployment where the government is unable or unwilling to protect.
- The protection of civilians mandate is a whole-of-mission activity, not only a military task, which embodies an active duty to protect.
- Protecting civilians is done in cooperation with humanitarian actors and with respect for humanitarian principles.
- The protection of civilians mandate is consonant with the principles of peacekeeping, including the consent of the host state, impartial mandate implementation and the use of force only in self-defence or as authorized by the Security Council.

---

[42] Holt, V., Taylor, G., & Kelly, M. (2009). *Protecting civilians in the context of UN peacekeeping operations: Successes, setbacks and remaining challenges.* Independent Study Jointly Commissioned by the Department of Peacekeeping Operations and the Office for the Coordination of Humanitarian Affairs, United Nations. https://reliefweb.int/sites/reliefweb.int/files/resources/B752FF2063E282B08525767100751B90-unocha_protecting_nov2009.pdf

[43] Ibid.

[44] United Nations. (2015). *Protection of civilians in UN peace keeping.* https://protectionofcivilians.org/wp/wp-content/uploads/2018/03/DPKO-DFS-2015-Policy-on-the-Protection-of-Civilians-in-United-Nations-Peacekeeping.pdf

- The protection of civilians mandate is a priority mandate, pursuant to Security Council resolutions".[45]

THE INTERNATIONAL COMMISSION ON INTERVENTION AND STATE SOVEREIGNTY

In September 2000, the Canadian government established the International Commission on Intervention and State Sovereignty (ICISS). In December 2001, the ICISS released its report 'The Responsibility to Protect'. The report, on its challenges, stated that if humanitarian intervention is considered an assault on sovereignty, how should we respond to gross and systematic violations of human rights.[46]

The ICISS report enunciated the idea that sovereignty entails not only rights but also responsibilities of a state to protect its people from major violations of human rights. In the event of a state being unwilling or unable to protect its people, the international community has a responsibility to intervene. It laid down the principle of responsibility to protect as follows: 'Where a population is suffering serious harm, as a result of internal war, insurgency, repression or state failure, and the state in question is unwilling or unable to halt or avert it, the principle of non-intervention yields to the international responsibility to protect'.[47]

2005: UN WORLD SUMMIT

In September 2005, more than 170 heads of state and governments met at a UN World Summit and adopted a wide-ranging agenda on development, security, human rights and reform of the UN.[48] Among

[45] United Nations. (2020). *Protection of civilians mandate*. https://peacekeeping.un.org/en/protection-of-civilians-mandate

[46] International Commission on Intervention and State Sovereignty. (2001). *The responsibility to protect: Report of the International Commission on Intervention and State Sovereignty*. International Development Research Centre. https://www.idrc.ca/en/book/responsibility-protect-report-international-commission-intervention-and-state-sovereignty

[47] Ibid.

[48] United Nations. (2005, September). *The 2005 world summit: High-level plenary meeting of the 60th session of the UN General Assembly* (14–16 September 2005, UN Headquarters, New York). Conferences, Meetings and Events. https://www.un.org/en/events/pastevents/worldsummit_2005.shtml

others, the World Summit agreed on the idea of responsibility to protect (paras 138 and 139 of the Summit document). The UN World Summit document restricted application of responsibility to protect to genocide, war crimes, crimes against humanity and ethnic cleansing. The document also reaffirmed the exclusive role of the Security Council in authorizing interventions.[49]

UN SECRETARY-GENERAL'S 2009 REPORTS

The UN Secretary-General issued two reports in 2009. The first was issued in January 2009 on 'Implementing the Responsibility to Protect' and the second in May 2009 on 'Protection of Civilians'.[50] The Secretary-General's report on protection of civilians is submitted annually for discussions at the Security Council.

SECRETARY-GENERAL'S REPORT ON IMPLEMENTING THE RESPONSIBILITY TO PROTECT

The Secretary-General called for a response strategy based on the agreement made by states in 2005 on the responsibility to protect. A consistent, fair and reliable response would generate confidence in the capacity of the UN to provide a credible multilateral alternative and help deter potential perpetrators of such crimes and violations. In his report, the Secretary-General referred to the concept of preventive deployment and cited the examples of former Yugoslavia, Republic of Macedonia, Burundi, Sierra Leone and the Democratic Republic of the Congo where consent-based international military forces were deployed to help prevent escalation of armed conflict (these deployments predate the acceptance of responsibility to protect concept in 2005).[51]

---

[49] Ibid.

[50] United Nations. (2001). *Report of the Secretary-General to the Security Council on the protection of civilians in armed conflict*. Protection of Civilians in Armed Conflict–SecGen Report, Security Council, S/2001/331. https://www.un.org/unispal/document/auto-insert-177959/

[51] United Nations Security Council. (2009). *Report of the Secretary-General on protection of civilians in armed conflict*. http://www.securitycouncilreport.org/atf/cf/%7B65BFCF9B-6D27-4E9C-8CD3-CF6E4FF96FF9%7D/POC%20S2009277.pdf

SECRETARY-GENERAL'S REPORT ON THE PROTECTION OF CIVILIANS

In May 2009, the Secretary-General issued a report on the protection of civilians to mark the 10th anniversary of the Security Council resolution 1265, which for the first time initiated discussion on the subject. The Secretary-General noted that despite the resolutions and actions taken in the last decade, the situation of civilians in conflicts 'is depressingly similar to that which prevailed in 1999'.[52]

The Secretary-General identified five core challenges: compliance with international law, compliance by non-state armed groups, resourcing UN peacekeeping missions, enhancing humanitarian access and enhancing accountability for violations. The Secretary-General welcomed the inclusion of protection activities in the mandates of peacekeeping missions. He called for the provision of additional capacity for robust protection mandates and the provision of required human and logistical and tactical capacity to ensure protection of civilians on the ground.[53]

An assessment on 20 years of protection of civilians in peacekeeping operations acknowledged that significant progress has been made, but there remains lot more to be done.[54]

AFRICAN UNION'S INITIATIVE ON THE PROTECTION OF CIVILIANS

Wars in Africa, particularly intrastate conflicts, have contributed to immense suffering for civilian populations. Studies have shown that nearly 90 per cent of victims of wars in Africa were civilians.[55] The human cost of numerous conflicts in Africa made the protection

---

[52] Ibid.

[53] Ibid.

[54] Hunt, C., & Zimmerman, S. (2020). Twenty years of the protection of civilians in UN peace operations—Progress problems and prospects. *Journal of International Peace Keeping, 23*(1–2), 50–81.

[55] Williams, P. D. (2010). *Enhancing civilian protection in peace operations: Insights from Africa.* Africa Center for Strategic Studies Research Paper No. 1. National Defense University Press.

of civilians a critical issue for the AU. As the protection of civilians emerged as a significant issue at the UN Security Council, the AU also deliberated on the subject. Beginning in the 1990s, AU's predecessor Organization of African Unity (OAU) began intervening in conflicts based on humanitarian concerns. Acknowledging that conflicts in Africa were intrastate conflicts, the OAU and later the AU started developing a legal and institutional framework for conflict management. A significant development was the adoption of the African Union Constitutive Act in July 2000. Article 4(h) of the Act stipulated the right to intervene in a Member State 'regarding grave circumstances, namely, war crimes, genocide and crimes against humanity'.[56] By adopting this Act, the AU changed its earlier position of non-interference. It deemed that the protection of civilians is a legitimate reason to interfere in the internal affairs of a Member State.[57] In 2006, based on its experience in dealing with the protection of civilians, AU developed a doctrine for its Peace Support Operations (PSOs). The doctrine, among others, stipulated that protection of non-combatant's life and dignity is fundamental to all PSOs. It also identified tasks such as the protection of aid agencies, safeguarding aid routes, the safety of refugee camps, curbing human rights abuses and apprehension of war criminals.[58] With varying support from the UN, exclusively, Africa-led peacekeeping operations to protect civilians were deployed in Liberia (1990–1997), Sierra Leone (1997–2000), Burundi (2003–2004) and Darfur in Sudan (2003–2007).[59] The UNAMID's 2010 strategy

[56] Constitutive Act of the African Union. (2000). https://au.int/sites/default/files/pages/34873-file-constitutiveact_en.pdf

[57] Bergholm, L. (2010). *The African Union, the United Nations and civilian protection challenges in Darfur* (Working Paper Series, No. 63). Refugee Studies Centre, Oxford Department of International Development, University of Oxford. https://www.rsc.ox.ac.uk/files/files-1/wp63-au-un-civilian-protection-challenges-darfur-2010.pdf

[58] Williams, P. D. (2010). *Enhancing civilian protection in peace operations: Insights from Africa* (Africa Center for Strategic Studies Research Paper No. 1). National Defense University Press.

[59] Bergholm, L. (2010). *The African Union, the United Nations and civilian protection challenges in Darfur* (Working Paper Series, No. 63). Refugee Studies Centre, Oxford Department of International Development, University of Oxford. https://www.rsc.ox.ac.uk/files/files-1/wp63-au-un-civilian-protection-challenges-darfur-2010.pdf

reflected AU's commitment to the protection of civilians by stressing two interconnected activities—physical protection and protection of humanitarian space.[60]

SOME OBSERVATIONS ON CIVILIAN COMPONENTS IN PEACEKEEPING OPERATIONS

Responding to situations on the field and normative developments at the global level, the UN integrated civilian components dealing with thematic and group concerns into peacekeeping operations. These include integration of human rights and the rule of law; women, peace and security; sexual and gender-based violence; children and armed conflict; and the protection of civilians in armed conflict. UNMISS provides an example of types of civilian components included in a mission. UNMISS includes the following civilian components: Child Protection, Civil Affairs, Gender Section, HIV/AIDS Unit, HRD, and the Relief, Reintegration and Protection (RRP) Section. In addition, UNMISS includes specialized service provided by the UN Mines Action Service (UNMAS).

All the above components have staff in the field, which means that a field office would have at least six international and corresponding national staff. Normally, some of the sections have several international civilian staff in each field office. In addition, each field office would also have administrative and other support staff. It means that the salary for the civilian staff in a field office comes to hundreds to thousands of US dollars. This is in a situation where 80 per cent of the South Sudanese population live on an equivalent of less than US$1 per day.

Security considerations may often restrict the movement of civilian staff and confine them to the office. It is not clear why a field office should have so many staff with often overlapping mandates. It is the same with most peacekeeping operations deployed in ongoing conflict

---

[60] Williams, P. D. (2010). *Enhancing civilian protection in peace operations: Insights from Africa* (Africa Center for Strategic Studies Research Paper No. 1). National Defense University Press.

situations. The integration of various thematic and group concerns in peacekeeping operations is a welcome step. However, in practice, it means each thematic or group mandate is vying to deploy as many staff as possible as a proof of its importance. Most often, it is based on templates. The deployment of numerous overlapping mandates creates managerial challenge for SRSG and the two deputies and distracts them from their core functions.

When a mission staff is evacuated for security reasons, most staff remain idle waiting for redeployment in the mission area which sometime takes several months. While the security of staff is fundamental, deployment of a large number of civilian staff adds to security problems and contributes to enormous wastage of resources. In response to the HIPPO report, the Secretary-General Ban Ki-moon proposed to the Security Council that

> With due consideration for the requirements of flexibility to respond to differing contexts, a dedicated capacity for specialized protection functions relating to child protection and conflict-related sexual violence will be consolidated within mission human rights components. The head of the component will be responsible, through the head of mission, for the implementation of those specialized mandates and ensure that the Special Representatives of the Secretary-General for Children and Armed Conflict and on Sexual Violence in Conflict have the engagement, information and support required for the delivery of their respective mandates.[61]

However, his proposal was opposed by some thematic mandates. In 2017, at the request of the Security Council, the Secretary-General initiated an independent assessment of UNAMI. The assessment report recommended the integration of Women's Protection Unit and Child Protection Unit into the Human Rights Office.[62] What is required

[61] United Nations. (2015, 2 September). *The future of United Nations peace operations: Implementation of the recommendations of the high-level independent panel on peace operations.* General Assembly Security Council, A/70/357-S/2015/682. https://www.securitycouncilreport.org/atf/cf/%7B65BFCF9B-6D27-4E9C-8CD3-CF6E4FF96FF9%7D/s_2015_682.pdf

[62] United Nations. (2017, 20 November). *Letter dated 15 November 2017 from the Secretary-General addressed to the President of the Security Council.* Security Council, S/2017/966. http://www.securitycouncilreport.org/atf/cf/%7B65BFCF9B-6D27-4E9C-8CD3-CF6E4FF96FF9%7D/s_2017_966.pdf

is a UN-initiated comprehensive study on civilian components and peacekeeping operations.

The Brahimi Report, HIPPO Report and Capstone Document provided guidance on macro issues and stressed the importance of civilian components in peacekeeping operations. Twenty years after the Brahimi Report, it is time to learn lessons from the deployment of civilian staff dealing with substantive issues. It would be valuable to particularly examine the overlap of mandates, their functions, evacuation and its impact on the work of civilian staff/resources and whether deployment of civilian staff could be sequenced and/or rationalized.

Human Rights Component in Operations

First Phase—1990–1998

Between 1990 and 1998, human rights were a part of peacekeeping operations in the following countries: El Salvador (1991), Cambodia (1992), Rwanda (1993), Guatemala (1994), Haiti (1993) and Angola (1995).[1]

EL SALVADOR AND GUATEMALA

Interestingly, El Salvador and Guatemala missions were initially set up for human rights monitoring/verification to create the conditions for peace agreement and deployment of a full-fledged mission.

During the 1980s, authoritarian regimes in Latin and Central American countries committed gross violations of human rights in their efforts to suppress both peaceful and armed opposition groups. Opposition groups, including armed opposition groups, demanded an end to human rights violations during the negotiations for a finalizing peace agreement.

El Salvador

In July 1990, the Salvadoran government and FMLN signed an agreement prior to agreeing on a ceasefire. The agreement signed in San Jose, Costa

---

[1] DPKO managed Cambodia and Angola. However, the Human Rights Field Operation in Rwanda (HRFOR) was managed by the High Commissioner for Human Rights, even though UNAMIR was present in the country. We are not examining OHCHR offices established during this period in Burundi (1996) and Colombia (1996). The presence in Croatia, Bosnia and Herzegovina and Republic of Macedonia (1995) was under OSCE. Rwanda (HRFOR) was the first human rights component that was under OHCHR while UNAMIR was deployed in the country.

Rica, was known as the 'Agreement on Human Rights' and provided for a verification mission to monitor nationwide respect for and the guarantee of human rights and fundamental freedoms in El Salvador.[2] In May 1991, the UN Security Council approved ONUSAL and the establishment of the Human Rights Division. Its mandate included actively monitoring the human rights situation in the country, investigating cases of alleged human rights violations and reporting to the UN General Assembly and Security Council. In January 1992, the parties signed a final peace settlement in Mexico City. After the signing of the final agreement, two new divisions, military and police, were added to ONUSAL.[3]

The San Jose Agreement provided ONUSAL with wide-ranging powers to verify observance of human rights. It had powers to receive communications regarding human rights violations from any individual, groups or body in El Salvador; visit any place or establishment freely without any prior notice; interview freely individuals or members of bodies or institutions; and hold meetings freely anywhere in the country. As part of the agreement, ONUSAL set up six regional and subregional offices and deployed over 100 human rights, police and military observers throughout the country. ONUSAL was unique in that for the first time, the UN had monitored the human rights situation in a Member State and certainly the first time such an undertaking had been attempted in the absence of a ceasefire.[4]

After the signing of the final agreement in January 1992, ONUSAL's human rights mandate was expanded to include judicial reform, elaboration of a new military doctrine, restructuring of the armed forces, formation of a National Civilian Police (PNC), establishment of an Office of the Human Rights Ombudsman (Procuraduria) and setting up a Truth Commission to investigate the abuses committed during the war.

---

[2] United Nations. (1990). *Background: Full text.* https://peacekeeping.un.org/en/mission/past/onusalbackgr2.html

[3] Ibid.

[4] Arnson, C., & Holiday, D. (1992, 2 September). *Peace and human rights: Successes and shortcomings of the United Nations observer mission in EL SALVADOR (ONUSAL).* News from Americas Watch. https://www.hrw.org/legacy/reports/pdfs/e/elsalvdr/elsalv929.pdf

A human rights expert observed that active monitoring of human rights created the conditions for peacebuilding by improving the country's internal situation.[5]

The Human Rights Division, through its 'active verification process', documented and meticulously verified information regarding human rights violations and sought remedies for them.[6] Verification of human rights violations did not end with mere denunciations; it resulted in strengthening institutions by seeking remedies for them, and, wherever necessary, assisting them in the process. HRD provided targeted assistance to institutions based on gaps identified through monitoring, and it was not done for the sake of providing technical assistance. 'Active verification' included proactive identification of issues and intervention.[7] Based on information regarding massive and systematic practice of arbitrary detentions, HRD conducted unannounced verification in 26 municipal and police jails throughout the country. The visits resulted in a range of legal, procedural and institutional reforms to prevent arbitrary detentions in the future.[8]

HRD contributed to reforming the process of appointment of judges of the Supreme Court and other procedural reforms to ensure independence of the judiciary at various levels. The constitutional amendments that were made as part of the peace agreement resulted in the establishment of the Office of the Human Rights Ombudsman (Procuraduria). HRD ensured that the Office of the Human Rights Ombudsman was given powers and resources to carry out its mandate. The Division assisted the Ombudsman Office in developing its procedures and tools.

The deployment of HRD led to a dramatic decrease in the number of gross violations of human rights between 1992 and 1994, including ending the practice of disappearances.[9]

---

[5] Garcia-Sayan, D. (1994). Human rights and peace-keeping operations. *University of Richmond Law Review*, *29*(1), 41–65. https://scholarship.richmond.edu/cgi/viewcontent.cgi?article=2118&context=lawreview

[6] Ibid.

[7] Ibid.

[8] Ibid.

[9] Ibid.

ONUSAL's other major achievement was the establishment of the Truth Commission for El Salvador. The Commission was mandated to determine the truth about the violence that took place during the internal war and make recommendations to prevent repetition of similar crimes in the future. The UN Secretary-General appointed three non-Salvadoran members to the Commission to ensure its impartiality.[10] The Commission concluded that the armed forces and paramilitary death squads supported by them were responsible for more than 90 per cent of the human rights violations committed since the 1980s. The Commission made numerous recommendations including on judicial reforms and for ensuring accountability.[11]

ONUSAL's Human Rights Division faced numerous challenges including violent attacks and lack of cooperation from the judiciary, police and other officials. The Division deployed a large number of human rights personnel due to the availability of experienced human rights workers within the country and in the region. The success of ONUSAL's HRD was attributed to its size and presence across the country, UN's prestige and moral authority and its ability to visit places without prior notice including barracks and detention centres.[12] The success was also due to the commitment of both parties to find negotiated settlement and implement the agreement in good faith.

The peace accords created favourable conditions for protection of human rights and to move from conflict to peace.[13]

---

[10] Commission members were Belisario Betancur, former president of Colombia and president of the Commission; Reinaldo Figueredo, former foreign minister of Venezuela; and Thomas Buergenthal, professor of law and honorary president of the Inter-American Institute for Human Rights in Costa Rica.

[11] Stein, S. (2012). *When do comprehensive peacekeeping operations succeed? The case of the un observer mission in El Salvador (onusal) and the un verification mission in Guatemala (minugua)* (Electronic Theses and Dissertations, 2004–2019). University of Central Florida. https://stars.library.ucf.edu/cgi/viewcontent.cgi?article=3328&context=etd

[12] Arnson, C., & Holiday, D. (1992, 2 September). *Peace and human rights: Successes and shortcomings of the United Nations observer mission in EL SALVADOR (ONUSAL)*. News from Americas Watch. https://www.hrw.org/legacy/reports/pdfs/e/elsalvdr/elsalv929.pdf

[13] Ibid.

Guatemala

In March 1994, the UN-sponsored peace talks led to an agreement between the government and URNG representing the rebels. The agreement was called the 'Comprehensive Agreement on Human Rights'; it was as an interim measure pending final peace agreement. The pact provided a structure for promoting human rights in Guatemala.

The UN Mission for the Verification of Human Rights and of Compliance with the Comprehensive Agreement on Human Rights in Guatemala (MINUGUA was mandated to verify and report on human rights violations. MINUGUA functioned as a verification mission till 1996, when both parties signed the final peace treaty. In January 1997, the Security Council authorized the addition of military observers to MINUGUA, and the name of the mission was changed to United Nations Verification Mission in Guatemala (the acronym MINUGUA remained) and expanded to implement a full-range peacekeeping operation.

MINUGUA deployed more than 250 human rights monitors throughout the country. It compiled reports based on investigations conducted on human rights complaints received from throughout the country. Some influential sections of the Guatemalan society opposed the deployment of MINUGUA. The mission faced harassment and threats. It also did not receive full support from the government and armed forces. Despite the challenges, MINUGUA contributed to reduction of human rights violations.

In June 1994, the parties agreed to establish the Guatemala's Commission for Historical Clarification. The Commission functioned from 1997 to 1999 with a mandate to clarify human rights violations committed between 1960 and 1996 and to foster tolerance and preserve memories of victims. The Commission was not to judge but to clarify the past. In 1999, the Commission issued a 12-volume report titled 'Guatemala: Memory of Silence'.[14] The Commission established that more than 200,000 people were killed or disappeared,

---

[14] Human Rights Data Analysis Group (HRDAG). (1999). *Gutemala-memory of silence: Report of the commission for historical clarification: Conclusions and recommendations 1999.* https://hrdag.org/wp-content/uploads/2013/01/CEHreport-english.pdf

and 83 per cent of the victims were Mayans. Paramilitary groups were responsible for 93 per cent of the violations. Former officials resisted prosecution based on the Commission's findings. A decade later, some progress was made with the UN assisting in the establishment of CICIG. CICIG's mandate was to conduct independent investigations, present criminal cases to a Public Prosecutor and function as a complementary prosecutor in criminal proceedings. In 2009, a retired colonel and three paramilitaries were successfully convicted for disappearances during the civil war.

Both ONUSAL and MINUGUA built on human rights tools used by civil society groups in the region. Both missions also contributed to the development of transitional justice concepts. Both were the first and the last UN operations with focus on human rights to create conditions for peace agreement. Subsequently, all UN peacekeeping operations included human rights but as a component of multidimensional missions.[15]

CAMBODIA

In 1992, the UN deployed UNTAC. It was the first large multidimensional peacekeeping operation in the post-Cold War period. The Pol Pot regime's policies and actions led to the death of 1.5–2.2 million Cambodians due to hunger, starvation and killings. The regime tortured its alleged opponents and developed various torture methods which became known after the regime was overthrown. Consequently, human rights became a major concern in the negotiations to end the conflict including the withdrawal of Vietnamese forces from Cambodia. However, major players involved in the peace agreement—the SOC that was ruling the country and Vietnam, China and the ASEAN governments—were not interested in human rights. The human rights aspect was included in the final peace agreement, mainly due to insistence by some Western governments and

---

[15] The UNMIN was preceded by the establishment of the OHCHR office. However, in El Salvador and Guatemala, human rights intervention was proposed as creating the conditions for peace accords. In Nepal, the OHCHR office was not proposed as laying the ground for peace agreement between the parties.

international human rights NGOs. UNTAC included a small human rights component. Initially, 10 HROs were deployed when UNTAC had about 20,000 personnel. Subsequently, the number increased with deployment of one HRO in each province and with several staff in the headquarters.[16]

The Human Rights Office mandate included investigation of allegations of human rights abuses, oversight of judicial and other institutions, general oversight of human rights aspects of UNTAC components and conduct of human rights education.[17] UNTAC human rights component's major contribution was the emergence of human rights and other NGOs in Cambodia; for example, the Association for Human Rights in Cambodia (ADHOC) and the Cambodian League for the Promotion and Defense of Human Rights were established at that time and continued to work for human rights in Cambodia under difficult circumstances. UNTAC's human rights component, in November 1992, organized an International Symposium on Human Rights in Cambodia to link the local NGOs with regional and international organizations to ensure continued support for local groups after the UNTAC period. It also established a Human Rights Trust Fund to assist local NGOs. UNTAC's human rights component, using traditional Khmer cultural media singers, puppets, comics and local artists, conducted extensive human rights education throughout the country.

UNTAC's human rights component faced numerous challenges. The Special Representative of the Secretary-General, Yasushi Akashi, was not supportive of seeking accountability for human rights violations. He did not encourage the human rights component to seek dismissal or transfer of officials who had committed human rights abuses. Despite running a transitional administration, Akashi considered the power to effect arrests or prosecute suspects to be the responsibility of enforcement authorities under the SOC or other factions. The SOC authorities refused to act against its officials.

---

16 The Human Rights Centre. (1998, 11–13 February). *Conference on the promotion and protection of human rights in acute crisis.* https://www1.essex.ac.uk/rightsinacutecrisis/default.htm

17 United Nations. (1990). *Background: Full text.* https://peacekeeping.un.org/en/mission/past/onusalbackgr2.html

The human rights component's proposal to establish a special prosecutor's office and deploy international judges faced internal opposition.[18] The human rights enforcement was, therefore, 'dilatory, sporadic and improvised'.[19] International human rights NGOs criticized UNTAC for the lack of progress in ensuring accountability for human rights abuses and argued that 'corrective action' envisaged in the UNTAC mandate included arresting and prosecuting perpetrators.[20] The human rights component suffered from the lack of resources. The UNTAC leadership was more concerned about political settlement to successfully conduct the elections rather than on state-building. Akashi took a position that in the context of Cambodia, it was unrealistic to seek robust accountability for past crimes.[21] The Cambodian judiciary was destroyed during the war, and the judicial system that emerged under the SOC was not independent. The human rights component conducted training for judges but was not able to revamp the system, consequences of which are still felt in the country.

The Head of UNTAC's human rights component, in his final report submitted in September 1993, concluded that UNTAC human rights mandate was not appreciated and was seen as conflicting with the mission's political and diplomatic efforts.[22] Finally, UNTAC was complicit in allowing Hun Sen (SOC) to share power with the opposition party that won the election. Hun Sen resorted to violence after the election, and UNTAC allowed him to share power even though he had lost the election.[23]

---

[18] United Nations. (1993, September). *Human rights component final report*. United Nations Transitional Authority in Cambodia. https://cambodia.ohchr.org/sites/default/files/report/other-report/Other_CMB091993E_0.pdf

[19] Findlay, T. (1995). *Cambodia: The legacy and lessons and UNTAC* (Stockholm International Peace Research Institute [SIPRI], Research Report No. 9). Oxford University Press. https://www.sipri.org/sites/default/files/files/RR/SIPRIRR09.pdf

[20] Ibid.

[21] Ibid.

[22] United Nations. (1993, September). *Human rights component final report*. United Nations Transitional Authority in Cambodia. https://cambodia.ohchr.org/sites/default/files/report/other-report/Other_CMB091993E_0.pdf

[23] Adams, B. (1998). UN Human rights work in Cambodia: Efforts to preserve the jewel in the peacekeeping crown. In A. H. Henkin (Ed.), *Honoring human rights from peace to justice*. Kluwer Law International.

Human Rights Watch was prophetic and stated that UN's weak support to human rights would lay the foundation for violence and impunity.[24] Twenty-seven years after UNTAC left, Hun Sen continues to rule Cambodia with an iron grip using violence and patronage to maintain his power. Despite UNTAC's success in conducting elections, the political arrangement that emerged at the end of its mission continues to haunt the international community with regard to ensuring democracy and human rights in Cambodia.

The UN Human Rights Commission approved UNTAC's proposal for continued human rights presence which remains in the country till now.[25] The Secretary-General appointed a Special Representative for Human Rights in Cambodia. The Special Representative's mandate was subsequently modified to include protection of human rights in collaboration with the Centre for Human Rights. Thus, the Special Representative's role was strengthened to include monitoring and engaging with the government on human rights issues. Hun Sen was critical of Human Rights Office's monitoring role and wanted it to limit its activities to education and training. In 1996, the Human Rights Commission adopted a resolution clarifying the monitoring role and ended the ambivalence surrounding its role of the Office.

The international community and the Human Rights Office were faced with the daunting task of rebuilding the country's non-existent or destroyed institutions. The police, prosecution, judiciary and legal profession needed to be built from scratch under a government that was least interested in human rights. The lack of human resources was a major obstacle as well. After UNTAC's departure, Cambodia witnessed disparate efforts to rebuild its institutions. In particular, the mangled legal and judicial system was superimposed with systems depending on which donor provided the assistance. The most famous (or infamous) programme was the USAID-funded International Human Rights Law Group's US$3 million, three-year project called the

---

[24] Findlay, T. (1995). *Cambodia: The legacy and lessons and UNTAC* (Stockholm International Peace Research Institute [SIPRI], Research Report No. 9). Oxford University Press. https://www.sipri.org/sites/default/files/files/RR/SIPRIRR09.pdf

[25] In 1993, the UN Human Rights Centre assumed responsibility for running the office, and it now functions as a stand-alone office of OHCHR.

Cambodian Court Training Project (CCTP). Brad Adams, a former staff of the Cambodia Human Rights Office, observed that most trainers were young American lawyers without any clue about the Cambodian situation. Their teaching had no basis to the Cambodian reality and caused confusion among the participants. The participants were more interested in the per diems and perks and considered the course a waste of time.[26]

Similarly, human rights education programme conducted by the office and the NGOs mainly focused on disseminating human rights treaties and standards. They suffered from the lack of clarity on how the standards could be applied in the Cambodian context, unimaginative teaching methods and problems in communicating in Khmer language through a local interpreter who was not familiar with the subject. Since its beginning, the Cambodia Office suffered from OHCHR's lack of experience in running a major field office. It faced leadership and administrative problems.[27]

The establishment of the Human Rights Office and the appointment of the Special Representative after the closure of UNTAC provided a valuable opportunity for the Cambodian government to build a country based on respect for human rights and the rule of law. However, Hun Sen was more interested in consolidating his power through violence and patronage and was least concerned about the human rights of Cambodians. The role of the Special Representative (beginning from 2000) and the office became increasingly marginal with Hun Sen having a free hand in suppressing the opposition and presiding over a corrupt system. The office presently remains as a symbol from the past waiting for a democratic change to pursue its original mandate.[28]

---

[26] Adams, B. (1998). UN human rights work in Cambodia: Efforts to preserve the jewel in the peacekeeping crown. In A. H. Henkin (Ed.), *Honoring human rights from peace to justice*. Kluwer Law International.

[27] The author worked at the Cambodia office from 1999 to 2002 in various capacities.

[28] Since its inception, several times, Hun Sen had threatened to close the office and not renew MoU with OHCHR. In December 2019, he refused to renew the agreement, accusing the office of interfering in internal political affairs. He signed an agreement in February 2020 to extend the office's term for two years.

ANGOLA

Starting in 1988, the UN deployed a series of missions in Angola. They were based on the agreement made between the Angolan government and the armed opposition group UNITA. In 1988, UNAVEM I was deployed to verify the withdrawal of Cuban troops. In 1992, UNAVEM II was deployed to monitor ceasefire and demobilization of forces. In 1995, UNVAEM III was deployed with an expanded mandate that included military, political, civilian police, humanitarian and electoral aspects. In 1997, UNAVEM III was replaced by MONUA. Both UNAVEM III and MONUA included a human rights component.

UNAVEM II was concerned with ceasefire monitoring and ignored human rights violations. It organized a high-profile International Symposium on Human Rights which seemed irrelevant in the prevailing context of human rights violations committed by the government and UNITA. The mission did not publish reports on human rights violations committed by both the parties. Human Rights Watch argued for a clean break from the past by making the Angolan leaders accountable for their abuses of human rights.[29]

UNAVEM III included a small human rights component. The Security Council, in August 1995, passed a resolution recognizing the role of human rights monitors and authorizing the Secretary-General to increase the strength of UNAVEM III's human rights unit.[30]

Following the Security Council's resolution, SRSG Alioune Blondin Beye sought the assistance of various foreign ministries for deployment of human rights experts. Denmark, France and Portugal provided three experts for six months in 1995 and the number increased to five. This formed the human rights unit which worked under the Political Affairs Division. Beye appointed Amadou Niang, a Malian, without much human rights experience but with family connections to Beye, to head the unit.[31]

---

[29] Human Rights Watch. (1999). *X. The United Nations*. https://www.hrw.org/reports/1999/angola/Angl998-10.htm

[30] Ibid.

[31] Ibid.

Though the human rights unit existed in Angola, not much serious monitoring work was done by it. Senior mission officials considered human rights too sensitive and did not even acknowledge its existence. Human rights experts on arrival were not briefed about their work and did not have office, computer or radios. Human rights staff posted in the field did not receive any support, feedback or guidance from the office in Luanda. According to Human Rights Watch, Amadou Niang, the head of UNAVEM's Human Rights Unit from 1995 to 1998, admitted that for most of 1995, human rights work had been on low priority. Human Rights Watch got access to a memo written by a staff member that stated that the mission's leadership showed little interest in reports prepared by HRD and the Division did not receive any feedback on its reports.[32]

In early 1996, the human rights unit deployed its staff in provinces including in UNITA-controlled areas. The unit's annual reports were about workshops and awareness building activities and did not contain information about human rights situation. In 1997, the unit was upgraded into a division within MONUA. In January 1998, the UN Secretary-General in his report on MONUA stated that HRD would investigate allegations of human rights violations and assist in capacity building of NGOs and sought more resources for the Division.[33]

Meanwhile, in 1997, the High Commissioner for Human Rights at the request of UNDPKO sent Ian Martin (former Secretary-General of Amnesty International and former head of human rights units in Rwanda and Haiti) to assess the work of the Human Rights Division. Martin in his report stated that for the peace process to succeed, human rights protection would be critical. Martin recommended that the Human Rights Division become proactive in working for the protection of human rights, including by assisting Angolan institutions. He proposed increasing the number of human rights staff and stressed the importance of hiring professional human rights monitoring staff.[34]

---

[32] Ibid.

[33] United Nations (1998, 12 January). *Report of the Secretary-General on the United Nations observer mission in Angola (MONUA)*. S/1998/17. https://documents-dds-ny.un.org/doc/UNDOC/GEN/N98/005/13/IMG/N9800513.pdf?OpenElement

[34] Martin, I. (1997, 2 February). *Report on the human rights activities of UNAVEM and proposals for an enhanced programme* (Unpublished Report). https://www.hrw.org/reports/1999/angola/Angl998-10.htm

In 1997, the Division continued to be marginal. It did not make efforts to link with Angolan NGOs or assist them. After a year-long search with three potential candidates turning down the offer, in May 1998, Nicholas Howen, former head of Amnesty International's legal department, became the head of the Division. Meanwhile, the peace process was heading to a collapse. SRSG Beye modified the mission strategy and encouraged human rights monitoring. The Human Rights Division, under Nicholas Howen, pursued a mandate focused on strengthening the justice system, monitoring human rights situation and strengthening civil society. The Division embarked upon outreach programmes by conducting creative human rights education initiatives. It also created local human rights committees to provide forums for victims to raise their concerns with local authorities.

In January 1999, the UN Secretary-General proposed ending MONUA's operation due to deteriorating security situation and lack of cooperation from both the parties. However, the UN continued its negotiations to ensure its presence to coordinate humanitarian situation which was dire. In June 1999, the Angolan government agreed for deployment of 30 UN personnel for coordinating humanitarian aid and strengthening the institutional capacity of the government in human rights. The government proposed that the UN personnel should be a part of the UNDP structures and not function independently. After further talks, the government agreed for establishment of the United Nations Office in Angola (UNOA) under the UN Political Affairs Department with a large human rights component. Through most of 1999, Human Rights Division's work was affected by the uncertainty about its existence and lack of resources. The Angolan War officially ended in August 2002. In February 2003, the UN mission ended its operations. OHCHR established a human rights office under the mandate of the UN Resident Coordinator. The office did not have monitoring mandate and was restricted to providing technical assistance.

HAITI

In 1986, Haitians mounted a massive protest against Baby Doc's corrupt rule, and he fled the country. Between 1986 and 1990, Haiti was ruled by short-lived military governments. In 1990, in an election conducted with the UN's assistance, National Front for Change and Democracy's Jean-Bertrand Aristide was elected as the president. His government was overthrown by a military coup in 1991. In September 1992, the OAS deployed a small civilian mission. From February 1993, the UN joined the OAS in what became a joint MICIVIH. The mission was mandated to monitor and investigate human rights violations.[35] In September 1993, it was followed by the establishment of UNMIH which operated till 1996.[36]

MICIVIH began deploying in the provinces by March 1993. Ian Martin, former Secretary-General of Amnesty International, served as the Director of the Human Rights Office. The Human Rights Office's mandate was to monitor human rights and make recommendations for the protection of human rights.[37] The Human Rights Office issued reports on violations, personnel involved in such violations and actions taken by the government. Despite threats by the army, thousands of civilians approached the mission staff to report human rights violations. Several human rights activists were tortured and/or killed for sharing information with the Human Rights Office. The human rights observers were authorized to visit any place where human rights violations may have occurred. The Haitian government was to guarantee the safety of mission members and ensure the security of persons who provided information or evidence regarding human rights violations. However, the governments failed to keep its commitment regarding safety of informants and the mission staff. The authorities even made weird allegations that the mission members were instigating demonstrations to report on police violence on such demonstrations.[38]

---

[35] United Nations. (2005). *Background: Summary*. https://peacekeeping.un.org/en/mission/past/unmihbackgr1.html

[36] Since then and till 2018, the UN had deployed five peace operations in Haiti: the UNSMIH (July 1996–July 1997), the UNTMIH (July 1997–November 1997), the MIPONUH (December 1997–March 2000), the MINUSTAH (2004–2017) and the MINJUSTH (October 2017–March 2018).

[37] Human Rights Watch. (1994, 1 April). *Terror prevails in Haiti: Human rights violations and failed diplomacy*. United Nations High Commissioner for Refugees. https://www.refworld.org/docid/3ae6a7f04.html

[38] Ibid.

In October 1993, when UNMIH personnel arrived by ship, armed militias prevented the ship from landing. Concerned about the safety of MICIVIH staff, the UN evacuated them also. The MICIVIH human rights staff's absence was felt in provincial towns where its presence had kept the military in check. In January 1994, the MICIVIH staff returned and began a gradual build-up.

During this period, the mission reported on human rights violations committed by military and its paramilitary entities. In July 1994, the military government ordered the international staff to leave the country within 48 h. Concerned about the safety of its staff, the UN evacuated them from Haiti. In September 1994, the Security Council authorized 20,000 strong international force led by the United States. After the force's intervention, the military rulers stepped down. In October 1994, MICIVIH returned to the country and resumed its monitoring and institution-building functions. In 1995, UNMIH took over from the multinational force and continued the stabilization process.[39]

Despite different mandates, MICIVIH and UNMIH complemented each other in the protection and promotion of human rights. The role of MICIVIH was modified to include police and prison reforms and assisting in the setting up of a Truth Commission and a new ombudsman. It also acquired the mandate to work closely with the Haitian human rights NGOs and strengthen their work. Despite dire economic situation, the mission was not mandated to work on economic, social and cultural (ESC) rights. The Haitians sought assistance for seeking jobs and development projects. To meet such requests, the mission provided technical advice on developing projects and fundraising to local organizations, particularly those that were established by the victims and internally displaced.[40] These activities came to an end with the reduction of staff in early 1996. MICIVIH pioneered the idea of setting up a medical unit for providing medical assistance to victims of past human rights abuses.

[39] United Nations. (2005). *Background: Summary*. https://peacekeeping.un.org/en/mission/past/unmihbackgr1.html

[40] Granderson, C. (1997). Institutionalizing peace: The Haiti experience. In A. H. Henkin (Ed.), *Honoring human rights and keeping the peace* (p. 227). Kluwer Law International.

MICIVIH was keenly aware of the close link between monitoring and technical cooperation activities. Based on its monitoring, it conducted studies on the judicial system (1994), on the criminal justice system (1996), on HNP after its first year of deployment (1996) and the Haitian penal system (1997). These studies provided the basis for donors to support projects for reforming these institutions. Based on its studies, MICIVIH was able to promote simple reforms like introduction of registers in police and prisons, which a first step towards protecting the rights of detained persons.

In the first phase in 1993, the human right component minimized human rights violations, assisted victims and drew the international community's attention to the situation. In 1994, with the military regime's lack of cooperation, the component, through its monitoring reports, played a role in influencing the debates in the UN and in the United States regarding ousting the regime. In the third phase under the constitutional government, it contributed to institution building, including in the establishment of a national civil police for the first time in the country.[41]

RWANDA

In October 1993, the UN Security Council deployed UNAMIR to monitor the Arusha Agreement signed between the Hutu-dominated Rwandan government and the armed opposition the Tutsi RPF. UNAMIR's mandate focused on monitoring ceasefire and referred to humanitarian assistance and repatriation of refugees. UNAMIR's mandate did not include reference to human rights.

In early April 1994, Hutu militia began systematically killing members of the Tutsi minority and moderate Hutus. In the killings and violence that lasted till mid-July, between 500,000 and 1 million persons lost their lives. RPF fought against the Rwandan military forces to halt the genocide and overthrow the Hutu-led government.

---

[41] The Human Rights Centre. (1998, 11–13 February). *Conference on the promotion and protection of human rights in acute crisis.* https://www1.essex.ac.uk/rightsinacutecrisis/default.htm

On 4 July, RPF captured the capital and more than two million Hutus fled to neighbouring countries. The RPF-led government detained a large number of persons for participating in the acts of genocide and other serious violations of human rights and humanitarian law. The justice system was in a total disarray with the killings of 80 per cent of judges and magistrates. Genocide was committed while UNAMIR was present in the country.

UNAMIR's Lack of Human Rights Mandate and Human Rights Response after the Genocide

The closest reference to human rights in UNAMIR's mandate was the wording 'to investigate and report on incidents regarding the activities of the gendarmerie and police'.[42] The Secretary-General appointed an independent inquiry commission to examine the UN's actions during the 1994 genocide in Rwanda. The Commission observed that the mission planning team was not aware of the disturbing report published only a couple of weeks before by the Special Rapporteur of the Commission on Human Rights on Summary and Extrajudicial Executions in which he had alerted about the possibility that a genocide was being committed in Rwanda.[43]

On 5 April 1994, the day after he assumed office, the High Commissioner José Ayala Lasso, was confronted with the violence in Rwanda. He convened an emergency session of the Human Rights Commission in May and visited Rwanda on 11–12 May 1994. He published his report on 19 May and stated that more than 200,000 civilians had been killed in a planned and concerted manner by the government and its supporters.[44]

The Security Council on 1 July 1994 established a Commission of Experts to examine and analyse information concerning responsibility

---

[42] Carlsson, I., Sung-Joo, H., & Kupolati, R. M. (1999). *Report of the independent inquiry into the actions of the United Nations during the 1994 genocide in Rwanda*. United Nations.

[43] Ibid.

[44] See note 54.

for serious violations of international humanitarian law committed in Rwanda, including genocide. The Commission concluded that the mass killings constituted 'genocide' within the meaning of the Convention on the Prevention and Punishment of the Crime of Genocide of 1948.[45] Based on the Commission's recommendations, the Security Council, in November 1994, created ICTR to prosecute those responsible for having committed genocide and other serious violations of international humanitarian law in the territory of Rwanda, and Rwandan citizens responsible for genocide and other such violations committed in the territory of neighbouring states during January–December 1994.

Deployment of Human Rights Observers

As proposed by the High Commissioner for Human Rights, in July 1994, a first group of human rights observers arrived in Rwanda. In August 1994, the Rwandan government and the High Commissioner concluded an agreement clarifying the status and mandate of HRFOR. The agreement included deployment of 147 human rights field officers, one for each of the country's communes. Even though UNAMIR continued its presence in Rwanda, HRFOR was under the authority of High Commissioner for Human Rights.[46]

HRFOR's mandate was (a) carrying out investigations into violations of human rights and humanitarian law, including possible acts of genocide; (b) monitoring the ongoing human rights situation and helping to prevent such violations through the presence of human rights field officers; (c) cooperating with other international agencies to re-establish confidence and facilitate the return of refugees and IDPs and the rebuilding of civil society and (d) implementing programmes of technical cooperation in the field of human rights, particularly in the area of the administration of justice, to help Rwanda rebuild its

[45] Carlsson, I., Sung-Joo, H., & Kupolati, R. M. (1999). *Report of the independent inquiry into the actions of the United Nations during the 1994 genocide in Rwanda.* United Nations.

[46] In our study, we are not examining OHCHR's stand-alone field offices. HRFOR is an exception since it was deployed in a conflict situation with the presence of UNAMIR.

shattered judiciary and to provide human rights education to all levels of the Rwandese society.[47]

The first task of HRFOR was to ensure that evidence was not lost or destroyed. HRFOR set up a Special Investigations Unit (SIU) to gather and safely store evidence. The High Commissioner for Human Rights sought the assistance of several governments to provide prosecutors, criminal investigators and forensic experts to collect and preserve evidence.

In addition to investigating past violations, the HRFOR staff monitored the RPF government's human rights practice. Its findings were shared with the UN Commission on Human Rights' Special Rapporteur on Rwanda and with other stakeholders. The RPF forces had detained more than 90,000 persons throughout the country. The lack of facilities in the prisons including overcrowding was a major concern. The HRFOR staff through regular prison visits ensured that the authorities followed legal procedures related to arrest and detention and dealt with prison conditions. HRFOR assisted the Rwandan government to organize an International Conference on Genocide held in Kigali from 30 October to 5 November in 1995. It also assisted the government's Inter-Ministerial Commission for the Memorial of the Genocide.

Initially, HRFOR lacked trained staff and funding. USAID, based on a field study conducted in early 1995, observed that many of the monitors appointed initially did not have relevant background and experience. They did not receive orientation or training on their arrival. The investigations unit lacked a well-defined purpose and direction. The USAID study also commented that SIU lacked clarity about its powers to request official records. The USAID report concluded that general perception was that the human rights operation has failed to meet its stated mission. HRFOR's poor performance was due to ambiguous mandate, lack of preparations of staff prior to deployment, inadequate resources, failure of leadership, incoherent

---

[47] United Nations. (1997, 4 April). *United Nations human rights field operation in Rwanda.* UN Office of the High Commissioner for Human Rights. https://reliefweb.int/report/rwanda/united-nations-human-rights-field-operation-rwanda

strategy, ineffective coordination between the field and headquarters and Rwandan government's hostility.[48]

Amnesty International and African Rights made stringent criticism against HRFOR.[49] Human Rights Watch criticized HRFOR's policy on distribution of its reports and the quality of information collected by it.[50]

In October 1995, Ian Martin was appointed as the chief of HRFOR to review and overhaul its work. Martin subsequently identified following challenges faced by HRFOR.[51]

The magnitude of victims (over half a million) and the sheer size of perpetrators (possibly hundreds of thousands) challenged the capacity of justice system to ensure accountability. HRFOR faced constant funding crisis since it was dependent on voluntary contributions made by states and was not funded by the UN's regular budget. Due to the lack of funding, the High Commissioner was dependent on assistance from the European Union (EU) and other countries for deployment of HROs. The EU's direct interference in the management of HRFOR created tensions in the smooth running of the office. HRFOR suffered from the lack of logistical support. HRFOR initially focused on investigating the genocide without direction or guidance. The OHCHR training and guidance notes provided to staff were inadequate. Only in 1996, a proper guidance manual was provided to the staff. While HRFOR was expanding its field presence, the Security Council established ICTR. Investigating for prosecution purposes was beyond the capacity of HRFOR staff. HRFOR's SIU

---

[48] Kumar, K., Tardif-Douglin, D., Knapp, C., Maynard, K., Manikas, P., & Sheckler, A. (1996, July). *Rebuilding postwar Rwanda: The role of the international community* (USAID Evaluation Special Study No. 76). Centre for Development Information and Evaluation. https://www.oecd.org/derec/unitedstates/50189461.pdf

[49] Ibid.

[50] Human Rights Watch. (1995, 1 January). *Human Rights Watch world report 1995-Rwanda*. United Nations High Commissioner for Refugees. https://www.refworld.org/docid/467fca9dc.html

[51] Martin, I. (1998). After genocide: The UN human rights field operation in Rwanda. In A. H. Henkin (Ed.), *Honoring human rights and keeping the peace*. Kluwer Law International.

that investigated the genocide suffered due to the lack of expertise. Experts who were seconded by governments to SIU functioned independently from HRFOR field staff and remained in the country only for short periods. ICTR was not willing to have a collaborative relationship with HRFOR. A collaborative relationship between the two could have defined the respective roles, with HRFOR preparing reports analysing the genocide and other grave violations without addressing individual guilt.[52]

Hutu insurgents based in refugee camps along Rwanda's borders mounted violent attacks against Tutsi local officials and civilians. HRFOR had warned the international community privately and publicly about the potential danger of allowing insurgents to operate from refugee camps on Rwanda's borders. The insurgents killed the international staff including five HRFOR staff in February 1997. The withdrawal of HRFOR staff from the provinces limited its ability to monitor the situation where it mattered the most.

The RPF forces' alleged reprisal attacks and killings of Hutus during the war emerged as a major concern. The UN Special Rapporteur on Rwanda asked HRFOR to investigate the allegations when HRFOR did not have the mandate or the capacity to carry out investigations of RPF's past abuses. HRFOR with its limited capacity was confronted with the issue of the RPF government's large-scale arrests of Hutus without legal procedures and the lack of capacity of prisons and conditions of prisons. HRFOR's reports on abuses committed by RPF forces strained its relationship with the government. The RPF government made efforts to end HRFOR's monitoring role. It took the position that the UN had lost its moral authority to condemn its actions since the UN did not intervene in the 1994 genocide.

HRFOR, from its inception, lacked staff experienced in human rights analysis and reporting. Only in mid-1995, a unit dedicated to reporting was established. HRFOR faced the tension of allocation of staff for monitoring/reporting and technical cooperation. To seek funding, HRFOR submitted reports to donors without sharing them

[52] Ibid.

with the government. The government complained that unsubstantiated reports were being circulated. In the late 1995, HRFOR initiated the practice of sharing in advance its monthly or bimonthly reports to relevant ministries, but the government was not keen to engage with HRFOR on concerns raised in the reports.

When HRFOR began implementing technical cooperation programmes, tensions emerged between UNDP and HRFOR because UNDP insisted that it was the lead agency. OHCHR managed the technical cooperation programmes directly from Geneva, creating difficulties for HRFOR staff to respond to urgent needs in the field. OHCHR's direct management of technical cooperation programmes further exacerbated the tension between monitoring and technical cooperation programmes and impacted on pursuing an integrated approach in the field.

The genocidal killings included personnel of leading human rights NGOs, both Tutsi and Hutu groups. Post-genocide, NGOs were divided mostly along ethnic lines. HRFOR's scope for working with NGOs was limited by political constraints and divisions within NGOs.

REFLECTIONS AND REVIEW OF HUMAN RIGHTS FIELD OPERATIONS ESTABLISHED BETWEEN 1990 AND 1998

The growing trend of deploying human rights components in peacekeeping operations in the 1990s led to reflection and assessment on them. In 1994, the Aspen Institute's Justice and Society Program convened a meeting to reflect on human rights components in peacekeeping operations in El Salvador, Cambodia and Haiti. The Aspen Institute followed it up with another conference in 1997 to reflect on the past missions (El Salvador, Cambodia and Haiti) and newer missions in Guatemala, Bosnia and Herzegovina and Rwanda. The conference proceedings also included a paper dealing with 'Smaller Missions, Bigger Problems' on human rights field presences in Abkhazia, Angola, Liberia, Mozambique, Burundi, Colombia and the Democratic Republic of the Congo. Former officers of human rights field missions, the UN staff and representatives of national and international human rights organizations attended these conferences. Aspen Institute published the papers submitted in 1995 and 1997 conferences and recommendations arising from the proceedings.[53]

THE 1998 REVIEW OF HUMAN RIGHTS FIELD OPERATIONS BY IAN MARTIN

Mary Robinson, the High Commissioner for Human Rights, appointed Ian Martin for six months (February–August 1998) as her Special Adviser on Human Rights Field Operations. Martin was tasked to review the role, functioning and support needs of the field operations of the OHCHR. Martin's report was based on his visits to field operations in Angola, Cambodia, Bosnia and Herzegovina, the Federal Republic of Yugoslavia (Serbia and Montenegro), Croatia, Colombia and Burundi. In addition, the report drew from his direct experience in running human rights offices in Rwanda and Haiti.[54]

Aspen Institute's reflections and Ian Martin's review provided valuable insights into human rights field operations and are still relevant.

SUMMARY OF ASPEN INSTITUTE'S CONCLUSIONS AND RECOMMENDATIONS

It is clear that the UN Secretariat's reforms are not enough. While the international community has come to recognize that massive human rights violations underlie most contemporary conflicts, and has, thus, included human rights in peacekeeping operations, human rights missions cannot be expected to succeed when the UN Member States do not provide the necessary political and financial backing.

---

[53] See Henkin, A. H. (1995). *Honoring human rights and keeping the peace: Lessons from El Salvador, Cambodia and Haiti*. The Aspen Institute; Henkin, A. H. (1998). *Honoring human rights: From peace to justice*. The Aspen Institute & Kluwer Law International.

[54] See Martin, I. (1998, August). *Final report of review of human rights field operations*. HCHR Special Adviser for Human Rights Field Operations.

ON INSTITUTION BUILDING

UN human rights missions were often asked to provide assistance to post-conflict governments in the reconstruction of national police forces and judicial and prison systems. The missions were asked to provide technical assistance to and human rights training for each of these institutions and to monitor their human rights record as reform efforts unfolded. While each required a different set of skills and approaches, they shared three critical challenges: to coordinate the work of a large number of actors, design sustainable programmes from the outset and plan for the long term. The sustainability of institution-building efforts after the departure of a UN human rights mission has been a concern everywhere. Host government's commitment has been weak and lacked strategy on building capacity in the national police and the judiciary.

Judiciary

Judicial reform has proven to be one of the most difficult institution-building areas in which to measure rapid progress. Judicial systems are destroyed in civil conflicts; they are dominated by jurists unwilling to modernize or are left to drift by governments unable or unwilling to commit to reform.

National Institutions

Some missions worked to support the development and institutional-ization of national human rights organizations (such as a human rights commission, ombudsman or legislative committee). Unfortunately, these new national institutions have not yet proven effective at promoting and defending human rights, and the UN support has not made a substantial difference in this outcome.

Non-governmental Organizations

In the past, missions' difficulties with the NGOs came from several sources. In some cases, the leadership did not give priority to the strengthening of NGOs. Some missions did not have any staff with relevant experience and, therefore, had difficulties understanding the NGO culture. NGOs were, at times, suspicious of a mission's commitment to human rights reporting when the mission was also engaged in institution-building activities. Although training has been the major focus for NGO support, UN missions should also include NGOs in the development and implementation of institution-building programmes. On balance, however, it is not clear how long the benefits of mission support (to NGOs) will endure. This concern over sustainability has to do, in part, with the lack of organizational development of NGO communities in many places.

Human Rights Education

Human rights education has been at the core of every mission's work, cutting across all monitoring and institution-building activities. Education activities tend to fall into three broad categories: human rights information for the general population, training programmes targeted at particular professional groups and promotion of the rights of particularly vulnerable populations, such as women and children. Unfortunately, few missions developed a strategic analysis of the general and specific education needs prior to taking the field. As a result, some found themselves without the staff and resources needed to launch significant education programmes once deployed. Finally, education and training follow-up was a consistent problem across missions. The long-term sustainability of a missions' education and training efforts was rarely addressed.

Addressing the Crimes of the Past

The legacy of past human rights abuses has shaped the current human rights and political climate in all mission states. While states must determine their own approach to the past, the UN can play a number of supporting roles. A mission can present options for dealing with the past which were/are utilized by other states as a way to assist a government to craft its own policy. It can provide direct technical assistance to a tribunal or a commission or monitor the fairness of efforts to address the past if neither its mandate nor the government authorizes a broader role.

The Relationship between Monitoring and Institution Building

Perhaps the most important operational lesson from the field mission experiences is the essential complementarity between human rights monitoring and institution building. Monitoring gave missions the ability to identify the sources and scope of human rights problems throughout the country. This information could then be used to design reform measures and training programmes. Finally, field monitoring provided direct feedback on the effectiveness of reform strategies or programmes as they were implemented. Attempting to integrate the two functions, though, was not without its challenges. Missions had to overcome the inevitable tensions between criticizing and assisting governments and the concern that one function might give way in importance to the other.

MAJOR POINTS FROM IAN MARTIN'S ASSESSMENT REPORT

Technical cooperation to develop national capacities can only be effective if there is a genuine commitment on the part of the government concerned to protect and promote human rights. Thus, it would be inadvisable to engage in technical cooperation while patterns of serious human rights violations exist, and there is no early prospect of their being adequately addressed by national institutions.

To identify the role of human rights field operations in contributing to human rights protection exclusively as monitoring is inadequate, a new language is needed. That role is first of all dissuasive or preventive: a local presence can have at least some inhibiting effect on those who may commit human rights violations. Then, when violations do occur, a local presence allows for early intervention to encourage corrective action. The third stage is the presentation of reports to the authorities at higher levels to enable them to take corrective and preventive action and to share information with other governments which maintain a dialogue with them on human rights issues. Fourth comes public reporting, since it is not conceivable that the UN should have a human rights presence where serious human rights violations are alleged, without reporting publicly on the human rights situation it is addressing.

The tendency to divide the work of field operations into monitoring and technical cooperation, at one time corresponding to organizational divisions between branches in the Centre for Human Rights, has had negative consequences for integrated structures in the field and for overall work planning, budgeting and administration.

The relationship of a field presence with the host government should be a principled partnership, neither confrontational nor compromised. This requires constant dialogue and the maximum transparency that can be reconciled with the respect for the confidentiality and security of others. The ideal is a regular formal forum, which does not preclude ready access at senior levels to those with real power including in the security forces.

Where field presences are monitoring and reporting on violations of humanitarian standards by armed opposition groups, a policy regarding contacts with their leadership is necessary. This will vary according to the extent to which the groups have an identifiable and accessible leadership or representation.

It should always be a high priority objective of any human rights field presence to support and encourage the work of national human rights NGOs, and it must consciously avoid, especially in the case of the larger field operations acting so as to displace them in any way.

The relationship with external NGOs is a sensitive one. Their role in maintaining scrutiny of the human rights situation is an important one, well recognized by the UN and properly extends to scrutiny of the role of the UN itself. However, the roles and responsibilities are not identical.

Field operations mounted in order to address human rights protection in conflict-related contexts have properly had as their priority the immediate violations of the right to life, integrity and security of the person, etc., and the deployment of human rights field officers is not an equally appropriate response to violations of ESC rights.

It is equally true that little has been done to integrate a gender perspective and priority attention to the human rights of women into field operations. A responsibility for the promotion of women's human rights has been assigned (at a junior level) within some larger operations (e.g., Rwanda), but a gendered perspective has not been integrated into their monitoring methodologies.

Training (of staff) cannot be separated from the development in the field of policy and guidance in relation to the actual human rights situation and mandate of each presence. It should be linked closely to the initial assessment mission and, thus, to the human rights situation and the mandate, objectives and strategy of the operation. It, thus, cannot be a package delivered from Geneva. Country-specific guidance manuals should be developed within each major operation, drawing upon the generic training manual and other materials available in Geneva.

The quality of personnel, especially those with managerial responsibility, is a key determinant of the success of field operations. The managerial demands of field posts, especially at the beginning of an operation, are in general greater than those of headquarter posts of equivalent seniority because field managers do not take over responsibility within an already fairly well-defined and functioning organizational structure; they have to create their own.

The delegation of decision-making authority to the field head also needs to be clarified. Field heads experience a schizophrenic attitude on the part of Geneva: lack of feedback (or requested response) and guidance on major policy matters, combined with overinvolvement and insistence on control over minor details. The principle should be maximum delegation to the field, commensurate with the seniority of the head, combined with rapid response where approval or guidance is sought.

Frequency of the Geneva briefing be reconsidered, and the nature and status of the reports presented clarified. The most important purpose of the preparation of regular reports by presences with a monitoring mandate is to have an effective dialogue with the government, and monthly is too frequent in most cases for this.

Field operations have never had adequate expertise in information handling, electronic data processing and archiving to ensure the responsible handling of confidential human rights information available to them. This requires a central capacity, as well as inclusion in the staffing of larger presences.

Human Rights Component in Operations

Second Phase—Post 2000*

MONITORING ROLE

In ongoing conflict situations, a human rights component's monitoring assumes great significance. UNMIS' monitoring role is discussed in the next section as a case study. The human rights component of the peacekeeping operation in the DRC[1] early on developed strategies to monitor human rights violations in an ongoing conflict situation.[2]

MONUC established human rights mobile teams to increase HRO's ability to cover areas in Eastern DRC where access was difficult for logistical and security reasons. The teams consisted of one HRO, one United Nations Volunteer, one national staff member in Eastern DRC and one United Nations Police (UNPOL) officer. The teams were intended to increase MONUC's capacity to provide early warning, effectiveness of investigations, outreach to the civilian population and follow-up of cases with civil, judicial and military authorities. The teams were equipped with special equipment such as mobile phones, laptops, GPS and camping gear. Presently, they spend about three to

---

* This is not an exhaustive report on human rights field presences in peacekeeping operations.

[1] United Nations. (2010). *United Nations organization stabilization mission in the Democratic Republic of Congo.* https://monusco.unmissions.org/en/background

[2] Some of the information on MONUC is based on the author's visit to the DRC as the director of UNMIS HRD to learn from MONUC HRD's experience in monitoring human rights violations in conflict situations. He was accompanied by UNMIS DARFUR HRO Team Leaders.

four days a week in the field and then return to a field office to provide headquarters with information and analysis.[3]

The role of the UNPOL officer in the team was to provide expertise in gathering physical evidence and monitoring re-establishment of law enforcement authority in areas under armed groups' control. The mobile teams liaise regularly with MONUC's military, which had appointed human rights focal points in each UN Military Observers' (MILOB) team site. One of the responsibilities of the focal points is to liaise with the mobile teams for purposes of information sharing and operational planning. MONUC's military provided the mobile teams with military escorts. The mobile teams also liaised with other civilian components to undertake joint missions in the field.

Since MILOBs were the primary source of information on human rights violations committed by Armed Forces of the DRC (Forces armées de la république démocratique du Congo [FARDC]), in 2006, the Force Commander assigned MILOB coordinators in team sites as focal points for interaction with the nearest MONUC human rights field office or mobile team. HROs trained MILOB coordinators on the basics of UN methodology for human rights investigation. HRD and the UN Force Commander's Office jointly developed a simple incident format for MILOBs to report on human rights violations. This information was submitted to the nearest human rights field office. MONUC's eastern and western military divisions were expected to submit daily reports on human rights violations to operations and to HRD.

MONUC HRD's SIU conducted investigations into serious violations of human rights and international humanitarian law and supervised the work of mobile teams. The purpose of SIU was to avoid overexposing its field officers, especially in violent situations. SIU gathered and stored evidence to support judicial investigations. The information gathered was normally handed over to the local judicial

---

[3] Mahony, L., & Nash, R. (2012). *Influence on the ground: Understanding and strengthening the protection impact of United Nations Human Rights field presences*. Fieldview Solutions. https://www.fieldviewsolutions.org/fv-publications/ Influence_on_the_Ground.pdf

authorities. HROs working with SIU received training on collection and storage of evidence from the Institute for International Criminal Investigations, based in the Netherlands, by attending its annual International Investigator Course. SIU pursued an interdisciplinary approach drawing on the relevant skills of the military and police components of MONUC.

OHCHR in collaboration with MONUC conducted a mapping exercise to document the most serious violations of human rights and international humanitarian law committed within the territory of the DRC between March 1993 and June 2003.[4] OHCHR deployed a 20-member mapping team to carry out the project. The mapping exercise officially began in July 2008. The 550-page report was completed in August 2010 and contained 617 alleged violent incidents that occurred in the DRC during the period.[5] Each of these incidents was related to the possible commission of gross violations of human rights and/or international humanitarian law. The mapping did not identify the perpetrators of violations and did not establish individual criminal responsibility for the crimes committed. However, the report identified the armed group(s) to which the alleged perpetrator(s) belong(ed).

The report became controversial with the Rwandan government. The report included allegations that Rwandan government's Tutsi troops might have killed thousands of Hutu refugees in the DRC in the mid-1990s, and those crimes might have constituted genocide. Before the report was officially released, based on a draft version, the Rwandan government called the report outrageous and damaging. In response to the report, the Rwandan government threatened to withdraw its peacekeepers from Darfur and South Sudan. The UN Secretary-General Ban Ki-moon visited Rwanda to persuade the

---

[4] United Nations Office of the High Commissioner for Human Rights. (2010). *Report of the mapping exercise documenting the most serious violations of human and international humanitarian law committee within the territory of the Democratic Republic of the Congo between March 1993 and June 2003, August 2010.* https://www.refworld.org/publisher,OHCHR,,,4ca99bc22,0.html

[5] Ibid.

Rwandan government from withdrawing its UN peacekeepers. The Secretary-General also proposed postponing the release of the report and include Rwandan government's comments in the final report.[6]

MONUC and MONUSCO under Chapter VII were mandated to use force to protect civilians.[7] In 2013, the UN Security Council authorized MONUSCO to deploy an intervention brigade to strengthen peacekeeping, to reduce the threats posed by armed groups and create conditions for carrying out stabilization activities.[8] The rebel militia did not consider the military component of MONUSCO and its intervention brigade as neutral forces, and both were targets of their attacks. The safety of MONUSCO civilian personnel, particularly HROs, was under threat.[9]

HUMAN RIGHTS DUE DILIGENCE POLICY

MONUSCO forces collaborated with the DRC armed forces (FARDC) whose members were accused of committing war crimes. However, the Security Council's resolution instructed MONUSCO forces to cooperate with DRC forces to neutralize armed groups. Cooperation between MONUSCO and DRC forces was problematic for HRD since it was monitoring abuses by all parties including FARDC. Based on HRD reports and criticism by international NGOs, MONUSCO in some instances suspended its cooperation with FARDC. However, it was done on an ad hoc manner, and the perception remained that the UN was collaborating with forces that had committed war crimes.

MONUSCO was not an isolated case; in several missions, cooperation between UN forces and government forces was problematic. OHCHR drafted a human rights due diligence policy on the UN's support to non-UN security forces. In March 2013, the UN

[6] Basheer, M. (2010). *UN Chief urges Rwanda not to withdraw Sudan peacekeepers*. https://www.voanews.com/africa/un-chief-urges-rwanda-not-withdraw-sudan-peacekeepers

[7] United Nations. (2010). *Background: United Nations organization stabilization mission in the Democratic Republic of Congo*. https://monusco.unmissions.org/en/background

[8] Ibid.

[9] Henry, E. (2015). *Use of force and peacekeeping operations*. https://www.academia.edu/37018831/Use_of_Force_and_Peacekeeping_Operations

Secretary-General transmitted the Human Rights Due Diligence Policy (HRDDP) to the General Assembly and the Security Council (A/67/775–S/2013/110).

HRDDP clarified that any support provided to non-UN forces must be consistent with the UN's responsibility to respect international humanitarian, human rights and refugee law. UN support cannot be provided if there is a real risk of receiving entities committing grave violations of international humanitarian, human rights and refugee law. The UN should intercede with the authorities to end such violations, and if it continues, the UN must suspend support to the offending elements.

The application of HRDDP was not a smooth process in DRC or in other countries. In Somalia, in December 2018, Nicholas Haysom, UN mission's SRSG, raised concerns about Somalia police's conduct in the arrest of a local leader in Baidoa and causing death to several persons when they protested the arrest. He observed that his concerns were based on HRDDP that governs UN's support to Somalia's police. In addition, donors (the EU, the UK and the Federal Republic of Germany) in a joint letter to the Minister of Interior raised similar concerns about the Somali police's conduct and suspended support to the Somalia police in the Baidoa region. In response, the Somalia government expelled SRSG on the allegation that he interfered in the sovereignty of Somalia.[10]

Several missions have developed standard operating procedures (SOPs) for applying HRDDP in their collaboration with the national army and police.[11] The other missions that have developed similar SOPs are UNMISS, UNAMID, MINUSMA, MINUSCA, MINJUSTH, MONUSCO, UNSMIL and UNSOM. MONUSCO has established a secretariat for coordination and monitoring HRDDP implementation.

---

[10] Bearak, M. (2019). Somalia expels top U.N. official after he criticizes crackdown on dissent. *The Washington Post*. https://www.washingtonpost.com/world/africa/somalia-expels-un-top-official-after-he-questions-crackdown-on-dissent/2019/01/02/ec1f89da-0e7d-11e9-831f-3aa2c2be4cbd_story.html

[11] Missions with SOPs are UNMISS, UNAMID, MINUSMA, MINUSCA, MINJUSTH, MONUSCO, UNSMIL and UNSOM.

The mission applies HRDDP for each joint military operation to vet the security forces participating in such operations.

PUBLIC REPORTING

Human rights components in peacekeeping operations issue public reports on human rights violations and other thematic issues. These reports range from electoral participation (UNSOM), conditions of migrants and refugees (UNSMIL), on mass graves (UNAMI), illegal use of force in the management of public demonstrations (MONUSCO), indiscriminate use of improvised explosive devices and their harm to civilians (UNAMA) and human rights in peace process (MINUSMA).

Public use of human rights information through media and other means is an effective tool against impunity. At times, human rights components use limited release of their reports to influential stake-holders like donors to encourage them to engage with the concerned government on human rights concerns. The risk in such approach is that the government might perceive it as a political use of information by the human rights component.

There have been instances when a human rights component's public report has led to major policy changes at the national level. In Liberia, UNMIL's human rights component issued a report on Liberian rubber industry and its impact on human rights. The report involved several months of detailed research on Liberian rubber industry including the involvement of foreign companies and the condition of plantation workers. The report resulted in the Liberian government renegotiating its agreements with foreign companies and enacting laws for the protection of plantation workers.[12]

Human rights component's report can have a positive or negative impact on their credibility and affect their work. A badly produced report might undermine their credibility with the concerned government and civil society groups. A study on OHCHR field presences identified several shortcomings on the content and process of issuing

---

[12] UN Mission in Liberia. (2006). *Human rights in Liberia's rubber plantations: Tapping into the future.* https://www.refworld.org/docid/473dade10.html

a public report. Often, issuing of reports becomes an end in itself without prior strategizing of how to effectively use the report. Lack of experience and planning on advocacy impacts the release of a report. Inadequate attention to producing a report with content and language that is suitable for the intended target audience is another weak area, in addition to the absence of planning for follow-up for short-term and long-term use of the report. The study identified a problem common to most human rights components such as lengthy approval process and delay in releasing the report impacting on its strategic value.[13]

REPORT ON CIVILIAN CASUALTIES

Increasingly, human rights components in peacekeeping operations are monitoring and reporting on civilian casualties in conflict. The civilian casualties report was first introduced in Afghanistan by UNAMA's human rights component. By mid-2000, UNAMA began systematically documenting civilian casualties caused by the Taliban, other Afghan militias and by ISAF. OHCHR assisted in developing guidelines for documenting civilian casualties. It became the main work for the human rights component of UNAMA, and its report on civilian casualties particularly those caused by ISAF attracted international publicity. UNAMA's reports on civilian casualties had an impact since there was international pressure on ISAF regarding its role in causing civilian casualties. Despite the specific context in which it emerged, casualty recording became a part of human rights component's work in other missions as well.[14]

OHCHR defines casualty recording 'as a system that seeks to methodically and comprehensively record and verify information on individuals killed (and possibly also on those injured) in a specific set

[13] Mahony, L., & Nash, R. (2012). *Influence on the ground: Understanding and strengthening the protection impact of United Nations Human Rights field presences*. Fieldview Solutions. https://www.fieldviewsolutions.org/fv-publications/Influence_on_the_Ground.pdf

[14] United Nations. (2019). *Guidance on casualty recording*. United Nations Human Rights Office of the High Commissioner. https://www.ohchr.org/Documents/Publications/Guidance_on_Casualty_Recording.pdf

of circumstances'.[15] Casualty recording impacts on human rights work by providing early warning, prevention and response. It provides a basis for advocacy on establishing accountability and development of policies on remedies and reparations.[16]

As explained by the UNSMIL HRD, the verification process involves contacting a wide range of sources of information and analysing them for reliability and credibility before conclusions are drawn.[17] Other than UNAMA, in other missions, the advocacy value of casualty reporting is not self-evident. It might provide cumulative data for the future. The risk is that after spending considerable resources on producing these reports, the data may not be used for any accountability purposes once a political settlement is arrived at or situation gets stabilized. On the other hand, victim-centred monitoring of human rights violations with identification of perpetrator(s) (individual and groups) might have long-term value of seeking justice by the victims. The classic example of it was that of Vicariate of Solidarity's meticulous monitoring done every single day for 16 years on Pinochet regime's atrocities in Chile in the 1970s. The information collected and documented during the military rule became a source for the Truth Commission, government investigators, victims' families and in prosecuting Pinochet and his generals. Human rights monitoring is not necessarily limited to civil and political rights violations as demonstrated by the UNMIL human rights component's report on Liberian rubber plantations. This observation does not mean abandoning casualty reporting but to stress the equal importance of traditional monitoring of human rights violations.

TECHNICAL COOPERATION

OHCHR, since 1995, has been engaged in conducting technical cooperation programmes to assist governments in their efforts in the promotion and protection of human rights. These programmes range

---

[15] Ibid.

[16] Ibid.

[17] United Nations. (2020). *Human rights report on civilian casuals, United Nations support mission in Libya*. https://unsmil.unmissions.org/human-rights-report-civilian-casualties-0

from strengthening national structures (judiciary, prosecution, police and national institutions) that have a direct impact on the observance of human rights. They also include human rights education, training and assistance to states that meet their treaty reporting obligations.[18] Most governments prefer technical cooperation programmes as a way of demonstrating their collaboration with OHCHR and their commitment to human rights. In peacekeeping operations, human rights components implement technical cooperation programmes with the support of OHCHR's technical cooperation funds. Thus, human rights components are better placed compared to other civilian components in providing specific assistance to governments and civil societies by using OHCHR funds.[19] Monitoring (pressure) and technical support (cooperation) of a human rights component is integrally linked.

REFLECTIONS ON HUMAN RIGHTS PRESENCES IN PEACEKEEPING OPERATIONS

Human rights' integration in the UN system on the ground, including in peacekeeping operations, normally face denial, indifference and opportunist acceptance. Human rights are often not considered for their intrinsic value. Post Rwanda genocide, a UN lesson–learned report stated that the presence of human rights component in the Rwandan mission (UNAMIR) would have helped in protecting civilians from political violence.[20] Trevor Findlay, however, considered it as a demonstration of 'naivety of the UN'.[21] Human rights components also

---

[18] United Nations Human Rights Office of the High Commissioner. (2010). *Technical cooperation in the field of human rights*. https://www.ohchr.org/EN/Countries/Pages/TechnicalCooperationIndex.aspx

[19] Peace operations do not allocate funds for civilian components to implement projects. Post Brahimi Report, funds are provided for Quick Impact Projects (QUIPs), which is not sufficient to cover the demands of military, police and civilian components of a mission.

[20] United Nations. (1996). *Comprehensive report on lessons learned from United Nations Assistance Mission for Rwanda (UNAMIR) October 1993–April 1996*. Lessons Learned Out, Department of Peacekeeping Operations.

[21] Findlay, T. (2002). *The use of force in UN peace operations*. Stockholm International Peace Research Institute (SIPRI). Oxford University Press. https://www.sipri.org/sites/default/files/files/books/SIPRI02Findlay.pdf

suffer from the approach that is common among senior UNDP officials which is based on the assumption that human rights would rock the boat and impact on their relationship with the host government. They tend to take at face value pronouncements made by governments, and human rights are an inconvenient truth for them.

As discussed previously, integration of human rights in peacekeeping operations has now been accepted in doctrine and practice. The present and past High Commissioners for Human Rights through their leadership have contributed to staking a claim on the high table and have strengthened the acceptance of human rights as an integral part of the UN-wide system. OHCHR's policy, tools and establishment of structures within the office to support field presences have contributed to an increased recognition of role of human rights components in peacekeeping operations. The following observations are made in good faith based on first-hand experience and on studies and reports on field presences in peacekeeping operations.

LEADERSHIP

Effective integration of human rights component in peacekeeping operations depends on (a) SRSG, (b) the structure of a mission and (c) the head of the human rights component.[22] Most present and former heads of human rights components would agree that the support provided by SRSG is vital for the effective functioning of a human rights component. In missions in which SRSG or his/her deputy have background in human rights and are committed to them, the component would be allowed to play a central role. It is also linked to the structure of the mission: if the human rights component is not part of the political pillar directly under SRSG or his/her deputy, then the human rights component remains marginal to the mission. In some instances, SRSG or his/her deputy would include the head of the human rights in his/her meetings with the host government, conveying a message about the importance given to human rights in the peacekeeping operation. In other instances, the head of the human rights would be discouraged

---

[22] Mansson, K. (2008). *A communicative act: Integrating human rights in UN peace operations, Dialogues from Kosovo and Congo* (PhD thesis submitted to the Irish Centre for Human Rights). Faculty of Law, National University of Ireland.

from meeting with senior government officials when a situation is perceived as a political task to be carried out by SRSG or his/her deputy. In the selection of SRSGs/DSRSGs, the commitment to human rights is taken into account. However, mostly SRSG's personality and his/her approach in dealing with the host government determines his/her relationship with the head of the human rights component.[23]

Correspondingly, the leadership and personality of the head of the human rights component impact the integration of the component in the peacekeeping operation. Heads of human rights should always bear in mind that they must negotiate with the mission leadership as much as they negotiate with the host government. Tact, diplomacy and proven leadership are required for running a human rights component. A badly run human rights component makes it easier for the mission leadership to marginalize it. The head of a human rights component may be committed to human rights, but his/her personality and style of functioning matters substantially while dealing with the mission leadership.[24] The head of a human rights component has dual reporting lines (SRSG and OHCHR) which helps in negotiating with the mission leadership, but maintaining a balance between the two requires some tact as well.

PROVIDING STRATEGIC LEADERSHIP ROLE

The head of a human rights component must demonstrate he/she is playing a strategic leadership role that advances the mandate of the mission. Coordination with other units is important, but it should be based on both the human rights units' priorities and that of the mission. As it happened during the initial deployment in Darfur in 2004, HROs were busy attending meetings of other UN agencies while neglecting their monitoring reporting work. It is the responsibility of the head of human rights to convey clearly to his/her staff priorities of the human rights office and guide the staff to pursue it.

[23] Ibid.

[24] In UNMIS, till I left the mission, human rights component was part of the senior management team and was invited to all senior management meetings. My successor who was highly committed to human rights alienated the mission leadership due to his style of functioning and was removed from the senior management team meetings.

STRATEGIC PROGRAMMES

Based on the mission's mandate and the country's context, the human rights component must design programmes that are relevant and strategic. Often, OHCHR tends to push for programmes that may not be relevant to the context or strategic. At times, human rights' heads face experiences similar to that of Sidney Jones in East Timor when OHCHR stressed the establishment of a national institution when it was not a feasible proposition due to the lack of political institutions.[25] Similarly, development of a national plan of action for human rights education would involve human and other resources without achieving much in a situation where institutions have been destroyed and past repression has not ended. Most human rights components often face the challenge of conducting programmes to fulfil OHCHR's priorities while remaining relevant on the ground.

RECRUITMENT AND DEPLOYMENT OF HUMAN RIGHTS STAFF

In the early days, recruitment and deployment of human rights staff faced resource constraints (funding came from voluntary sources) and delay. The establishment of PMSS within OHCHR and creation of a roster to identify potential staff to some extent have mitigated some of the problems faced previously. However, heads of human rights components still face the challenge of timely deployment of staff with relevant experience and commitment. Sidney Jones' observation in 2000 continues to remain valid. According to her, OHCHR seems to assume that anyone who had served in a mission would automatically qualify as a staff in another mission. OHCHR needs to evaluate staff before sending him/her from one mission to another. Previous mission experience may be relevant at senior levels but not for all staff.[26]

OHCHR should rethink its policy of redeploying staff from one mission to another particularly at the level of staff holding P2 and

[25] Jones, S. (2003). East Timor: The troubled path to independence. In A. H. Henkin (Ed.), *Honoring human rights and keeping the peace*. Kluwer Law International.

[26] Ibid.

P3 positions.[27] Peacekeeping operations or OHCHR should not become employment generating agencies. At the level of P2 and P3, contract should be offered for a period of two to three years. A break must be insisted before they apply for a position in the same level or the next level. This would ensure recruitment of new staff (new blood) with diverse experience. OHCHR should also make efforts including modifying its recruitment process to attract national staff working in various OHCHR offices. At the Uganda OHCHR office, most of the national staff were more knowledgeable and resourceful than the international staff (P3 level).[28] Initially, OHCHR may encounter some challenges in rotating staff every two to three years. However, once the system is established, it might have long-term effect of OHCHR contributing to the emergence of a large number of persons with experience in a peacekeeping operation, working in various capacities nationally or internationally.

ENGAGEMENT WITH THE HOST GOVERNMENT

A human rights component's priority is to deal with human rights concerns and, towards that end, maintain systematic communication with the host government. It remains a major challenge. However, the success of maintaining a critical and constructive relationship with the host government is also dependent on the way a component is run. A component through its work should establish its reliability and credibility. It should be consistent in its approach that its objective is to seek remedies and/or strengthen the host government's efforts to deal with human rights concerns.[29]

Even with a difficult host government, certain calmness and respect must be maintained while engaging with it. Care should be taken to

---

[27] I am not sure if I would now re-employ some of the P2 and P3 staff I recruited in Sudan in 2005. After 15 years, I doubt they have learnt new skills and or have retained the same commitment they had when they joined the mission as fresh candidates.

[28] Author spent six months as the Director of OHCHR Uganda Office in 2010.

[29] Mahony, L., & Nash, R. (2012). *Influence on the ground: Understanding and strengthening the protection impact of United Nations Human Rights field presences*. Fieldview Solutions. https://www.fieldviewsolutions.org/fv-publications/Influence_on_the_Ground.pdf

ensure that no disparaging comments are made by the staff on the government or the country to avoid the risk of it being conveyed to the government. A human rights component should avoid giving the impression that it is supporting the national staff who are critical of the government or those who belong to opposition parties. To ensure systematic communication in a formal setting, a human rights component should seek establishment of a mechanism to pursue dialogue with the government authorities.[30] However, a human rights component should be aware of the danger of a government creating a toothless forum for engaging with it.

REPORTING INCLUDING PUBLIC REPORTING

A human rights component's reporting obligations are often demanding. In addition to numerous reports and submission made to the mission, a component has to meet OHCHR's reporting requirements as well. OHCHR and the human rights component, considering the context and the available resources (staff), should agree on a realistic plan for types and duration of reports to be submitted to OHCHR. As proposed by Peter Bouckaert, Head of the Human Rights Watch Emergency Team, the stress should be on production of analytical reports (identifying the state of human rights and trends in abuses/violations) and not the type of unanalytical 'kitchen sink' reports.[31]

PUBLIC REPORTING

Now, issuance of public reports by human rights components has become routine. A public report issued particularly by OHCHR creates awareness on the situation at the national and international levels. A well-researched, quality report enhances the credibility of a human rights component. Often, the head of a human rights component needs to consider the mission's response and the government's response to

---

[30] See case study on UNMIS regarding the use of a joint mechanism to conduct dialogue with the government.

[31] Bouckaert, P. (2004). *Submitted a note to director on reporting strategy.* UNMIS HRD Staff.

a report. In some cases, it might lead to frictions within the mission. In some other cases, governments may limit the dialogue or take the extreme step of expelling the human rights staff (including creating security risk for the staff) from the country. In the latter instance, support of the mission leadership would be crucial to re-establish communication with the government and minimize the impact on the functioning of the component.

In this regard, a human rights component must consult and strategize (however difficult it may be) with the mission leadership regarding the issuance of a public report. It should begin from the moment when an investigation is initiated on an issue or theme to develop a report.[32] OHCHR should allow freedom to the human rights component to select the focus of a public report and to plan how the report would be used for advocacy purposes. OHCHR should not seek reports from a human rights component as a routine, and it should be a part of a strategy (including mission strategy) for strengthening human rights in the country.[33] Reports should not become an end in themselves 'rather than conceived of as elements of comprehensive and targeted strategies'.[34] Reporting process should also be a part of strengthening the role of civil society and should take into account the safety and security of NGOs who collaborate with the human rights office in the preparation of the report.

[32] In UNMIS, when HRDs came across the use of women as sex slaves by some armed groups, the mission was informed about it and the need for issuing a public report on it. Mission agreed and DSRSG was involved in planning for the consequences once the report is made public.

[33] In Libya, OHCHR was keen on a report on detention while the mission and the human rights component believed that a report advocating transitional justice would be more relevant at that point of time.

[34] Mahony, L., & Nash, R. (2012). *Influence on the ground: Understanding and strengthening the protection impact of United Nations Human Rights field presences*. Fieldview Solutions. https://www.fieldviewsolutions.org/fv-publications/Influence_on_the_Ground.pdf

Human Rights Component in Operations

Case Studies of Timor-Leste, Sudan and Libya*

TIMOR-LESTE (EAST TIMOR)

In August 1999, the East Timorese voted for independence from Indonesia in a UN-conducted 'popular consultation'. In October 1999, the Security Council established UNTAET.[1] UNTAET was set up as a multidimensional peacekeeping operation with responsibility to administer East Timor during the transition to independence.[2] On 20 May 2002, UNTAET handed over its powers to the East Timorese. Timor-Leste (the official name of the territory under the Constitution) was recognized internationally as an independent country. The Security Council on 20 May 2002 authorized the establishment of UNMISET to replace UNTAET. Both UNTAET and UNMISET included human rights components. UNMISET ended its operations in May 2005.

The East Timorese articulated their struggle for independence as human rights struggle to counter the Indonesian occupation since 1975 and the Indonesian army's atrocities during the occupation. Post-independence, the East Timorese sought accountability for human rights violations during the occupation and the violence unleashed

---

* Author was the director of Human Rights Division's in East Timor (UNAMET), (Sudan UNMIS) and Libya (UNMISL).

[1] See Chapter 2 for historical and political background that led to the UN's involvement and deployment of peacekeeping operations in East Timor.

[2] United Nations. (1999, 25 October). *Security council establishes United Nations transitional administration in East Timor for initial period until 31 January 2001*. Meeting Coverage and Press Releases.

before and after the 1999 popular consultation. The UN International Inquiry Commission on East Timor[3] in its report stressed that the UN had a special responsibility to ensure respect for the East Timorese human rights to justice, compensation and the truth.[4]

UNTAET's mandate was unprecedented and complex. In implementing its mandate, UNTAET was 'empowered to exercise all legislative and executive authority'.[5] UNTAET's human rights role was not specified except to develop an 'independent Timorese human rights institution'. It did not mention investigations into past crimes. Absence of a clear human rights mandate was compounded by the lack of clarity on human rights' place within the mission structure. Initially, an Office of Human Rights Affairs was made part of SRSG's executive office. The human rights office did not have a separate budget. Its 13 field staff in districts came under the governance and public administration unit. The head of the human rights office had no supervisory role over HROs in the district.[6] UNTAET's human rights office was planned with a focus on the establishment of a national human rights institution (NHRI) in a country that was still in transition with non-existent judicial and other institutions. According to the first head of the Human Rights Office, UNTAET planners had an understanding that East Timorese wanted justice for past violations more than anything else. 'A human rights unit that did not have full access to information about and some meaningful involvement in the investigations was going to be the object of ridicule'.[7]

UNTAET as an interim administration faced the problem of legal vacuum in carrying out its functions. The Brahimi Report referring to

[3] Author was the secretary of the Inquiry Commission. In that capacity, he collected testimonies from numerous victims and witnessed first-hand the destruction of East Timorese homes and infrastructure.

[4] United Nations. (2000). *Report of the International Commission of Inquiry on East Timor.* https://reliefweb.int/report/indonesia/report-international-commission-inquiry-east-timor

[5] United Nations. (1999, 25 October). *Security Council establishes United Nations transitional administration in East Timor for initial period until 31 January 2001.* Meeting Coverage and Press Releases.

[6] Jones, S. (2003). East Timor: The troubled path to independence. In A. H. Henkin (Ed.), *Honoring human rights and keeping the peace.* Kluwer Law International.

[7] Ibid.

the problems faced by UNTAET stressed that the pressing problem of 'applicable law' must be addressed.[8] In particular, in situations like East Timor, local judicial and legal capacity were found to be non-existent.[9] UNTAET faced the challenge of establishing the judicial system to bring to trial those detained for committing crimes after the popular consultation. To expedite the process, UNTAET appointed East Timorese as judges after providing them with a crash course. These judges were expected to deal with serious crimes such as crimes against humanity. The UNTAET staff raised concerns about the ability of the East Timorese judges with very little experience or training to conduct cases on serious crimes. Under UNTAET's Judicial Mentoring Program, international jurists sat along with the local judges and assisted them in their work. However, it faced the problem of international jurists communicating through interpreters which made the whole process cumbersome. Another problem was the enormous disparity between the local judges and the international judges. It led to the local judges going on strike. The situation was resolved, but the underlying tensions remained.[10]

Initially, UNTAET's human rights office was mostly staffed with persons who had worked for many years on the issue of East Timor prior to its independence. Therefore, the office had good links with East Timorese NGOs who had a long track record. After independence, NGOs mushroomed, especially with numerous donors assisting NGOs in East Timor. In its work with NGOs, the human rights office focused on working with them to disseminate material on human rights norms for wider circulation to the public and assisting them with provision of materials. Since UNTAET's other units also engaged with local NGOs, there was considerable duplication and wastage of resources.

UNTAET established Special Panels of the Dili District Court to try serious criminal offences committed in 1999. The panels consisted

---

[8] *United Nations. (2000). Report of the international commission of inquiry on East Timor*. United Nations. https://reliefweb.int/report/indonesia/report-international-commission-inquiry-east-timor

[9] United Nations. (2000, 21 August). *Report of the panel on United Nations peace operations*. A/55/305-S/2000/809. United Nations. https://undocs.org/A/55/305

[10] Jones, S. (2003). East Timor: The troubled path to independence. In A. H. Henkin (Ed.), *Honoring human rights and keeping the peace*. Kluwer Law International.

of an East Timorese judge and two international judges. A similar panel was set up as a Court of Appeal to hear appeals from ordinary and serious crimes courts. UNTAET transferred the Serious Crimes Unit (SCU) from the Human Rights Unit (HRU) to the Prosecutor General's Office. The human rights office had extensive contacts with local NGOs who had documented violations committed in 1999. SCU that was run mainly by the police investigators did not trust NGOs, and the lack of involvement of local NGOs affected the investigation process.

The UN's recruitment process also delayed the appointment of judges for the Special Panels. Most of the judges did not have adequate experience in dealing with international crimes. Gender balance was not maintained with only one of the international judges being a female. None of the Timorese judges had prior judicial experience except for the President of the Court of Appeal.

SCU did not have a clear prosecution strategy which led to the criticism that SCU prosecuted only low-level crimes. SCU faced the major challenge of prosecuting majority of suspects who were in Indonesia beyond its jurisdiction. Out of the 391 indicted, 309 were in Indonesia. The Indonesian government did not cooperate in handing over the suspects despite signing an MoU with UNTAET.

The ICTJ in its study of the Serious Crimes Process concluded that it was not clear what the UN expected from the process. Its success was dependent on Indonesia's cooperation, and when it did not materialize, UNTAET did not modify its approach. Despite spending US$20 million, neither did it contribute to justice nor did it leave a lasting legacy in building the local justice system.[11]

The human rights office played a major role in the establishment of the Commission on Reception, Truth and Reconciliation (CAVR). The office was instrumental in facilitating consultations across the country about the proposed Commission. Its initiatives made it a genuine consultation and contributed to amending the statute of the

---

[11] Reiger, C., & Marieke, W. (2006). *The serious crimes process in Timor-Leste: In retrospect.* International Center for Transitional Justice. https://www.ictj.org/sites/default/files/ICTJ-TimorLeste-Criminal-Process-2006-English.pdf

proposed commission.[12] CAVR began functioning from January 2002 and submitted its final report in 2005 entitled 'Chega!', Portuguese for 'no more, stop, enough'. CAVR held 8 national hearings and 52 local hearings and provided urgent reparations to 712 victims. Through its innovative community reconciliation programmes, it contributed to grassroots reconciliation process and prevented large-scale revenge attacks by victims. CAVR established a national archive and contributed to shared understanding of the country's tumultuous past.[13] It was an example of national initiative succeeding despite confronted with enormous challenges. The human rights office deputed two senior staff to work with CAVR from its inception to its closure.

United Nations Mission of Support in East Timor Human Rights Office

In May 2002, UNTAET was replaced by UNMISET which included a human rights office. Some of the human rights staff from UNTAET continued to work in the new mission.[14] In UNMISET too, the human rights office continued to remain a marginal unit. Despite increasing the role of the national police and the military in maintaining internal security, the human rights office's mandate did not allow for monitoring their functioning. On 4 December 2002, a student demonstration against the arrest of some students the previous day erupted into large-scale riots with burning of government buildings, vehicles and looting. Five reportedly died, and more than 20 people were injured due to firing by the police. The government and UNMISET attributed the violence to elements trying to destabilize the country. UNMISET police was responsible for enforcing security in Dili, and the Timorese questioned its role in managing the conflict and in the death of protestors. UNMISET conducted an inquiry which was prolonged for several months. The human rights office was completely kept out of

---

[12] International Center for Transitional Justice. (2016, 23 February). *After 10 years, CAVR report still resonates in Timor-Leste and around the world.* https://www.ictj.org/news/10-years-cavr-report-timor-leste-truth

[13] Ibid.

[14] Author was the director of UNMISET Human Rights Office, from October 2003 to February 2005.

the inquiry, and its report on the incident was not taken into account. The human rights office was mainly confined to work with NGOs and with CAVR. The human rights office tried to make itself relevant by initiating various projects. In collaboration with the UN Police, it initiated a project for establishment of an accountability mechanism within the Timor-Leste police department. It developed a training programme for parliamentarians on legal drafting. It also brought experts from the OHCHR office to assist the government to meet its treaty reporting obligations. The human rights office had more staff than it was required for carrying out its limited activities.

The office reported to Sukehiro Hasegawa, DSRSG, who was keen to avoid any negative reports on the Timor-Leste government.[15] In a week, DSRSG convened several meetings with the human rights senior staff mainly to monitor its activities without in any way contributing to the work of the office. It was not surprising that UNTAET, UNMISET and UNOTIL leadership came under scrutiny for the 2006 crisis.[16] The International Crisis Group in a report published after the 2006 crisis made the following harsh comment, 'Sukehiro Hasegawa, the Special Representative of the Secretary-General (SRSG of UNOTIL), was widely seen as a well-meaning man, eager to avoid conflict, but put in a position beyond his depth and an uncomprehending bystander as the forces that erupted in 2006 gathered strength'.[17]

SUDAN: UNITED NATIONS ASSISTANCE MISSION IN SUDAN

The Sudan Civil War (between the Muslim North and the Christian/animist South) began in 1955. After prolonged talks lasting two decades, the GoS and the armed opposition group, SPLM, agreed to

[15] The Secretary-General's report on UNMISET's work (2002 to 2005) did not include any mention of the human rights office or its work.

[16] In April–June 2006, the country faced a serious political and security crisis. The conflict began with dissatisfied elements of the military alleging discrimination, followed by a coup attempt, and it ended in widespread violence across the country.

[17] International Crisis Group. (2006). *Resolving Timor-Leste's crisis* (Asian Report No. 120). https://www.crisisgroup.org/asia/south-east-asia/timor-leste/resolving-timor-leste-s-crisis

resolve the conflict. In 2004, with the prospect of a peace agreement between the parties, the UN deployed an advance mission (UNAMIS) to prepare for the deployment of a full mission.

OHCHR Involvement in Sudan Including Developments in Darfur

In 1993, the Human Rights Commission appointed a Special Rapporteur on Sudan, and since then, OHCHR has been involved in the country. In 2000, OHCHR established an office focusing on technical cooperation (no monitoring mandate). In March 2005, OHCHR ended its technical cooperation programme in Sudan. Independent Sudanese civil society groups were critical of the OHCHR technical cooperation programme. They questioned the value of OHCHR which conducted hundreds of training programmes for police, judges and officials while the human rights situation was deteriorating. The office remained marginal when the Darfur conflict broke out in 2003. It was the UNDP resident coordinator who alerted about the Darfur conflict and human rights violations committed there.[18]

As a result of conflict in the Darfur region by 2004, more than a million people were internally displaced and several thousand had fled to the neighbouring Chad. OHCHR on its own initiative (no Security Council resolution) deployed a team to Chad to investigate/assess the conflict in Darfur. The acting High Commissioner briefed the Security Council on the situation in Darfur. In July 2004, the UN Secretary-General Kofi Annan visited Darfur and signed a joint communique with the GoS in which the GoS committed to providing humanitarian and human rights access to Darfur.[19]

---

[18] Mukesh Kapila, UN Resident Coordinator, spoke publicly about rape and other human rights violations committed in Darfur by the Sudanese army and its militia. In April 2004, the Sudanese government expelled him because of his statements regarding the conflict in Darfur.

[19] Human Rights Watch. (2004, 11 August). *Empty promises? Continuing abuses in Darfur*. Human Rights Watch. https://www.hrw.org/report/2004/08/11/empty-promises/continuing-abuses-darfur-sudan

Based on this commitment, OHCHR in August deployed the first team of human rights staff in Darfur. In September 2004, the Security Council requested the Secretary-General to create a Commission of Inquiry to investigate reports of violations of human rights and humanitarian law in Darfur by all parties. The resolution also called for increase in the human rights monitors deployed in Darfur [UN Doc. S/RES/1564 (2004)]. Since the international human rights' NGOs did not have access to Darfur, they expected OHCHR's presence to play an important role in documenting and publicizing the violations in Darfur. In August 2004, Human Rights Watch called for rapid and sufficient number of OHCHR human rights monitors to be deployed, and they regularly provide the Council with human rights information.[20]

OHCHR's deployment in Darfur came amidst the transition in Geneva with the appointment of Louis Arbour in July 2004 as the High Commissioner for Human Rights. By September, OHCHR had deployed about 12 HROs in Darfur. The deployment initially was apparently managed by the Desk Officer (Tunisian). Done in a hurry, the initial deployment was badly handled. The staff, deployed without any briefing or training and without any logistical support, also suffered from acute lack of living and office space in Darfur. The choice of staff deployed in Darfur seemed random. A staff who was working in Guatemala for many years was deployed in Darfur to provide an opportunity to serve in another mission. Several had limited background in human rights work, and most had no previous field experience. OHCHR did not sufficiently check the background of staff deployed in Darfur. OHCHR deployed a former UNHCR staff with Sudan experience without knowing that UNHCR Sudan had previously dismissed him for serious misconduct.[21]

Initially, without any supervision, most human rights staff attended meetings convened by the humanitarian agencies on topics ranging from IDP's nutrition to protecting animal husbandry. Due to the lack

---

[20] Ibid.

[21] After he spent six months in Darfur, his dismissal from UNHCR was unearthed while recruiting him as UNMIS staff.

of experience, guidance and lack of logistical support, they were not able to monitor the situation and produce reports regularly.

Under pressure, in December 2004, Louise Arbour sent Ian Martin as her Special Adviser to strengthen the human rights presence in Darfur.[22] Ian Martin's intervention stabilized the situation of human rights staff in Darfur (focus and logistical support). He organized structured training programmes for the human rights staff to brief them about the situation and on monitoring tools. Ian Martin in his end of mission report, dated 15 March 2005, concluded that only a start has been made in professionalizing the Darfur human rights presence. OHCHR must improve its ability to support a challenging human rights presence such as in Darfur.[23]

Meanwhile, Louise Arbour appointed Fabrizio Hochschild with vast field experience (with UNHCR, including in Sudan) as the Chief of Field Operations and Technical Cooperation Department in Geneva. Fabrizio Hochschild's appointment led to increased coordination between Geneva and Khartoum including in the recruitment of HROs.

North–South Peace Agreement

While the Darfur conflict was occupying the world media, both the UN and the regional organizations continued their efforts to finalize the peace agreement on the North-South conflict. Kofi Annan made it clear that settling the North-South conflict was essential for resolving the Darfur conflict.[24]

In January 2005, GoS and SPLM signed CPA. In March 2005, the Security Council established UNMIS. It was a large (with 10,000 military personnel) and complex mission with wide-ranging tasks

---

[22] In September, Louise Arbour visited Darfur and briefed the Security Council on her visit.

[23] See Ian Martin's end of mission report submitted to the High Commissioner for Human Rights on 15 March 2005 (Unpublished; copy with the author).

[24] United Nations. (2004, 4 October). *Report of the Secretary-General on the Sudan pursuant to paragraph 15 of Security Council resolution 1564 (2004) and paragraph 6, 13 and 16 of Security Council resolution 1556 (2004)*. S/2004 787. United Nations. https://digitallibrary.un.org/record/532668?ln=en#record-files-collapse-header

including protection of human rights (see Chapter II for details of UNMIS mandate and its operations). In April 2005, the OHCHR Darfur presence was integrated into the UNMIS HRD.[25] The region of UNMIS's human rights presence included Khartoum, Darfur and the South including the three areas.

UNMIS HUMAN RIGHTS DIVISION (APRIL 2005–NOVEMBER 2007)

Deployment and Orientation of Staff

The UNMIS SRSG Jan Pronk was fully engaged with the Darfur conflict and encouraged HRD's work in Darfur. OHCHR was demanding increased reporting on the situation in Darfur. HRD, as a priority, established four offices in Darfur in El Fasher, Nyala, El Geneina and Zalingei. UNMIS' recruitment process was initially slow.[26] By September 2006, HRD had deployed a total of 37 international officers in Darfur: El Fasher (9), Nyala (13), El Geneina (10) and Zalingei (5). In addition, the Khartoum office had 13 international staff including the Director. In September 2007, HRD had 105 staff including 40 national staff. In addition to Khartoum, human rights presence included four offices in Darfur and seven offices in the South.

Training of Staff

Based on the lessons learnt from OHCHR's initial deployment, HRD developed a plan for continuous training of its staff. Through several meetings, it identified training needs of HROs (and plans were made for meeting those needs. The training was a continuous process provided as and when new staff arrived in the mission. A guidance manual was prepared as a reference document for all staff. The manual included the mandate and structure of UNMIS; human rights context

---

[25] I joined UNAMIS in February 2005 to coordinate the human rights presence in Darfur. I continued as the Director of UNMIS Human Rights Division from April 2005 to November 2007.

[26] Deputy SRSG Taye Zerihoun, who was responsible for HRD, intervened to expedite the recruitment process.

and challenges; HRD's mandate, structure and activities with detailed guidelines on major activities; and information on various administrative matters.[27]

Strengthening Human Rights Officers' Monitoring Capacity

Most HROs (including the newly recruited) did not possess adequate experience and skills on monitoring human rights violations in an ongoing conflict situation. Understanding the legal system was essential in their monitoring work, but all the international staff lacked adequate understanding of the Sudanese legal system. The regime had modified the original common law system by introducing Islamic law in an ad hoc manner. HRD engaged Dr Amin Mekki Medani, a leading Sudanese human rights lawyer, to conduct a series of workshops for HROs on the legal system. This was followed by the development of a manual on Human Rights Violations in Sudan. The manual defined human rights violations and clarified international human rights standards that form the basis of each human rights violation. In the manual, the human rights violations were organized per right. It included a summary sheet for quick reference on human rights definitions. The manual used as a reference was the OHCHR Manual on Human Rights Monitoring and the OHCHR Manual on Human Rights for Judges, Prosecutors and Lawyers. The development of this manual was a learning process for HROs, and it ensured greater uniformity in the monitoring and reporting of violations. The manual's language and style were simple to make it accessible to the national staff as well. In addition to the manual, as and when required, brief policy notes were circulated to HROs to assist them in their monitoring work; for example, a policy note was issued on monitoring rape cases and social and health consequences of rape victims.

---

[27] Bela Kapur, who was Ian Martin's Special Assistant, continued to work with UNMIS HRD. Bela Kapur made valuable contributions during the start-up period. She was responsible for recruitment, planning, development of strategy, initial training of HROs and preparation of the guidance manual.

Capacity Building of Human Rights Officers in the South

The situation in South Sudan was different from Darfur. War had ended, and SPLM had assumed control over the territory. Institutions in the South were weak and/or non-functioning. Monitoring human rights violations was not a major priority. People in the South were impoverished and lacked access to basic health care, education, housing and water. In consultations with HROs based in the South, HRD decided that ESC rights should be the focus. All HROs based in the South required clarity on ESC rights and on relevant interventions to be made to advance these set of rights. An expert conducted intensive training for HROs on ESC rights and strategies on applying them in the South Sudan context.[28] In addition to ESC rights training, HROs in the South were briefed about various relevant issues such as customary law, prison systems and the judiciary. HROs in the South assisted the emerging civil society by providing training and creating forums for them to work together.

The human rights presence in the South faced the challenge of working in a situation of weak institutions, extreme poverty and weak civil society groups. The human rights presence in the South also suffered from high turnover of staff (most staff members wanted to be based in Darfur which was more glamorous), lack of experience of incoming staff and insufficient support provided by the HRD Director.[29]

UNMIS was established to implement CPA, and HRD should have focused on the South, but it did not happen till the end of 2007 when UNAMID was established. In the South, HRD was not equipped to deal with a situation where there were no massive violations (2005–2007) by the state. On hindsight, instead of deploying HROs as per a staffing plan negotiated by OHCHR, a gradual approach of using experts/consultants would have been more beneficial. More rigorous planning

---

[28] Ann Blyberg, author of *Circle of Rights—A Manual on ESC Rights*, conducted the training.

[29] Only towards the middle of 2007, a P5 was appointed in Juba to assist the Director and coordinate the work in the South.

process including thorough consultations with experts on South Sudan, even if it meant delaying the deployment of HROs in South, would have saved resources that were spent on staff salary.

Engagement with the Government of Sudan

The GoS under President Bashir had scant respect for human rights. In Darfur, its forces and a militia (Janjaweed) unleashed violence against civilians to suppress the insurgency. The UN Independent Commission of Inquiry on Darfur concluded that the GoS and the Janjaweed were responsible for widespread and systematic violations of international human rights law and international humanitarian law, which may well amount to war crimes and crimes against humanity. The GoS was antagonistic to UNMIS and HRD. However, HRD by creating a formal forum managed to systematically engage with middle-level officials on various human rights concerns.

In July 2004, the UN Secretary-General Kofi Annan signed a joint communique with the GoS that included the establishment of a high-level Joint Implementation Mechanism (JIM) co-chaired by the Minister of Foreign Affairs and SRSG Jan Pronk. After the initial meeting, the GoS did not convene JIM.[30] However, the GoS had agreed for setting up a Sub-Joint Implementation Mechanism (Sub-JIM) to focus on human rights which was to be co-chaired by the Head of the Advisory Council for Human Rights and the Director of UNMIS HRD.[31] The Sub-JIM meetings were attended by the GoS officials and representatives of the AU and embassies of the UK, the United States, the Netherlands and France.

Amending Regulations

The Sub-JIM was a useful forum for engaging with the GoS on human rights violations and for seeking its intervention. Sub-JIM's major contribution was the reform of criminal procedure relating to rape.

---

[30] The relationship between SRSG Jan Pronk and the Sudanese government deteriorated to the extent that he was declared persona non grata in October 2006.

[31] The Advisory Council was GoS' focal point for human rights.

The Sudanese criminal procedure required the completion of a standardized form, known as Criminal Form 8, by a registered doctor in cases of rape and other serious violent crimes such as murder and physical assault. Form 8 procedure prevented rape victims from directly accessing medical treatment without going through the police to fill the form. The procedure denied rape victims access to private medical facilities, also including those run by NGOs. The procedure had major implications for women victims in Darfur where large number of rape victims suffered due to Form 8 procedure. At Sub-JIM, HRD raised the issue of Form 8 and proposed amendments to the procedure. After prolonged negotiations, in October 2005, the Ministry of Justice issued a circular amending the procedure.

The amendment clarified the procedure for the collection of medical evidence and prohibited harassment of medical providers for treatment of victims of sexual violence. The amendment confirmed the right of victims of sexual abuses, including rape survivors, to receive medical treatment without first reporting to the police and completing Form 8 and stipulated that medical providers may not be harassed by government authorities after treating the victims of rape. The GoS also agreed to widely disseminate the amended procedure, particularly in Darfur.

Sexual and Gender-based Violence

HRD also raised the issue of sexual and gender-based violence (SGBV) in Darfur and sought the GoS' intervention to prevent it. Based on the discussions at Sub-JIM with the contribution of concerned UN entities, the GoS on 28 November 2005 launched the Action Plan to Eliminate Violence against Women in Darfur. A unit to combat violence against women was created within the Ministry of Justice to oversee the implementation of the Action Plan. Many of the measures proposed in the Acton Plan were based on key recommendations contained in HRD public report titled 'Access to Justice for Victims of Sexual Violence'. Dr Attiat Mostafa, Director of the National Unit to Combat Violence against Women and Children, briefed Sub-JIM on its implementation.

Access to Prisons and Detention Facilities

The issue of HRO's access to prisons and detention facilities was discussed at Sub-JIM too, and after several meetings on the subject, the GoS agreed to provide UNMIS HROs full, free and unfettered access to detention facilities in Sudan, including national security and military intelligence detention facilities. However, despite commitments by the government to provide unfettered access to all detention facilities, the UNMIS Human Rights was not granted access to military intelligence detention facilities. HROs accessed other prisons and detention facilities, particularly in Darfur.

Protection of Non-governmental Organizations

HRD at Sub-JIM consistently raised the issue of harassment of NGOs by various security agencies and sought the GoS' intervention to end them. HRD, through Sub-JIM, made efforts to reform the Humanitarian Aid Commission (HAC) which was the GoS' focal point for humanitarian NGOs. HAC often restricted the work of humanitarian NGOs, particularly in Darfur. HRD was not successful in reforming HAC but succeeded in mitigating major problems faced by humanitarian NGOs.

Joint Field Visits

The Sub-JIM made several field visits to Darfur, and HRD organized these visits and helped GoS representatives to understand the situation on the ground.

Visit to Mornei Internally Displaced Persons Camp (18 December 2005)

The Sub-JIM conducted a mission to Mornei, West Darfur, on 18 December 2005. The delegation included members of the GoS, UNMIS HR, representatives from diplomatic missions and the AU. The objective of the visit was to verify the allegations regarding human rights violations committed by members of the Central Police Reserve based at the camp. The delegation also assessed whether GNU officials in Mornei were abiding by the criminal procedure for investigating gender-based violence. The HRD team leader in El Geneina had repeatedly raised with the state governor the issue of human rights violations committed by the Central Police Reserve in Mornei. The local authorities did not take any credible step to end the violations in Mornei. The Sub-JIM visit surprised both the governor and the Commander of the Central Reserve Police, and both promised to act against the perpetrators. The visit reassured the victims, and they came forward to file complaints which were followed up by the El Geneina team.[32]

Visit to the South Darfur State Committee (6–7 March 2006)

On 6–7 March 2006, a delegation of the Sub-JIM conducted a visit to the South Darfur State Committee on gender-based violence to assess its functions and examine ways to strengthen it. The delegation was headed by Dr Attiat Mostafa, Director of the National Unit to Combat Violence against Women and Children, and included the Director of UNMIS Human Rights, representatives of diplomatic missions, the AU and UNFPA. The delegation conducted a visit to Kalma IDP Camp in Nyala where they met with a number of IDP women. During the meeting, the women were vocal and complained about incidents of rape and expressed their lack of confidence in the Sudanese police. Ms Mostafa was a supporter of Bashir and was unwilling to accept the concerns raised by the women. Ms Mostafa had no remorse about the situation of women living in camps. She accused UNMIS HRD of supporting women who opposed the government. The visit demonstrated the gulf between the Khartoum elite and the people of Darfur living in miserable conditions.

Visit to Three Darfur States for the Dissemination of the Amended Criminal Circular 2 (March 2005)

From 21 to 24 March 2005, a Sub-JIM delegation visited the three states of Darfur to disseminate to the local authorities the content of the amended circular regarding the requirements for filing Criminal

---

[32] Joanna Oyediran was the team leader in El Geneina. She demonstrated remarkable leadership in ensuring cohesion in her team, responding to concerns of victims and in maintaining good communication with the local authorities including the governor.

Form No. 8. The delegation included officials from the Ministry of Justice, Ministry of Health and Ministry of Interior, as well as the Director of UNMIS HRD. The delegation met with the governor, deputy governor, State Ministers of Health, police commissioners, General Prosecutors, Prosecutors and senior police officers from the towns and outlying areas.

The government suspended Sub-JIM meetings in August 2006 for unknown reasons and resumed them in August 2007. However, the meetings were not productive, and the GoS was unwilling to engage with UNMIS as it did previously.

Human Rights Division's Response to Sexual and Gender-based Violence in Darfur

The GoS denied and reacted strongly to accusations of systematic rape and other forms of sexual violence in the Darfur conflict. However, UNMIS HR officers continued to document multiple cases of sexual violence on a weekly basis. Women victims faced legal hurdles to reporting on sexual crimes including the possibility that the rape victim herself can face capital charges. If an unmarried woman is pregnant and cannot prove that she was raped, she can be charged with the capital crime of adultery (Zina). UNMIS HRD in private and publicly raised with the authorities the issue of sexual abuse and rape of women. In July 2005, Louise Arbour, the High Commissioner for Human Rights, issued a public report on 'Access to Justice for Victims of Sexual Violence' prepared by UNMIS HRD (OHCHR, 2005). It was followed by issuance of weekly, monthly and annual reports with information on SGBV. These reports provided the basis for advocating for accountability and reforms to end SGBV.

UNMIS HRD did not stop with its advocacy with the government, but it also made efforts to empower Darfurian men and women. In March and April 2006, two experts Amal Abdel Hadi, a well-known Egyptian women leader and trainer, and Nadia El Afify Hanfy, an Egyptian doctor providing assistance to women victims of violence, conducted workshops in all the four Darfur states. The participants were mostly members of local NGOs and lawyers assisting women victims. It was the first time that the issue of violence against women committed by men within the community and outsiders in Darfur was systematically discussed.

Encouraged by the response, HRD organized a Training of Trainers' (ToT) workshop for men and women including those who attended the sessions in March–April 2006. March workshops were conducted on-site at IDP camps. ToT was proposed to bring a small group of participants (15) to a centralized location and provide a six-day residential course.

In November 2007, two experts, Ms Madhavi Kukreja (an expert trainer on violence against women) and Ms Huma Khan (a former HRD Darfur staff on SGBV issues), conducted the training. Most of the participants had no formal education, but due to creative methods and material used by the trainers, they showed keen interest to learn and communicate the ideas to the others in their respective communities. It provided an opportunity for men to reflect on gender, status of women in Darfur society and violence against women. On completion of the course, the participants conducted practice sessions in their respective IDP camps. Resource persons observed these sessions to assist and mentor the trainers.

Unlike the March–April session, the organization of a residential course was a logistical nightmare. The Darfur HRD team did a tremendous job in organizing the workshops despite the challenges involved.[33]

Khartoum Monitoring Unit

In the beginning of 2005, HRD did not assign staff to monitor the human rights situation in Khartoum and the surrounding areas. However, the events following the death of Sudan's Vice-President John Garang in a helicopter accident, on 30 July 2005, showed the vulnerability of the Southerners living in Khartoum. The increasing

---

[33] By 2008, UNAMID mission was deployed in Darfur. UNMIS HRD's programmes and initiatives were not followed up by the UNAMID Human Rights Office. Most of the work done in Darfur between 2004 and 2007 was lost without any follow-up.

number of cases brought to the attention of UNMIS Human Rights and the events following the death of John Garang led to the establishment of a unit to monitor cases in Khartoum and the surrounding areas including the situation in IDP camps.

The Khartoum unit monitored the excessive use of force by the police in prisons including cases of arbitrary arrests, torture or ill-treatment.[34] The Khartoum team also monitored the situation arising from the construction of two major hydroelectric dams by the government in Kajbar and Merowe regions. These two construction projects were a source of numerous human rights violations.

Prison and Court Monitoring

Despite the varying degrees of access to detention facilities, UNMIS HR gathered a significant amount of information about detention and detention abuses in Darfur and other regions of Sudan.[35] Many of the prisons that were accessed had been previously closed to independent monitors. Each team had a focal point for prison and court monitoring, and regular meetings were conducted for focal points to share their experiences and strengthen their strategy.

HROs, based on their prison visits, followed up on cases of arbitrary arrests and denial of access to justice. In El Fasher, during visits to the prisons in remote areas, HROs found that the prisoners were held without trial since the local courts did not have a judge, prosecutor and lawyer. No official was willing to travel to that area to conduct trials. The UNMIS Human Rights team based in El Fasher persuaded

[34] Rafeef Dajani headed the Khartoum team. Her effective monitoring work including investigations into torture in a national security prison led to her expulsion from Sudan by GoS.

[35] Prisons accessed in Khartoum: Dar el Thoba prison, Omdurman men's prison, Omdurman women's prison, Dabak prison, Juvenile Rehabilitation Center (Al Jereif) and the Juvenile Rehabilitation Centre (Bahri). Prisons visited in East Sudan: Kassala prison, Gedaref prison and Port Sudan prison. In South Sudan: Juba Federal prison, Rumbek State prison, Torit County prison and Yei County prison. In Darfur: El Geneina prison, Shalla prison Al Fasher and Zalengei Big Prison. UNMIS Human Rights in South Darfur has also gained access twice to National Security facilities in Nyala. UNMIS has been denied access to military intelligence detention facilities throughout Sudan.

the governor to facilitate deployment of personnel to these courts. The El Fasher team organized UN transport for judges, prosecutors and lawyers to reach these remote areas and conduct trials. The reviving of local courts helped in the trial of numerous cases including in the acquittal of many who had spent several months awaiting trial.[36]

In March 2005, the Security Council referred Sudan to the ICC and the ICC began investigating war crimes committed in Darfur. In June 2005, the Chief Justice of Sudan, Molana Jalaedine Mohamed Osman, announced the creation of the Special Criminal Court on the Events in Darfur (the 'Court'). The GoS indicated that the Court had been established to deal with major criminal offences which have occurred in the Darfur states and which have been characterized as war crimes or crimes against humanity. The Court was proposed as an alternative to the ICC to meet its principle of complementarity. This principle meant that the Court would complement, but not supersede, the national jurisdiction. National courts would continue to have priority in investigating and prosecuting crimes committed within their jurisdictions, but the ICC would act when national courts were 'unable or unwilling' to perform their tasks.[37]

The international community was concerned about the credibility of the Special Courts and their effectiveness in ensuring the justice for Darfur victims. HRD through its monitoring and analysis of the Court's functioning submitted regular reports to SRSG. HRD concluded that there was a lack of systematic and transparent case selection process. It was unclear how cases were selected and why the Court tried ordinary crimes; the cases selected did not reflect the major crimes committed during the 2003–2004 Darfur conflict. Major militia attacks against civilians were not being prosecuted; cases were not brought against high-level government officials; and the Court failed

[36] Boehme, J. (2008). *Human rights and gender components of UN and EU peace operations: Putting human rights and gender mandates into practice*. German Institute for Human Rights. https://www.refworld.org/pdfid/4ecd10ed2.pdf

[37] Carter, L. E. (2010). The principle of complementarity and the international criminal court: The role of Ne Bis in Idem. *Santa Clara Journal of International Law, 8*(1), 165–198. https://digitalcommons.law.scu.edu/cgi/viewcontent.cgi?referer=https://www.google.com/&httpsredir=1&article=1079&context=scujil

to address command responsibility. HRD's reports provided valuable assessment to the international community on the functioning of the Special Court. UNMIS HRD was not authorized to submit information directly to the ICC. However, on ICC's request, the Office of Legal Affairs in New York forwarded them to the ICC. In May 2006, ICC Prosecutor Luis Moreno Ocampo, in a cable addressed to Jean-Marie Guéhenno, Under the Secretary-General of UNDPKO, acknowledged the receipt of UNMIS HRD reports and stated that his staff found them tremendously helpful in the context of ongoing admissibility analysis. He also sought copies of several specific reports such as UNMIS HRD's consolidated weekly reports.[38]

Reporting and Analysis Unit

The reporting and analysis unit was responsible for a number of activities which went beyond mere reporting. It functioned as a support cell for the HRD Director and as focal point of information for both HRD field teams and other sections within UNMIS and external partners (UN agencies, donor community, OHCHR, etc.). Based on the monitoring done by HROs, it provided analyses on human rights issues and assessed their impact on the human rights situation in Sudan, while also monitoring political and social developments.

In September 2005, to develop a coherent policy on its reporting including its reporting obligations, HRD requested Peter Bouckaert, Head of the Human Rights Watch Emergency Team (he was a UNMIS HRD staff in Darfur), to develop a note on the state of information gathering and reporting by the UNMIS Human Rights.[39]

He acknowledged that compared to 2004, HRDs reports have considerably improved including capacity to produce reports. Information provided by field offices has valuable information. Consolidated weekly reports of Darfur field offices are more analytical compared to

---

[38] Ocampo Luis Moreno (2006), Cable Addressed to Jean—Marie Guehenno, Under-Secretary-Genera, UNDPKO, New York, NY (Unpublished; Copy with the author).

[39] Bouckaert Peter (2005), A Note on Information Collection by UNMIS Human Rights Staff, Sudan (Unpublished; copy with the author).

earlier reports. Appointment of focal points on thematic areas such as SGBV and access to justice have increased information gathering in these areas. Establishment of focal points on specific thematic areas is a positive example for future human rights field presences in peacekeeping operations. HRD should prioritize production of thematic reports rather than issuing six-monthly overview reports that lack analytical insight and rigour. However, there is a need for regular overview reports on developments in Sudan, but they should not be of 'unanalytical kitchen sink reports'.[40]

Human Rights Database

Between April 2005 and November 2007, HRD produced 124 consolidated weekly reports (based on weekly reports submitted by all HRD sections), 85 incident reports from the field, 8 public reports issued by the High Commissioner for Human Rights and 8 reports submitted for inclusion in the Secretary-General's report. In addition, HRD also submitted monthly updates to OHCHR and provided inputs to the reports by the UN Special Rapporteur on Sudan and other rapporteurs.

HROs' monitoring generated information on a vast number of cases that needed to be systematically stored for safety and for retrieval purposes. Initially, HROs stored data in an ad hoc manner. UNMIS HRD failed in its efforts to engage an external expert to visit Sudan and assist in the establishment of a database. HRD then developed an interim database using the expertise of its staff. The OCHA Humanitarian Information Centre (HIC) offered its services to set up the database programme, which started running in November–December 2005. However, HIC ended its support due to staff shortage. The HRD staff continued to maintain the database. In February 2007, OHCHR proposed a common database for all field presences and began working on it.[41]

---

[40] Bouckaert, P. (2004). *Submitted a note to Director on reporting strategy.* UNMIS HRD Staff.

[41] When I left in the end of 2007, the OHCHR database was still under construction. Meanwhile UNAMID was established in Darfur with a Human Rights Division. It is possible that valuable data may have been lost in the transition process.

Technical Cooperation and Capacity Building

UNMIS HRD had established a separate unit (based in Khartoum) to coordinate its technical cooperation and capacity-building programmes.

Summary of Various Projects and Programmes Implemented by United Nations Assistance Mission in Sudan Human Rights Division

1. **Provision of small grants**

   UNMIS HRU provided a grant of US$11,000 to the South Darfur State Committee on Combating Gender Violence. The purpose of the project was to strengthen its secretariat to effectively implement its activities identified in the six-month work plan. The grant was made to strengthen a state institution focusing exclusively on SGBV.

   UNMIS HRD, under the mission's Quick Impact Projects (QUIPS), provided US$17,000 to build two large shelters at Kuria Prison in Nyala. During prison monitoring visits, HROs found that prisoners, during the day, were not able to spend time in the prison's open areas because there was no shade. The shelters provided Kuria inmates much needed protection from extreme heat and sun when they were allowed to step out of their cells.

2. **Focus on laying the foundations for institutions in the South Sudan Human Rights Commission**

   In January 2006, UNMIS Human Rights appointed two national consultants. The national consultants held dialogues and meetings with civil society groups, political actors, academics and professional groups in South Sudan to develop HRD's strategy in South Sudan. In April 2006, the GoS set up a task force for drafting a bill on the South Sudan Human Rights Commission (SSHRC). UNMIS Human Rights provided background materials including NHRI model laws for the task force. HRD dedicated a HRO to conduct regular consultations with members of the task force for drafting the legislation. In June 2006, a workshop was held in Juba to discuss the mandate and role of the proposed SSHRC. Prior to formulating a law on SSHRC, the President of the South Sudan appointed the Chairperson, Deputy Chair and members of the SSHRC through a presidential decree on 26 June 2006. UNMIS HR began working with the Commission members to assist in drafting of the law and to develop SSHRC's programmes and structures. In July 2006, an international expert on NHRIs was appointed to provide advisory and technical assistance, in particular, to assist in the drafting of the law and procedures of SSHRC. In August 2006, HRD organized an induction workshop that was attended by all the five members of SSHRC as well as by members from the Ministry of Legal Affairs and Constitutional Development, the Ministry of Labour, Public Service and Human Resource Development, the Ministry of Parliamentary Affairs, the Human Rights Committee of the Legislative Assembly of South Sudan and members of the civil society. In October 2006, SSHRC, in cooperation with UNMIS Human Rights, conducted a preparatory workshop to develop a strategic plan and annual budget for the year 2007. In November, SSHRC organized a strategic planning workshop, which was attended by civil society groups. In November 2006, SSHRC conducted a study tour to Uganda with the support of HRD and the British Embassy in Khartoum. In November 2006, a national consultant was appointed for a period of four months to assist SSHRC to establish its secretariat and implement its programmes. In March 2007, the members of SSHRC conducted a study tour to South Africa with the support of HRD and the British Embassy in Khartoum. In April 2007, a consultant was appointed to support the SSHRC secretariat. In May 2007, HRD and SSHRC signed an MoU for the organization of a one-month-long training programme for SSHRC monitors.

Working with the National Assembly

In 2006 and 2007, UNMIS Human Rights focused on the capacity building of National Assembly, South Sudan Legislative Assembly and State Assembly for the promotion and protection of human rights in all parts of Sudan.

Realization of ESC Rights through Human Rights Approach to Budgeting

In 2005 and 2006, UNMIS Human Rights organized two workshops on 'Human Rights Approaches to National Budgeting', which were attended by 100 members of the National Assembly. Both the workshops helped the National Assembly members to understand technical aspects of national budget and examine it from the perspective of human rights. Wealth sharing between parties was an essential element of CPA, and the workshop helped the National Assembly members to understand the budget process and the budget as a whole. The third workshop on the same topic took place in November 2007.

Workshop on Human Rights Treaties for National Assembly Members

UNMIS Human Rights organized a four-day workshop on international human rights treaties in June 2006. Forty-five members of the National Assembly, particularly members of the Legislative Standing Committee and Human Rights Standing Committee, attended the workshop. The objective of the workshop was to enhance the capacity of Assembly members to understand the rights and freedoms enshrined in international human rights treaties. In early 2007, UNMIS Human Rights facilitated dialogues between civil society organizations and the Human Rights Committee of the National Assembly on human rights issues. UNMIS Human Rights provided technical support to the Human Rights Committee of the National Assembly for developing a programme for the Committee to receive and act on complaints related to human rights abuse. In December 2005, a three-day workshop was organized on the role of South Sudan Legislative Assembly to introduce the members to human rights treaties and how the members could contribute to the protection of human rights in South Sudan.

Strengthening the Law Reform Process

In October 2005, the Federal Ministry of Justice initiated a law reform process. A committee was formed to study CPA and review the relevant national laws to determine if they were in harmony with CPA and the Interim Constitution. The Committee identified 60 laws for reform. The Legislative and Justice Standing Committee of the National Assembly was responsible for reviewing these laws. In 2006, UNMIS Human Rights provided a consultant to the National Assembly to work on law reform issues. The purpose was to ensure that Sudan's national laws were reformed in conformity with the international human rights standards. The consultant provided technical assistance with a particular focus on laws relating to national security, human rights commissions and criminal procedure. In June 2007, UNMIS Human Rights supported the National assembly to organize two workshops on the harmonization of national laws with international human rights instruments. At the end of the workshop, the Human Rights Committee of the National Assembly submitted a set of recommendations for law reform to the Speaker of the National Assembly.

In early 2007, a workshop on reform of laws related to rape and other sexual violence was organized to enhance awareness among the National Assembly members. UNMIS Human Rights provided the Human Rights Committee critical comments on laws, including commentaries and critical reviews on the NGO Act, 2006, the National Human Rights Commission (NHRC) Bill, the Police Forces Act, 1999, certain provisions of the Criminal Procedure Act, 1991, Criminal Act, 1991 and laws related to rape and sexual violence.

Working with Law Enforcement Agencies

UNMIS Human Rights appointed an international expert to develop a comprehensive human rights training plan for the Sudanese police. The expert conducted two missions to Sudan in April and August 2006. Two separate reports were published on UNMIS Human Rights' strategy on capacity building of police forces in the northern and southern Sudan. The reports provided a valuable source for the UN Police and others to integrate human rights into their ongoing efforts at strengthening the law enforcement agencies.

In 2006 and 2007, UNMIS Human Rights conducted 13 human rights awareness workshops for various levels of police officers in

Khartoum. Three hundred and ninety-five police officers attended these workshops. UNMIS Human Rights also continued to support the UN Police for the implementation of their training programmes for police forces in the North and South. UNMIS Human Rights, in collaboration with the Advisory Council of Human Rights (ACHR) and Police Training Department of the Ministry of Interior, developed a human rights training manual for the Sudan Police Force (SPF). The manual was produced for use by Police Academy trainers. A similar project was initiated in the South for the development of a separate human rights manual for the southern SPF. An international consultant deployed by HRD assisted in the drafting of the manual.

Assistance for Establishing a National Human Rights Commission in Sudan

In view of the lack of GoS' human rights commitment, HRD was reluctant to assist in setting up a NHRC. However, it was a priority area for OHCHR, and UNMIS HRD was not able to avoid it. HRD, therefore, decided that it would pursue a two-pronged approach: first, to support drafting a credible law for the establishment of a national institution and, second, to involve the civil society in the process. The GoS-established preparatory committee drafted a bill for the establishment of a national institution.

UNMIS Human Rights held a workshop on 6 May 2006 for civil society organizations to discuss the draft bill and identify areas of concerns. ACHR and HRD jointly organized a consultation workshop on the draft bill on 8 May 2006. Representatives from civil society organizations, human rights organizations and women rights organizations, along with academics and parliamentarians, attended the workshop. In September 2006, a workshop was organized to assist civil society groups to develop their strategy for advocating the establishment of NHRC. On November 19, the National Constitutional Review Commission (NCRC), entrusted with finalizing the drafts laws on various commissions including NHRC, organized a workshop to consult with various social and political groups on the draft law. The workshop was organized with the support of UNDP and UNMIS HRD.

In December 2006, the coordination committee of the civil society groups organized a workshop to comment on the final draft law on NHRC submitted to the government by NCRC. The workshop, organized with the assistance of UNMIS HRD, was attended by civil society groups. In January 2007, HRD organized a consultation workshop at the National Assembly on the final draft of the NHRC Bill. In May 2007, HRD organized a consultation meeting with civil society groups to engage them more actively in the advocacy for the establishment of NHRC. (In 2009, the drafting was completed, and in 2012, the Sudan National Human Rights Commission came into existence. It was not independent at the time but was expected to be an independent institution after the overthrow of Bashir in 2019.)

Working with Sudanese Civil Society

Since 2005, UNMIS Human Rights has worked with the civil society and human rights groups and conducted 33 human rights awareness programmes. HRD supported the efforts of the Sudanese civil society to work with the Human Rights Treaty Bodies. In July 2006, Sudan submitted its third periodic report on ICCPR to the UN Human Rights Committee. Members of Sudanese civil society expressed an interest in submitting an alternative report on ICCPR. UNMIS Human Rights conducted a series of training sessions on ICCPR and on drafting an alternative report. About 30 representatives of civil society organizations participated in the training. HRD appointed a national consultant to coordinate the project.

Women's Human Rights

In July 2006, UNMIS Human Rights organized a consultation meeting with civil society groups to discuss reforming legal provisions concerning rape and sexual violence. In the July 2006 workshop, civil society groups submitted recommendations to amend relevant sections of the Criminal Act of 1991 and the Evidence Act. UNMIS Human Rights continued to organize dialogues with women's organizations and decision-makers on this issue. Two more workshops were organized on a similar topic in 2007, and they were attended by members of the National Assembly and legal professionals. In 2006 and 2007, HRD conducted eight workshops on women's human rights.

International Human Rights Treaty Ratifications and Reporting Obligations

In 2007, UNMIS Human Rights initiated the process for supporting ACHR for drafting and submitting its overdue report to the Committee on Economic, Social and Cultural Rights. In 2007, two workshops were organized to expedite the process of ratification of CAT and CEDAW (Convention on the Elimination of All Forms of Discrimination against Women). UNMIS Human Rights also continued to support civil society groups to create awareness on ratification of CEDAW.

Human Rights Day Events

Since 2005, every year on the Human Rights Day on 10 December, HRD held a number of creative activities across Sudan; for example, in Kadugli, the local community with the support of HRD organized an exhibition and a dancing and singing celebration which showcased cultural traditions of several tribes from South Kordofan. In Wau, UNMIS HR organized a march through the town with the presence of the police band and a song festival performed by several choirs and musical groups from the town. In Abyei, UNMIS released the Universal Declaration of Human Rights in Dinka. In Juba, members of SSHRC in collaboration with HRD conducted programmes with civil society groups and members of the local community. In Zalingei, West Darfur, public information material on human rights issues was distributed to the local authorities and IDPs. In Nyala, South Darfur, the observation focused on the issue of violence against women. A play on the topic was performed at Nyala Theatre, with about 300 students from high schools and Nyala University attending the event.

HRD published 6,000 posters in Arabic and English relating to the International Human Rights Day and the Universal Declaration of Human Rights. These posters were distributed in various parts of Sudan. In 2007, UDHR was translated into two South Sudanese languages, Dinka and Bari. The Dinka translation of UDHR was officially published on the OHCHR Web.

Development of a Manual on Sudanese Administration of Criminal Justice

In 2006, two consultants (international and national) were contracted to develop a manual on the Sudanese legal and judicial system with a particular focus on the administration of criminal justice system. The consultants conducted research and later developed a manual which provided HRD and local human rights NGOs with basic information regarding legal framework and structures relevant to the administration of justice. UNMIS also published 1,50,000 simplified version of 7 human rights treaties. In 2006, UNMIS Human Rights reprinted 10,000 copies of OHCHR's expanded pocket handbook on human rights and policing in both Arabic and English for distribution to the Sudanese police in the northern and southern Sudan. In 2007, a pocket leaflet on Human Rights Principles for Law Enforcement was published.

United States Agency for International Development Support

In April 2006, UNMIS, United States Agency for International Development (USAID) and OHCHR entered into a funding agreement for conducting programmes on the theme of SGBV. HRD organized a series of training seminars for the members of IDP communities. It provided human rights training to lawyers, local NGOs and selected IDP camp residents. Using USAID funding, HRD organized a visit by the Khartoum-based Human Rights Committee of the National Assembly to all the three states in Darfur to expose them to human rights situation on the ground.

Security Challenges

Systematic monitoring of violations in a conflict situation posed several challenges, including challenges pertaining to the security situation. UNDSS, for security reasons, imposed restrictions on HROs' movement to monitor human rights violations. In Darfur, if UNDSS received information concerning clashes in the mission area, it would impose restrictions on the movement of all mission staff until it conducted an assessment mission to verify the situation. Due to the limited staff, UNDSS was often not able to promptly conduct assessment missions. In some instances, HROs would be grounded for several days (especially if UNDSS considered the clashes to be serious) and were not able to promptly visit areas where clashes involving civilian casualties had occurred. Delayed visits affected the collection of evidence and tracing of victims. HRD sought the intervention of UNMIS SRSG to authorize UNDSS to include HROs in their initial assessment missions. SRSG, as the Designated Official for UNMIS Security, issued a policy note to that effect and soon HROs also joined UNDSS' initial assessment missions. It helped HROs to make contacts with affected communities and if required follow-up with a longer visit for producing a detailed report. A similar arrangement was made with the African Mission in Sudan (AMIS) for providing transportation and security to HROs.[42] Maintaining a balance between UNDSS' security concerns and HROs' access to collect information continued to be a challenge.

Limited Resources

UNMIS had the greatest number of civilian components—Civil Affairs, Human Rights, Rule of Law, Protection of Civilians, Child Protection, Gender, Political Affairs and Public Information. In Darfur, each sector included staff from Civil Affairs, Human Rights, Rule of Law, Protection of Civilians, Gender and Child Protection units. Office space was limited and resources such as interpreters and translators were scarce. In particular, access to vehicles was a major problem. Staff of all the civilian components conducted field visits, and in some cases, due to security situation, field visits were allowed only with convoys increasing the demand for vehicles.

---

[42] Since 2004, the AU had deployed AMIS in Darfur to provide security to the civilian population in close coordination with UNMIS.

OHCHR and the international community expected HRD to provide regular reports on the human rights situation in Darfur. Without vehicles, it was not possible to undertake field visits. HROs were also frustrated since they were not able to respond to the situations promptly. HRD, with the authorization of UNMIS DSRSG, sought USAID's assistance since it was keen to fund human rights programmes in Darfur. The HRD Director and the USAID representative developed a project to strengthen HROs' work in Darfur. Under this project, in April 2006, UNMIS Human Rights was provided with US$2 million for the procurement of 20 Minimum Operation Security Standard (MOSS) compliant vehicles and IT and communication equipment. HRD was fortunate in obtaining funds from USAID, and the mission leadership was supportive of this initiative.[43]

Coordination between Civilian Components

In Darfur, with more than a million people living in camps, it was difficult to accept the idea of several well-paid UN staff spending time in front of their computers due to the lack of vehicles. Finding solutions to logistics was easier than sorting out the confusion regarding the role of some of the components. It was the first time that the Protection of Civilians staff was deployed in a mission (The Civilian Protection Division had an approved staffing level of 27 in headquarters and 42 for field locations including child protection officers). The CPD staff, including the Child Protection staff, did not have clarity about their role and functions. Overlapping functions between different civilian components confused both the victims and the local authorities.

In December 2005, the UN Office of Internal Oversight Services (OIOS) audited UNMIS' civilian components. In its report, it stated that UNMIS has four offices which deal with quite closely similar functions relating to human rights and rule of law—HRD, Rule of Law Unit, UN Police and Protection of Civilian Division. Also, Political Affairs and Civil Affairs have roles that deal with the rule of law in some respects. All of them have similar functions. They deal with

---

[43] DSRSG Taye Zerihoun supported the initiative and authorized UNMIS to provide patrol and service the vehicles.

some aspects of capacity building, training, reporting and monitoring of human rights violations, state prisons and correction services and courts and judges. There is potential for overlap and duplication in this scenario. The report also identified other UN agencies based in Sudan with overlapping functions with the UNMIS components. The report recommended better coordination between human rights, civilian protection and the rule of law functions.[44]

Subsequently, UNMIS set up several coordination mechanisms to ensure smooth functioning among the civilian components. UNMIS set up a Human Rights and Protection Steering Committee with UNMIS Human Rights coordinating it. The Protection Steering Committee developed a policy note identifying various sections involved in protection activities and defined their respective roles. In addition, UNMIS established working groups and task forces to increase coordination on thematic areas such as SGBV, child protection and gender. These mechanisms helped in coordination among heads of divisions even as confusion and duplication often continued in the field.

LIBYA: UNITED NATIONS SUPPORT MISSION IN LIBYA

In September 2011, the Security Council established a political mission without peacekeepers called the UNSMIL. The Libyan revolution against Qadhafi's long, repressive rule was based on demands for restoration of rights and freedoms. NTC that assumed power during the transition committed itself to building a new Libya based on human rights and the rule of law. UNSMIL's mandate stressed human rights and included assisting in setting up of a TJ process, human rights monitoring and reporting and rebuilding the rule of law institutions.

The UN Secretary-General appointed Ian Martin as his Special Representative to head UNSMIL. From the outset, Ian Martin insisted on national ownership and a light footprint. In view of his extensive experience in human rights and TJ, he assembled a four-person human

[44] Office of Internal Oversight Services Internal Audit Division I, Audit no: AP2005/600/16, 12 December 2005 (copy with the author).

rights team.[45] The team reflected the immediate priorities of HRD. Unlike other missions, UNSMIL did not have a separate Rule of Law unit. It was part of the Human Rights, Transitional Justice and Rule of Law Division. During the final planning process, an OHCHR representative visited Libya and proposed a staffing table with 54 human rights staff. SRSG in consultation with HRD approved 17 international staff and 6 national staff.[46] OHCHR may not have been happy with the reduction, but on hindsight, given the security situation and lack of institutions, it was the right decision.

UNSMIL HRD's priorities were concerning conflict-related detentions, strengthening the emerging civil society groups, violence against women, violations of rights of minorities and migrant workers, providing assistance to the Libyan authorities for ensuring accountability for past crimes committed by the Qadhafi regime, support for rebuilding an independent judicial system, reviving prison administration, tracing of missing persons and assisting in the establishment of a national TJ process.

Conflict-related Detentions

The Libyan revolutionaries (thuwar), during the armed conflict against Qadhafi, captured large number of Qadhafi forces and his alleged supporters. These persons were detained in makeshift detention centres that were controlled by different revolutionary armed groups. Revolutionary groups tortured and ill-treated the detainees under their control. By October 2011, it was estimated that there were about 8,000 detainees held by revolutionaries in detention centres in various parts of the country. HRD, as a priority, engaged with NTC and

---

[45] Author joined as the director of HRD. The team included Marieke Wierda, Senior Human Rights Officer, who came from the ICTJ and had extensive global experience on transitional justice. Ahmed Ghanem as a staff of UNODC had lived and worked in Libya before the revolution and had strong links with the members of the Libyan judiciary, prosecution and the legal profession. Samira Bouslama had worked in post-conflict situations and was deployed by Amnesty International to monitor and report during the revolution.

[46] It included officers for transitional justice, rule of law, corrections, judicial affairs, child protection, gender, reporting and outreach.

proposed that NTC assume control over the detainees. NTC issued Law No. 38, which ordered the Ministry of Interior, the Ministry of Defence and Ministry of Justice to assume control over all conflict-related detainees. However, the transfer did not take place due to the lack of coordination among the three ministries, non-functioning of courts and destruction of prisons during the conflict. Moreover, the revolutionaries used the detainees as a way of demonstrating their power in their effort to stake a claim in the new order.

While the interim government was engaged with the revolutionaries to exercise its jurisdiction over the detainees, HRD pursued a multi-dimensional strategy to tackle the issue. The first and most important was to monitor torture and ill-treatment of detainees and the conditions of detention centres. Monitoring helped in engaging with NTC and often with the revolutionaries to ensure the safety, security and well-being of the detainees. HRD trained local groups on human rights monitoring so that they could visit the detentions centres regularly and report on the situation of detainees. HRD mapped the detention centres to identify centres that required frequent visits to prevent torture or ill-treatment of detainees.[47]

The second was to assist the Prosecutor General to develop a prosecutorial strategy to bring to justice those detainees who had committed human rights violations before, during and after the revolution. HRD, with the help of experts,[48] trained more than 100 prosecutors to screen the detainees' files to discard evidence that was taken in breach of their fundamental rights and identify cases for immediate release or for further investigations based on the objective criteria.[49]

A third strategy was to assist the government in rebuilding the correctional system. UNSMIL initiated a bilateral programme with the

---

[47] HRD was careful not to duplicate the work of ICRC since it had expertise to deal with the abuse of detainees.

[48] The experts were Luc Côté from Canada and Iskander Ghattas and Mohamed Khalef from Egypt.

[49] Even after several years, detention centres controlled by armed groups continue to exist. The issue of detainees reflected legal, institutional and political challenges of the transition. It is a symptom of a non-functioning state and persistence of conflicts between various communities.

Jordanian Rehabilitation and Corrections Department to assist in the restoration of Libyan corrections system. A high-powered Jordanian delegation visited Libya and planned assistance for prison reform including infrastructure needs, institutional restructuring, legislative and regulatory reform and capacity-building needs. The Jordanian assistance included training and professional development of Judicial Police to effectively manage and operate prisons in line with regional and international human rights standards.

UNSMIL HRD's approach to dealing with conflict-related detentions demonstrates the effectiveness of integrating rule of law within HRD. The Libyan authorities dealt with a single entity. It avoided setting up a coordination mechanism within the mission for ensuring coordination between human rights and rule of law initiatives saving time and resources. Advocacy for release of detainees, training the prosecutors and judges to deal with conflict-related detentions and rebuilding the correctional system was carried out in a seamless manner. UNSMIL HRD saw the role of UNDP as contributing to long-term development of rule of law institutions in the country and developed joint programmes accordingly.

Strengthening Civil Society

Qadhafi did not permit independent civil society groups to function and targeted them by detaining their members, torturing them and at times hanging them in public.[50] Post revolution, many, particularly young men and women, formed local organizations to engage in social activities. HRD with the aim to strengthen such groups reached out to them in many parts of Libya. In all the four provinces, HRD assisted in the strengthening of local groups and provided regular training and human rights materials. It trained local groups to monitor human rights violations and report on them. They were also introduced to TJ principles so that they could contribute to the TJ process in Libya.

---

[50] Woodward, B. (1984, 23 April). Hangings in Tripoli focus attention on Libyan dissent. *The Washington Post.* https://www.washingtonpost.com/archive/politics/1984/04/23/hangings-in-tripoli-focus-attention-on-libyan-dissent/9c2481e3-1b2d-4b74-8d69-4304afe24ed1/

These groups played an important role in monitoring and providing information regarding the conditions of conflict-related detainees and were instrumental in preventing abuse in detention centres. Some of them contributed to the local-level reconciliation process by bringing together communities that fought for and against Qadhafi.

Transitional Justice[51]

In the immediate aftermath of the Libyan revolution, there was general support for moving forward with reconciliation and dealing with the past. NTC considered TJ a priority.[52] Among others, NTC faced the challenge of addressing past crimes and crimes committed during the revolution by Qadhafi forces and revolutionaries.

The revolutionaries had raised the expectation of the population that the detainees held by them would be punished for their crimes. In addition, during Qadhafi's regime, thousands of persons were involved in carrying out his oppressive policies and had committed human rights abuse. The post-revolution Libya did not have the legal framework, institutional capacity or human resources to conduct credible trials of all the detainees and other numerous perpetrators. Moreover, the revolutionaries were suspicious of judges and prosecutors since they had functioned under Qadhafi. When judges and prosecutors began their work, they were intimidated by the revolutionaries. Consequently, the courts did not function in most parts of the country.

As for the trial of leading former regime figures, the UN Security Council had referred the Libyan situation to the ICC and the ICC Prosecutor had issued arrest warrants against Qadhafi and his close associates. After the revolution, the ICC Prosecutor requested the Libyan authorities to handover Qadhafi's son Saif al-Islam against whom the ICC had issued a warrant. The Libyans were reluctant to involve the ICC in prosecuting Saif al-Islam and other leading

---

[51] SRSG Ian Martin had a strong background in TJ, and he recruited Marieke Wierda, a former senior staff from the ICTJ, to coordinate as a HRD staff member.

[52] Wierda, M. (2015). Confronting Qadhafi's legacy: Transitional justice in Libya. In C. Peter & B. McQuinn (Eds.), *The Libyan revolution and its aftermath.* C. Hurst & Co.

figures. The ICC's Pre-Trial Chambers ruled that the Libyan authorities were unable to carry out proceedings against Saif al-Islam and established its jurisdiction over his case. Despite the ICC's ruling, the trial of Saif-al Islam continued with several substantive and procedural inadequacies. Another factor that complicated addressing past crimes was the issue of accountability of revolutionaries for the crimes committed by them during the revolution. Revolutionaries considered themselves to be martyrs. NTC encouraged this narrative and even offered money to keep them under control. It laid the ground for their impunity.[53]

Transitional Justice Law and Truth Seeking

HRD worked closely with the Libyan committee that was drafting the transitional justice law. It repeatedly requested NTC to seek wider consultation on the transitional justice law. In February 2012, NTC adopted the law without broad public consultation. Based on the comments made by HRD and others, in 2013, GNC modified the NTC law and established a Fact-Finding and Reconciliation Commission. The Commission focused on individual cases and avoided truth-seeking process. It was formal and entirely run by male judges. Ordinary Libyans did not engage with it.[54] In the absence of a systematic truth-seeking process, reparations for victims also suffered. NTC and GNC continued Qadhafi's policy of using payments to appease specific groups. They made ad hoc payments to victims without developing a reparation programme.

Missing Persons

Post revolution, there was a demand for knowing the plight of those who had gone missing during the Qadhafi regime. There were known cases like the relatives of those killed in Abu Salim prison seeking

---

[53] After the election, in 2012, the GNC adopted a law criminalizing torture and other crimes committed by revolutionaries during the revolution. It was not implemented.

[54] Wierda, M. (2015). Confronting Qadhafi's legacy: Transitional justice in Libya. In C. Peter & B. McQuinn (Eds.), *The Libyan revolution and its aftermath*. C. Hurst & Co.

information about their loved ones. Most post-conflict situations face the problem of finding the plight of missing persons, and Libya was not an exception. Globally, diverse experiences were available on tracing, including forensic techniques to identify the remains of missing persons. In Libya, during the revolution, some prominent scientists with relevant knowledge and skills initiated a programme on missing persons. NTC recognized their work by making them a part of the official Commission on the Search and Identification for Missing Persons. GNC dissolved this Commission and established a Ministry for the Affairs of Families of Martyrs and Missing Persons. The minister responsible for the ministry reportedly came from a radical Islamic group and did not have much experience on the question of missing persons or TJ. He focused on the martyrs (revolutionaries who were killed during the revolution) and immediately began a scheme for compensating the families of martyrs that distracted from the difficult job of tracing and identifying missing persons. The Ministry embarked on ad hoc efforts to identify missing persons by conducting exhumation and collection of DNA samples without adequate expertise or legal framework.

International assistance provided to the Ministry by governments and NGOs suffered due to the lack of coordination; for example, an NGO in Bosnia offered to verify DNA samples and the Ministry sent the samples to them without applying proper protocols. HRD made efforts to assist the Ministry in the development of a legal framework and protocols. However, the Minister was more interested in finding a quick fix to what was otherwise a complex process. It was an area where HROs including OHCHR did not have expertise in. HRD sought the assistance of international organizations with forensic and other relevant expertise and with experience in several countries. However, engaging them required large funding. In the absence of the Ministry's commitment to seek assistance from experts, it was not possible to deploy them in Libya.

Marieke Wierda subsequently observed that the issue of missing persons illustrated the challenges faced in implementing a TJ programme in Libya. Due to high expectations from the public, policymakers made impossible promises and pursued popular causes like assistance to martyrs than deal with issues concerning both Qadhafi supporters and opponents.[55]

Reconciliation

The reconciliation process suffered in the absence of a vision for pursuing TJ in Libya. Dormant conflicts between communities had become latent during the revolution. In some instances, they manifested as supporting or opposing the revolution. NTC was keen to pursue reconciliation. It engaged local leaders to deal with some of the ongoing conflicts between communities. In the initial euphoria after the revolution, some of the conflicts were temporarily reconciled. NTC also organized large national conferences on reconciliation with the participation of local elders and religious leaders. On the other hand, revolutionaries considered reconciliation as nothing but compromising with the supporters of the former regime. Instead of reconciliation, the effort was to isolate or exclude those associated with the former regime. Due to public pressure, particularly from the revolutionaries who went to the extent of occupying the Ministry of Justice, GNC adopted a law in 2013 on 'political isolation' of those associated with the former regime from 1 September 1969 till 23 October 2011.[56]

It barred persons associated with the former regime for 10 years from holding wide-ranging positions, including in the government and the legislature. The broad criteria for identifying persons for exclusion affected not only the Qadhafi regime officials but a large number of people. UNSMIL criticized the law as flawed and discriminatory. The law may have reflected Libya's desire to break from the past, but it was shaped by internal power struggle between groups rather on TJ principles.[57]

---

[55] Ibid.

[56] The debate regarding the isolation law started in 2011, and HRD was engaged in ensuring that it does not violate human rights. HRD also provided experience from Iraq and other countries that had gone through a similar process.

[57] Wierda, M. (2015). Confronting Qadhafi's legacy: Transitional justice in Libya. In C. Peter & B. McQuinn (Eds.), *The Libyan revolution and its aftermath*. C. Hurst & Co.

Human Rights Division's Initiatives on Transitional Justice in Libya (2012)

HRD, in addition to assisting the official TJ initiatives, carried out its own programmes to contribute to the process. It integrated TJ in its training module for civil society groups. It also focused on the role of women in TJ, since men mostly dominated the formal process. The process was also handicapped by the lack of participation and consultation with cross-section of Libyan. HRD took the initiative to facilitate broad-based discussions on TJ in Libya.

'Envisioning Reconciliation' Project

UNSMIL, in May 2012 and in collaboration with the National Consultancy Group (a Libyan think tank) and the embassies of South Africa and Switzerland, implemented the 'Envisioning Reconciliation' project with the following objectives:

1. Raise awareness on what a reconciliation process based on implementing holistic TJ strategy may offer to the Libyan society.
2. Enhance the capacity of the Libyans to formulate a strategy to achieve TJ and reconciliation.
3. Share lessons learnt and best practices through reflections from actors with global experience in reconciliation.

The project had the following components:

1. The visit of six international experts to Libya to share their experience and expertise on TJ.[58]
2. A two-day workshop for opinion makers on TJ in Tripoli, preceded by the public viewing of the film 'Confronting the Truth' and followed by discussion.
3. Experts' visit to Sabha, Zintan, Misrata and Benghazi, where they met with the local council and military council members (in Sabha and Zintan), community leaders and civil society.

---

[58] The experts were Yasmin Sooka, Farid Esack and Graeme Simpson from South Africa; Sofia Macher from Peru; Mo Bleeker from Switzerland and Claudio Cordone representing the International Center for Transitional Justice.

4. A half-day workshop at the High Judicial Institute for judges and lawyers.
5. A debriefing of the international diplomatic community.

Conclusions and Recommendations of the Transitional Justice Experts

1. Throughout the various meetings, many participants stressed that criminal justice should precede reconciliation. At the same time, public expectations that large numbers of persons associated with the former regime ought to be tried are unrealistic and need to be addressed. The Libyan justice system is still weak and will not be able to deliver criminal justice beyond a limited number of cases. More public debate is needed in Libya on the limitations of criminal justice and the additional measures needed, in particular, in relation to victims, truth seeking or institutional reform. More discussion is also needed on how these measures should be sequenced to form a part of an integrated approach.
2. In general, there is a dearth of conversation among Libyans on TJ and reconciliation. Much more dialogue is needed to craft an approach that is domestically owned and driven and best suited to the Libyan context. This approach should use a language that people understand, bearing in mind that the local 'languages' in Libya centre around religion and group solidarity. Religious, cultural and educational institutions can all play a role in stimulating such a discussion, including civil society organizations, which ought to play a key role.
3. A large number of participants stressed the flaws in the current legislative framework, including the law on TJ. When a new National Congress is elected, it should reconsider the legislative framework for TJ in Libya.
4. TJ should be closely connected to other processes that are consolidating democracy in Libya and contributing towards a vision of Libyan society in the future, in particular, immediate steps on disarmament and improvements to security but also crucially important processes such as the drafting of the new Constitution.
5. TJ and reconciliation in Libya should not just encompass crimes such as murder, disappearances and torture but should also seek

to address root causes such as basic inequalities and patterns of exclusion and various forms of discrimination that exist within the society, in addition to issues such as land disputes and corruption.

6. While the crimes of the former regime form the major challenge and focus of TJ and reconciliation, violations committed during the conflict or in recent times should also be addressed. There should be no impunity for serious crimes, no matter which side has committed them. The new Libya should be based on values that connote justice for all, delivered by strong state institutions.

7. The Fact-Finding and Reconciliation Commission, when it starts, will be an important development, but many Libyans do not know about it. The Commission should have a sufficiently focused mandate and a carefully selected, representative membership.

Public Report on Transitional Justice in Libya

On 12 September 2012, UNSMIL SRSG Ian Martin and the High Commissioner for Human Rights Navanethem Pillay issued a public report 'Transitional Justice–Foundation for a New Libya'. The report stated that the successful conduct of the 7 July election and the establishment of the GNC represented major milestones in the transition to building a new Libya; the success of which, however, required addressing past human rights violations and facilitating reconciliation. The report noted that Libya was at a critical juncture in its history, and there was an opportunity for the country to lay solid and lasting foundations for a just society based on human rights.

The report provided an overview of the challenges facing TJ in Libya and made the following recommendations:

1. The new GNC and the new government commit to implementing a comprehensive TJ process.

2. The new GNC considers instituting an official public consultation on TJ.

    (1) TJ should encompass not just criminal justice but also truth seeking, reparations and reforms.

3. The legal framework currently in place, both the Transitional Justice law and the amnesty laws, be revisited.

4. Arbitrary detention of those suspected of committing crimes during the conflict must end as soon as possible, and all cases should be screened and designated for further investigation or release.

5. A prosecutorial strategy be formulated to ensure that those with a high degree of responsibility will be tried for serious crimes, and a screening is done to determine who needs to be further investigated and who should be released.

6. Trials should serve to strengthen the rule of law.

7. Post-revolution local conflicts should be addressed through TJ processes which take into account historical root causes of conflict.

8. The relatives of missing persons should have an active involvement in the search and identification process.

9. Civil society organizations that seek to support victims and human rights are facilitated and fostered.

Postscript

By 2014, Libya witnessed a breakdown of political arrangement that emerged after the July 2012 election. Two governments sought to rule the country amidst violent clashes between different groups. In 2015, UNSMIL evacuated its staff and set up its operations in the neighbouring Tunisia. Ian Martin left the mission in October 2012, and his successors were focused on political negotiations to resolve the crisis in Libya. HRD was not able to continue most of its work except for monitoring by receiving information from local contacts or by making short visits to Libya. In the end of 2015, SRSG Martin Kobler instructed HRD to monitor civilian casualties, thereby affecting its ongoing work on monitoring human rights violations such as torture, extrajudicial executions, trafficking and violence against migrant workers. HROs working on justice system, prisons and TJ did not have much work to do. In effect, several highly paid staff were whiling away their time waiting to return to Libya as and when the crisis ends.

In 2015, HRD was tasked with facilitating mediation between the Misratans and the Tawerghans. Misrata is the third largest city in Libya, and the town of Tawergha is located about 40 km south of Misrata. During the 2011 revolution, Misrata was under siege and faced indiscriminate shelling by Qadhafi's forces. Tawergha was the staging post, and many Tawerghans allegedly participated in the attack against Misrata. The Misratans accused the Tawerghans of committing crimes against civilians that including rape. By mid-August 2001, the Misratans had broken the siege and their assault on Tawergha resulted in the flight of all its residents.

The mediation was to arrive at a settlement to ensure the safe return of Tawerghans to their town.[59] HRD was successful in persuading both the parties to formulate a road map document as a basis for implementing their agreement. The road map document demonstrated a shift away from a narrow focus on reparations/compensations as proposed by Misratans as a quid pro quo for the return of Tawerghans. The document acknowledged TJ principles as well as conditions required for ensuring returns in safety and dignity.

The Misratan and Tawerghan mediation process demonstrated that if NTC and GNC had implemented a robust TJ process, many of the local conflicts may have been resolved, which in turn would have contributed towards increased stability. It also showed that the UN and other international actors' efforts to resolve the Libyan political crisis must be accompanied by a bottom-up process of facilitating dialogue between warring local groups.

[59] Author as a consultant with UNSMIL facilitated the mediation process from September 2015 to April 2016.

BIBLIOGRAPHY

Adams, B. (1998). UN Human Rights work in Cambodia: Efforts to preserve the jewel in the peacekeeping crown. In A. H. Henkin (Ed.), *Honoring human rights from peace to justice.* Kluwer Law International.

Adhikari, A. (2008, 1 October). Shackled or unleashed UNMIN in Nepal's peace process. *Himal Southasian.* https://www.himalmag.com/shackled-or-unleashed-unmin-in-nepals-peace-process

Africa Watch Committee. (1990). *Somalia: A government at war with its own people* (An Africa Watch Report). Human Rights Watch. https://www.hrw.org/sites/default/files/reports/somalia_1990.pdf

African Union. (2000). Constitutive Act of the African Union. https://au.int/sites/default/files/pages/34873-file-constitutiveact_en.pdf

African Union Mission in Somalia. (2007). *AMISOM background.* https://amisom-au.org/amisom-background/

Akashi, Y. (1995). The use of force in a United Nations peace-keeping operation: Lessons learnt from the safe areas mandate. *Fordham International Law Journal, 19*(2), 312–323. https://ir.lawnet.fordham.edu/cgi/viewcontent.cgi?referer=https://www.google.com/&httpsredir=1&article=2223&context=ilj

Aline, L. (2008, 5 March). *Sierra Leone: List of extremely violent events perpetrated during the war, 1991–2002.* Mass Violence and Resistance (Online). https://www.sciencespo.fr/mass-violence-war-massacre-resistance/en/document/sierra-leone-list-extremely-violent-events-perpetrated-during-war-1991-2002

Aljazeera Media Network. (2011). *Timeline: Ivory coast.* News Agencies. https://www.aljazeera.com/news/africa/2010/12/2010121971745317811.html

Aljazeera Media Network. (2020). *Challenges ahead as UN set to extend 'most dangerous' mission.* https://www.aljazeera.com/news/2020/6/26/challenges-ahead-as-un-set-to-extend-most-dangerous-mission

Armed Forces Division. (2020, 29 May). *United Nations Peacekeepers Journal, 6*(6), Bangladesh. https://www.afd.gov.bd/sites/default/files/journal/UN%20Day%20Journal%202020-converted.pdf

Arnson, C., & Holiday, D. (1992, 2 September). *Peace and human rights: Successes and shortcomings of the United Nations observer mission in EL SALVADOR (ONUSAL)*. News from Americas Watch. https://www.hrw.org/legacy/reports/pdfs/e/elsalvdr/elsalv929.pdf

Ashton, B. (1997). Making peace agreements work: United Nations experiment in the former Yugoslavia. *Cornell International Law Journal, 30*(3), 769–788. https://scholarship.law.cornell.edu/cgi/viewcontent.cgi?article=1417&context=cilj

Bangkok Post. (2020, 17 March). UN report calls for political mission in Darfur. https://www.bangkokpost.com/world/1880560/un-report-calls-for-political-mission-in-darfur

Barnett, K., & Jefferys, A. (2008, September). *Full of promise: How the UN's monitoring and reporting mechanism can better protect children*. Commissioned and Published by the Humanitarian Practice Network at ODI (Network Paper, No. 62). Overseas Development Institute. https://odihpn.org/wp-content/uploads/2008/09/networkpaper062.pdf

Basheer, M. (2010). *UN Chief urges Rwanda not to withdraw Sudan peacekeepers*. https://www.voanews.com/africa/un-chief-urges-rwanda-not-withdraw-sudan-peacekeepers

BBC News. (2006). *Timeline: Break-up of Yugoslavia*. http://news.bbc.co.uk/2/hi/europe/4997380.stm

BBC News. (2011). *Libya profile: Timeline*. https://www.bbc.com/news/world-africa-13755445

BBC News. (2015). *Sierra Leone profile: Timeline*. http://www.bbc.co.uk/news/mobile/world-africa-14094419

BBC News. (2017). *Who are Somalia's al-Shabab?* https://www.bbc.com/news/world-africa-15336689

BBC News. (2018). *El Salvador profile: Timeline*. https://www.bbc.com/news/world-latin-america-19402222

BBC News. (2018). *Iraq profile: Timeline*. https://www.bbc.com/news/world-middle-east-14546763

BBC News. (2018). *Rwanda profile: Timeline*. https://www.bbc.com/news/world-africa-14093322

BBC News. (2019). *Afghanistan profile: Timeline*. https://www.bbc.com/news/world-south-asia-12024253

BBC News. (2019). *Democratic Republic of Congo profile: Timeline*. https://www.bbc.com/news/world-africa-13286306

BBC News. (2019). *Haiti profile: Timeline*. https://www.bbc.com/news/world-latin-america-19548814

BBC News. (2019). *Ivory coast profile: Timeline*. https://www.bbc.com/news/world-africa-13287585

BBC News. (2019). *Sudan Coup: Why Omar al-Bashir was overthrown*. https://www.bbc.com/news/world-africa-47852496

BBC News. (2020). *Mali profile: Timeline*. https://www.bbc.com/news/world-africa-13881978

Bearak, M. (2019). Somalia expels top U.N. official after he criticizes crackdown on dissent. *The Washington Post.* https://www.washingtonpost.com/world/africa/somalia-expels-un-top-official-after-he-questions-crackdown-on-dissent/2019/01/02/ec1f89da-0e7d-11e9-831f-3aa2c2be4cbd_story.html

Bellamy, A. J., & Hunt, C. T. (2015). Twenty-first century UN peace operations: Protection, force and the changing security environment. *International Affairs, 91*(6), 1277–1298. https://doi.org/10.1111/1468-2346.12456

Bellamy, A. J., & Williams, P. D. (2011). The new politics of protection? Côte d'Ivoire, Libya and the responsibility to protect. *International Affairs, 87*(4), 825–850. https://doi.org/10.1111/j.1468-2346.2011.01006.x

Bergholm, L. (2010). *The African Union, the United Nations and civilian protection challenges in Darfur* (Working Paper Series, No. 63). Refugee Studies Centre, Oxford Department of International Development, University of Oxford. https://www.rsc.ox.ac.uk/files/files-1/wp63-au-un-civilian-protection-challenges-darfur-2010.pdf

Berkeley, B. (1993, August). Zaire: An African horror story. *The Atlantic.* https://www.theatlantic.com/magazine/archive/1993/08/zaire-an-african-horror-story/305496/

Bildt, C. (2013). *Dag Hammarskjöld and United Nations peacekeeping.* UN Chronicle. https://www.un.org/en/chronicle/article/dag-hammarskjold-and-united-nations-peacekeeping

Blackburn, P. (1984). Zaire's Mobutu rules through balance of respect ad repression. *The Christian Science Monitor.* https://www.csmonitor.com/1984/1203/120344.html

Boehme, J. (2008). *Human rights and gender components of UN and EU peace operations: Putting human rights and gender mandates into practice.* German Institute for Human Rights. https://www.refworld.org/pdfid/4ecd10ed2.pdf

Bouckaert, P. (2004). *Submitted a note to director on reporting strategy.* UNMIS HRD Staff.

Bowcott, O., & Borger, J. (2017). Ratko Mladi convicted of war crimes and genocide at UN tribunal. *The Guardian.* https://www.theguardian.com/world/2017/nov/22/ratko-mladic-convicted-of-genocide-and-war-crimes-at-un-tribunal

Carlsson, I., Sung-Joo, H., & Kupolati, R. M. (1999). *Report of the independent inquiry into the actions of the United Nations during the 1994 genocide in Rwanda.* United Nations.

Carter, L. E. (2010). The principle of complementarity and the international criminal court: The role of Ne Bis in Idem. *Santa Clara Journal of International Law, 8*(1), 165–198. https://digitalcommons.law.scu.edu/cgi/viewcontent.cgi?referer=https://www.google.com/&httpsredir=1&article=1079&context=scujil

Chanda, N. (1986). *Brother enemy: The war after the war. A history of Indochina since the fall of Saigon.* Harcourt Brace Jovanovich.

Chesterman, S. (2002). *Tiptoeing through Afghanistan: The future of UN state-building.* International Peace Academy. United Nations Plaza. https://www.ipinst.org/2002/09/tiptoeing-through-afghanistan-the-future-of-un-statebuilding-simon-chesterman

Cole, P., & MaQuinn, B. (Eds.). (2015). *The Libyan revolution and its aftermath.* C. Hurst & Co.

Cook, T. D. (2007). *Lost in the middle of peace: An exploration of citizen opinion on the implementation of the CPA in the three areas of Abyei, Southern Kordofan and Blue Nile.* Findings from Focus Groups with Men and Women in the Three Areas: Conducted April 26–July 2, 2006. National Democratic Institute for International Affairs.

Dahir, A. L. (2020, 31 August). Sudan signs peace deal with rebel alliance. *The New York Times.* https://www.nytimes.com/2020/08/31/world/africa/sudan-peace-agreement-darfur.html

Danticat, E. (2017, 19 October). A new chapter for the disastrous United Nations mission in Haiti? *The New Yorker.* https://www.newyorker.com/news/news-desk/a-new-chapter-for-the-disastrous-united-nations-mission-in-haiti

De Waal, A. (2007). Darfur and the failure of the responsibility to protect. *International Affairs, 83*(6), 1039–1054. http://guillaumenicaise.com/wp-content/uploads/2013/10/Darfur-and-the-failure-of-the-R2p.pdf

De Waal, A. (2010). Sudan's choices: Scenarios beyond the CPA. In Heinrich Böll Foundation (Ed.), *Sudan—No easy ways ahead* (Vol. 18, pp. 9–30, English ed., Publication Series on Democracy). Heinrich Böll Foundation.

De Waal, A. (2014). *Violence and peacemaking in the political marketplace.* https://reliefweb.int/sites/reliefweb.int/files/resources/Accord25_ViolenceAndPeacemaking.pdf

De Waal, A. (2019, 2 August). *Sudan's political marketplace and the prospects for democracy.* The London School of Economics and Political Science. https://blogs.lse.ac.uk/africaatlse/2019/08/02/sudan-political-marketplace-democracy/

Doherty, B. (2019). Why are there violent clashes in Papua and West Papua? *The Guardian.* https://www.theguardian.com/world/2019/aug/22/why-are-there-violent-clashes-in-papua-and-west-papua-explainer

Duica , A.-F. (2016). *The role of the United Nations Security Council in the evolution of peacekeeping.* Case Studies: Congo and Somalia. University of Bucharest. https://www.academia.edu/31629054/The_role_of_the_United_Nations_Security_Council_in_the_evolution_of_peacekeeping_Case_Studies_The_Congo_and_Somalia

Durch, W. J., Holt, V. K., Earle, C. R., & Shanahan, M. K. (2003). *The Brahimi report and the future of UN peace operations.* The Henry L. Stimson Center. https://www.stimson.org/wp-content/files/file-attachments/BR-CompleteVersion-Dec03_1.pdf

Emmanuel, O. O. (2018, August). *Peacekeeping operations and the United Nations Security Council.* Essay submitted to the Faculty of Law, Osun State University, Ifetedo Campus, Nigeria in Partial Fulfilment of the Requirements for the Award of Bachelor of Law (L.L.B. Hons) Degree. https://www.academia.edu/40397927/PEACEKEEPING_OPERATIONS_AND_THE_UNITED_NATIONS_SECURITY_COUNCIL20190919_46081_1' :noun?auto=download&email_work_card=download-paper

Eriksson, J., Adelman, H., Borton, J., Christensen, H., Kumar, K., Suhrke, A., Tardif-Douglin, D., Villumstad, S., & Wohlgemuth, L. (1996). *The international response to conflict and genocide: Lessons from the Rwanda experience: Synthesis report*. Joint Evaluation of Emergency Assistance to Rwanda.

Felbab-Brown, V. (2018, 14 November). *Developments in Somalia*. Brooking. https://www.brookings.edu/testimonies/developments-in-somalia/

Findlay, T. (1995). *Cambodia: The legacy and lessons and UNTAC* (Stockholm International Peace Research Institute [SIPRI], Research Report No. 9). Oxford University Press. https://www.sipri.org/sites/default/files/files/RR/SIPRIRR09.pdf

Findlay, T. (2002). *The use of force in UN peace operations*. Stockholm International Peace Research Institute (SIPRI). Oxford University Press. https://www.sipri.org/sites/default/files/files/books/SIPRI02Findlay.pdf

Forti, D., & Connolly, L. (2018). *The mission is gone, but the UN is staying: Liberia's peacekeeping transition*. International Peace Institute. https://www.ipinst.org/wp-content/uploads/2018/12/1812_Liberias-Peacekeeping_-Transition.pdf

Fukuyama, F. (2018). *Identity: The demand for dignity and the politics of resentment*. Profile Books.

Garcia-Sayan, D. (1994). Human rights and peace-keeping operations. *University of Richmond Law Review, 29*(1), 41–65. https://scholarship.richmond.edu/cgi/viewcontent.cgi?article=2118&context=lawreview

Gascoigne, B. (2005). *History of Sierra Leone: Slavery and freedom: 17th–19th century*. http://www.historyworld.net/wrldhis/plaintexthistories.asp?historyid=ad45

Geneva Academy. (2019, 5 February). *DRC: A mapping of non-international armed conflicts in Kivu, Kasai and Ituri*. http://www.rulac.org/news/democratic-republic-of-the-congo-a-mapping-of-non-international-armed-confl

Global Policy Forum. (2007). *UN role in Iraq*. https://archive.globalpolicy.org/security/issues/iraq/unindex.htm

Granderson, C. (1997). Institutionalizing peace: The Haiti experience. In A. H. Henkin (Ed.), *Honoring human rights and keeping the peace* (p. 227). Kluwer Law International.

Guéhenno, J.-M. (2018). *The fog peace. Taken from Alexandra Novosseloff 'The many lives of a peacekeeping mission: The UN operation in Côte d'Ivoire'*. Center on International Cooperation.

Hatto, R. (2013). From peacekeeping to peacebuilding: The evolution of the role of the United Nations in peace operations. *International Review of the Red Cross, 95*(891/892), 495–515. https://www.icrc.org/en/doc/assets/files/review/2013/irrc-891-892-hatto.pdf

Hayner, P. (2007). *Report: Negotiating peace in Sierra Leone: Confronting the justice challenge*. Centre for Humanitarian Dialogue. https://www.files.ethz.ch/isn/55192/SierraLeoneReportrevise_1207.pdf

Henkin, A. H. (1995). *Honoring human rights and keeping the peace: Lessons from El Salvador, Cambodia and Haiti*. The Aspen Institute.

Henkin, A. H. (1998). *Honoring human rights: From peace to justice*. The Aspen Institute & Kluwer Law International.

Henry, E. (2015). *Use of force and peacekeeping operations.* https://www.academia. edu/37018831/Use_of_Force_and_Peacekeeping_Operations

History.com Editors. (2009). *Rwandan genocide.* A & E Television Networks. https://www.history.com/topics/africa/rwandan-genocide

Hobsbawm, E. J. (1994). *Age of extremes: The short twentieth century, 1914–1991.* Michael Joseph; Viking Penguin.

Holt, V., Taylor, G., & Kelly, M. (2009). *Protecting civilians in the context of UN peacekeeping operations: Successes, setbacks and remaining challenges.* Independent Study Jointly Commissioned by the Department of Peacekeeping Operations and the Office for the Coordination of Humanitarian Affairs, United Nations. https://reliefweb.int/sites/reliefweb.int/files/resources/ B752FF2063E282B08525767100751B90-unocha_protecting_nov2009.pdf

Human Rights Data Analysis Group (HRDAG). (1999). *Gutemala-memory of silence: Report of the commission for historical clarification: Conclusions and recommendations 1999.* https://hrdag.org/wp-content/uploads/2013/01/ CEHreport-english.pdf

Human Rights Watch. (1994). *Human rights developments.* https://www.hrw.org/ reports/1994/WR94/Africa-10.htm

Human Rights Watch. (1994, 1 April). *Terror prevails in Haiti: Human rights violations and failed diplomacy.* United Nations High Commissioner for Refugees. https://www.refworld.org/docid/3ae6a7f04.html

Human Rights Watch. (1995, 1 January). *Human Rights Watch world report 1995-Rwanda.* United Nations High Commissioner for Refugees. https://www. refworld.org/docid/467fca9dc.html

Human Rights Watch. (1999). *The United Nations.* https://www.hrw.org/ reports/1999/angola/Angl998-10.htm

Human Rights Watch. (1999). *Shocking war crimes in Sierra Leone: New testimonies on mutilation, rape of civilians.* https://www.hrw.org/news/1999/06/24/ shocking-war-crimes-sierra-leone

Human Rights Watch. (2004, 11 August). *Empty promises? Continuing abuses in Darfur.* https://www.hrw.org/report/2004/08/11/empty-promises/ continuing-abuses-darfur-sudan

Human Rights Watch. (2005). *MONUC: A case for peacekeeping reform.* https:// www.hrw.org/news/2005/02/28/monuc-case-peacekeeping-reform

Human Rights Watch. (2006, 1 August). *Democratic Republic of Congo: On the brink.* Finest Finance. https://www.hrw.org/news/2006/08/01/ democratic-republic-congo-brink

Hunt, C., & Zimmerman, S. (2020). Twenty years of the protection of civilians in UN peace operations—Progress problems and prospects. *Journal of International Peace Keeping, 23*(1–2), 50–81.

International Center for Transitional Justice. (2010). *Background: Confronting ethnic division, addressing impunity.* https://www.ictj.org/our-work/ regions-and-countries/c%C3%B4te-divoire

International Center for Transitional Justice. (2012). *Exploring the legacy of the special court for: Sierra Leone.* https://www.ictj.org/sites/default/files/subsites/scsl-legacy/about-project/

International Center for Transitional Justice. (2016, 23 February). *After 10 years, CAVR report still resonates in Timor-Leste and around the world.* https://www.ictj.org/news/10-years-cavr-report-timor-leste-truth

International Commission on Intervention and State Sovereignty. (2001). *The responsibility to protect: Report of the International Commission on Intervention and State Sovereignty.* International Development Research Centre. https://www.idrc.ca/en/book/responsibility-protect-report-international-commission-intervention-and-state-sovereignty

International Criminal Court. (2005, March). *Darfur, Sudan. Situation referred to the ICC by the United Nations Security Council.* https://www.icc-cpi.int/darfur

International Crisis Group. (2004). *Darfur raising: Sudan's new crisis* (ICG Africa Report No. 76). https://www.crisisgroup.org/africa/horn-africa/sudan/darfur-rising-sudans-new-crisis

International Crisis Group. (2006). *Resolving Timor-Leste's crisis* (Asian Report No. 120). https://www.crisisgroup.org/asia/south-east-asia/timor-leste/resolving-timor-leste-s-crisis

International Crisis Group. (2011, 13 December). *Nepal's peace process: The end-game nears* (Briefing No. 131). Crisis Group Asia.

International Crisis Group. (2012, 22 August). *Towards a post-MINUSTAH Haiti: Making an effective transition* (Report No. 44). https://www.crisisgroup.org/latin-america-caribbean/haiti/towards-post-minustah-haiti-making-effective-transition

International Crisis Group. (2019, 4 December). *A new approach for the UN to stabilize the DR Congo* (Briefing No. 148). Multilateral Diplomacy. https://www.crisisgroup.org/africa/central-africa/democratic-republic-congo/b148-new-approach-un-stabilise-dr-congo

International Crisis Group. (2019, 29 August). *Iraq: Evading the gathering storm* (Crisis Group Middle East Briefing No. 70). https://www.crisisgroup.org/middle-east-north-africa/gulf-and-arabian-peninsula/iraq/070-iraq-evading-gathering-storm

International Crisis Group. (2020, 29 January). *Honouring commitments to end Libya's Civil War.* Commentary/Middle East & North Africa. https://www.crisisgroup.org/middle-east-north-africa/north-africa/libya/honouring-commitments-end-libyas-civil-war

International Crisis Group. (2020). *What will peace talks Bode for Afghan Women?* https://www.crisisgroup.org/asia/south-asia/afghanistan/what-will-peace-talks-bode-afghan-women

International Crisis Group. (2020, 30 March). *Are the Taliban serious about peace negotiations?* (Briefing Note). https://www.crisisgroup.org/asia/south-asia/afghanistan/are-taliban-serious-about-peace-negotiations

International Crisis Group. (2020). *Rescuing Iraq from the Iran–U.S. crossfire* (Document #2022398). European Country of Origin Information Network. https://www.ecoi.net/en/document/2022398.html

Jezequel, J.-H. (2020). *Crisis group role*. International Crisis Group. https://www. crisisgroup.org/who-we-are/people/jean-herve-jezequel

Jones, S. (2003). East Timor: The troubled path to independence. In A. H. Henkin (Ed.), *Honoring human rights and keeping the peace*. Kluwer Law International.

Kandeh, J. D. (1992, April). Politicization of ethnic identities in Sierra Leone. *African Studies Review, 35*(1), 81–99. https://www.cambridge.org/core/journals/african-studies-review/article/politicization-of-ethnic-identities-in-sierra-leone/9C608170100D0F3B576C8495128AAEB0

Karlsrud, J. (2015). The UN at war: Examining the consequences of peace-enforcement mandates for the UN peacekeeping operations in the CAR, the DRC and Mali. *Third World Quarterly, 36*(1), 40–54. https://www.tandfonline.com/doi/full/10.1080/01436597.2015.976016

Katunga, J. (2007). *Minerals, forests, and violent conflict in the Democratic Republic of the Congo*. Report from Africa: Population, Health, Environment, and Conflict, ECSP Report, Issue 2. https://www.wilsoncenter.org/publication/minerals-forests-and-violent-conflict-the-democratic-republic-the-congo

Khalil, M. A. (2018). *The world needs robust peacekeeping not aggressive peacekeeping*. International Committee of the Red Cross. https://reliefweb.int/report/world/world-needs-robust-peacekeeping-not-aggressive-peacekeeping

Klot, J. (2012, October). *The impact of armed conflict on children*. Humanitarian Practice Network. https://odihpn.org/magazine/the-impact-of-armed-conflict-on-children/

Kumar, A. (2017, 10 March). *UN plan to stop peacekeeper abuse puts victims first: Focus on Victims a refreshing change*. Human Rights Watch. https://www.hrw.org/news/2017/03/10/un-plan-stop-peacekeeper-abuse-puts-victims-first

Kumar, K., Tardif-Douglin, D., Knapp, C., Maynard, K., Manikas, P., & Sheckler, A. (1996, July). *Rebuilding postwar Rwanda: The role of the international community* (USAID Evaluation Special Study No. 76). Centre for Development Information and Evaluation. https://www.oecd.org/derec/unitedstates/50189461.pdf

Labuda, P. I. (2015, 2 September). UN peace operations: Tracking the shift from peacekeeping to peace enforcement and state-building. *EJIL: Talk! Blog of the European Journal of International Law*. https://www.ejiltalk.org/un-peace-operations-tracking-the-shift-from-peacekeeping-to-peace-enforcement-and-state-building/

Lewis, P. (1992). *A short history of United Nations peacekeeping*. https://www.historynet.com/short-history-united-nations-peacekeeping.htm

Lupis, I., & Pitter, L. (1995). *The fall of Srebrenica and the failure of UN peacekeeping: Bosnia and Herzegovina*. Human Rights Watch. https://www.hrw.org/report/1995/10/15/fall-srebrenica-and-failure-un-peacekeeping/bosnia-and-herzegovina

Lyall, G. (2017). *Rebellion and conflict minerals in North Kivu.* Conflicts Trends 2017/1. ACCORD. https://www.accord.org.za/conflict-trends/rebellion-conflict-minerals-north-kivu/

MacAskill, E., & Borger, J. (2004, 16 September). Iraq war was illegal and breached UN charter, says Annan. *The Guardian.* https://www.theguardian.com/world/2004/sep/16/iraq.iraq

Maguire, R. (2009, November). *USI peace briefing: What role for the United Nations in Haiti?* United States Institute of Peace. https://www.usip.org/sites/default/files/haiti_united_nations_pb_0.pdf

Mahony, L., & Nash, R. (2012). *Influence on the ground: Understanding and strengthening the protection impact of United Nations Human Rights field presences.* Fieldview Solutions. https://www.fieldviewsolutions.org/fv-publications/Influence_on_the_Ground.pdf

Mahony, C., & Sooka, Y. (2015). The truth about the truth: Insider reflections on the Sierra Leonean truth and reconciliation commission. In K. Ainley, R. Friedman, & C. Mahony (Eds.), *Evaluating transitional justice* (pp. 35–54). Palgrave Macmillan.

Mamdani, M. (2001). *When victims become killers: Colonialism, nativism and the genocide in Rwanda.* Fountain Publishers.

Mansson, K. (2008). *A communicative act: Integrating human rights in UN peace operations, Dialogues from Kosovo and Congo* (PhD thesis submitted to the Irish Centre for Human Rights). Faculty of Law, National University of Ireland.

Martin, I. (1997, 2 February). *Report on the human rights activities of UNAVEM and proposals for an enhanced programme* (Unpublished Report). https://www.hrw.org/reports/1999/angola/Angl998-10.htm

Martin, I. (1998). After genocide: The UN human rights field operation in Rwanda. In A. H. Henkin (Ed.), *Honoring human rights and keeping the peace.* Kluwer Law International.

Martin, I. (1998, August). *Final report of review of human rights field operations.* HCHR Special Adviser for Human Rights Field Operations.

Martin, I. (2001). *Self-determination in East Timor: The United Nations, the ballot, and international Intervention.* Lynne Reinner Publishers.

Martin, I. (2008, 28 August). Nepal: A remarkable peace. *The Guardian.* https://www.theguardian.com/commentisfree/2008/aug/28/nepal.humanrights

Martin, I. (Ed.). (2010). *Nepal's peace process at the United Nations* (Vol. 1). Himal Books.

Martin, I. (2015). The United Nations role in the first year of the transition. In P. Cole & B. McQuinn (Eds.), *The Libyan revolution and its aftermath.* C. Hurst & Co.

Martin, I., & Mayer-Reickh, A. (2005). The United Nations and East Timor: From self-determination to state-building. *International Peacekeeping, 12*(1), 125–145.

Meiloud, A. (2015). *Foreign actors and the Libyan civil war.* Middle East Eye. https://www.middleeasteye.net/big-story/foreign-actors-and-the-libyan-civil-war

Mosely, A. L. (1998). *Sudan's contested national identities.* Indiana University Press.

News & Resources. (2001). *Crisis in Sudan.* https://web.archive.org/web/20041210024759/http://www.refugees.org/news/crisis/sudan.htm

Novosseloff, A. (2018). *The many lives of a peacekeeping mission: The UN operation in Côte d'Ivoire.* International Peace Institute. https://www.ipinst.org/wp-content/uploads/2018/06/1806_Many-Lives-of-a-Peacekeeping-Mission.pdf

Novosseloff, A., Abdenur, A. E., Mandrup, T., & Pangburn, A. (2019). *Assessing the effectiveness of the United Nations Mission in the DRC/MONUC–MONUSCO.* Norwegian Institute of International Affairs.

Office of the High Commissioner for Human Rights. (2011). *A preliminary report on human rights violations.* During Armed in Southern Kordofan. https://reliefweb.int/report/sudan/preliminary-report-violations-international-human-rights-and-humanitarian-law-southern

Office of the Historian. (1990). *The breakup of Yugoslavia, 1990–1992.* https://history.state.gov/milestones/1989-1992/breakup-yugoslavia

Paddon, E. (2013, 18 April). *The perils of peacekeeping without politics: MONUC and MONUSCO in the DRC* (Briefing Paper). Rift Valley Institute.

Peralta, G. A. (2005). *Anatomy of the accords and levels of compliance.* Irenees.net a Website of Resources for Peace. http://www.irenees.net/bdf_fiche-analyse-797_en.html

Prunier, G. (2005). *Darfur: The ambiguous genocide.* C. Hurst & Company.

Reiger, C., & Marieke, W. (2006). *The serious crimes process in Timor-Leste: In retrospect.* International Center for Transitional Justice. https://www.ictj.org/sites/default/files/ICTJ-TimorLeste-Criminal-Process-2006-English.pdf

Reuters Staff. (2008, 28 May). TIMELINE: Milestones in political history of Nepal. *World News.* https://uk.reuters.com/article/us-nepal-chronology/timeline-milestones-in-political-history-of-nepal-idUKL281216020080528

Reynaert, J. (2011). *MONUC/MONUSCO and civilian protection in the Kivus.* Interns & Volunteers Series. https://monusco.unmissions.org/sites/default/files/monuc-monusco_and_civilian_protection_in_the_kivus_0.pdf

Rhoads, E. P., & Laurence, M. (2019). Peace operations, principles, and doctrine. In R. Oliver & V. Gëzim (Eds.), *The Palgrave Encyclopedia of peace and conflict studies.* Palgrave Macmillan.

Roberts, A. (2000). Humanitarian issues and agencies as triggers for international military action. *International Review of the Red Cross, 82*(839), 673–698. https://www.cambridge.org/core/journals/international-review-of-the-red-cross/article/abs/humanitarian-issues-and-agencies-as-triggers-for-international-military-action/C7D1B849CDA3DDFCFB7DC34EA978380C

Robinson, G. (2000). With Unamet in East Timor: A historian's personal view. *Bulletin of Concerned Asian Scholars, 32*(1), 23–26. https://www.researchgate.net/publication/295388252_With_Unamet_in_East_Timor_A_historian's_personal_view/link/5939d9f9a6fdcc58aea31b69/download

Rogier, E. (2005). *The (Un-) Comprehensive peace agreement. From the report No More Hills Ahead? The Sudan's tortuous ascent to heights of peace* (Chapter 4). Clingendael Institute.

Ruggie, J. G. (1993, November/December). Wandering in the void: Charting the UN's new strategic role. *Foreign Affairs, 72*(5), 26–31. https://www.jstor.org/stable/20045810?origin=crossref&seq=1

Rutting, T. (2019, 15 April). *Women and Afghan peace talks: 'Peace consensus' gathering left Afghan women without reassurance.* Report War and Peace, Afghanistan Analysts Network. https://www.afghanistan-analysts.org/en/reports/war-and-peace/women-and-afghan-peace-talks-peace-consensus-gathering-left-afghan-women-unassured/

Shagalov, V. A., Letyaev, V. A., Grishin, Y., & Vladimirova, M. M. (2018). Dag Hammarskjold's role in the development of peacekeeping. *Revista Publicando 5, 16*(1), 606–616. https://pdfs.semanticscholar.org/41df/60a0c1372dfdbe07e3cec07885a0eb1f3f76.pdf

Smith, D. (2011, 6 June). UN admits peacekeepers dialed in Sudan clashes. *The Guardian.* https://www.theguardian.com/world/2011/jun/06/un-admits-sudan-peacekeepers-failure

Soderlund, W. C., Briggs, E. D., Najem, T. P., & Roberts, B. C. (2013). *Africa's deadliest conflict: Media coverage of the humanitarian disaster in the Congo and the United Nations Response, 1997–2008.* Wilfrid Laurier University Press. http://muse.jhu.edu/books/9781554588787

South African History Online. (2015). *The Angolan civil war (1975–2002): A brief history.* https://www.sahistory.org.za/article/angolan-civil-war-1975-2002-brief-history

Stearns, J. (2012). *North Kivu: The background to conflict in North Kivu province of Eastern Congo.* The Usalama Project, RIFT Valley Institute. https://www.refworld.org/pdfid/51d3d5f04.pdf

Stein, S. (2012). *When do comprehensive peacekeeping operations succeed? The case of the un observer mission in El Salvador (onusal) and the un verification mission in Guatemala (minugua)* (Electronic Theses and Dissertations, 2004–2019). University of Central Florida. https://stars.library.ucf.edu/cgi/viewcontent.cgi?article=3328&context=etd

Stern, J. (2015, September). *Establishing safety and security at protection of Civilians sites: Lessons from the United Nations peacekeeping in South Sudan* (Civilians in Conflict, Policy Brief No. 2). Stimson Centre. https://www.stimson.org/wp-content/files/file-attachments/CIC-Policy-Brief_2_Sept-2015.pdf

Strangio, S. (2014). *Hun Sen's Cambodia.* Yale University Press.

Study.com. (2017). *Humanitarian intervention in Somalia.* https://study.com/academy/lesson/humanitarian-intervention-in-somalia.html

Suma, M. (2019, 1 January). *Côte d'Ivoire's continued struggle for justice and reconciliation.* International Center for Transitional Justice. https://www.ictj.org/news/cote-d'ivoire's-continued-struggle-justice-and-reconciliation

The Carter Center. (2011). *Carter Center urges political parties and Blue Nile popular consultation commission to ensure genuine dialogue on key issues in Blue Nile state.* https://www.cartercenter.org/news/pr/sudan-032111.html

The Centre for Justice & Accountability. (2010). *El Salvador.* https://cja.org/where-we-work/el-salvador/

The Henry L. Stimson Center. (2002, June). *Rebuilding Afghanistan: The United Nations Assistance Mission in Afghanistan (UNAMA).* Peace Operations Backgrounder. https://www.stimson.org/wp-content/files/file-attachments/UNAMAbackgrounder_1.pdf

The Human Rights Centre. (1998, 11–13 February). *Conference on the promotion and protection of Human Rights in acute crisis.* https://www1.essex.ac.uk/rightsinacutecrisis/default.htm

The Irish Times. (1997, 9 September). Mobutu leaves legacy of chaos and corruption. https://www.irishtimes.com/news/mobutu-leaves-legacy-of-chaos-and-corruption-1.104463

Uma, J. N. (2011, 30 March). S. Kordofan elections: Carter Center concerned over low voter registration. *Sudan Tribune: Plural News and Views on Sudan.* https://sudantribune.com/S-Kordofan-elections-Carter-Center,38427

UN Mission in Liberia. (2006). *Human Rights in Liberia's rubber plantations: Tapping into the future.* https://www.refworld.org/docid/473dade10.html

UNAMI/OHCHR. (2014). *Report on the protection of Civilians in the non international armed conflict in Iraq: 5 June–5 July 2014.* https://www.ohchr.org/Documents/Countries/IQ/UNAMI_OHCHR_POC%20Report_FINAL_18July2014A.pdf

United Nations. (1945). *Charter of the United Nations and statue of the International Court of justice* (Chapter VII). https://upload.wikimedia.org/wikipedia/commons/a/a4/Uncharter.pdf

United Nations. (1945). *Charter of the United Nations and Statue of the International Court of justice* (Article 2(4)). https://upload.wikimedia.org/wikipedia/commons/a/a4/Uncharter.pdf

United Nations. (1945). *Charter of the United Nations and Statue of the International Court of Justice* (Article 24 & 26). https://upload.wikimedia.org/wikipedia/commons/a/a4/Uncharter.pdf

United Nations. (1945). *Charter of the United Nations and Statue of the International Court of Justice* (Chapter VII, Article 45 & 47). https://upload.wikimedia.org/wikipedia/commons/a/a4/Uncharter.pdf

United Nations. (1945). *Charter of the United Nations and Statue of the International Court of Justice* (Chapter VI, Article 33(1)). https://upload.wikimedia.org/wikipedia/commons/a/a4/Uncharter.pdf

United Nations. (1945). *Charter of the United Nations and Statue of the International Court of Justice* (Chapter VI, Article 33). https://upload.wikimedia.org/wikipedia/commons/a/a4/Uncharter.pdf

United Nations. (1945). *The United Nations and decolonization.* https://www.un.org/dppa/decolonization/en/about

United Nations. (1962). *West New Guinea—UNSF: Background.* https://peacekeeping.un.org/en/mission/past/unsfbackgr.html

United Nations. (1964, March). *UNFICYP fact sheet: United Nations peacekeeping force in Cyprus.* United Nations Peacekeeping. https://peacekeeping.un.org/en/mission/unficyp

United Nations. (1989). *Namibia–UNTAG: Background.* https://peacekeeping.un.org/sites/default/files/past/untagS.htm

United Nations. (1990). *Background: Full text.* https://peacekeeping.un.org/en/mission/past/onusalbackgr2.html

United Nations. (1992, 17 June). *An agenda for peace: Preventive diplomacy, peacemaking and peace-keeping.* Report of the Secretary-General pursuant to the statement adopted by the Summit Meeting of the Security Council on 31 January 1992, A/47/277–S/24111. https://www.un.org/ruleoflaw/files/A_47_277.pdf

United Nations. (1992). *Somalia-UNOSOM I: Background.* https://peacekeeping.un.org/mission/past/unosom1backgr2.html

United Nations. (1992). *The responsibility of the Security Council in the maintenance of international peace and security.* https://www.un.org/en/sc/repertoire/89-92/Chapter%208/GENERAL%20ISSUES/Item%2028_SÇ%20respons%20in%20maint%20IPS.pdf

United Nations. (1993). *Graça Machal and the impact of armed conflict on children.* https://childrenandarmedconflict.un.org/about-us/mandate/the-machel-reports/

United Nations. (1993, September). *Human rights component final report.* United Nations Transitional Authority in Cambodia. https://cambodia.ohchr.org/sites/default/files/report/other-report/Other_CMB091993E_0.pdf

United Nations. (1994). *Document retrieval: Comprehensive agreement on Human Rights.* United Nations Peacemaker. https://peacemaker.un.org/guatemala-humanrightsagreement94

United Nations. (1995). *El Salvador—ONUSAL: Mandate.* https://peacekeeping.un.org/en/mission/past/onusalmandate.html

United Nations. (1996). *Comprehensive report on lessons learned from United Nations Assistance Mission for Rwanda (UNAMIR) October 1993–April 1996.* Lessons Learned Out, Department of Peacekeeping Operations.

United Nations. (1996). *The United Nations and Rwanda 1993–1996.* UN Department of Public Information.

United Nations. (1996). *United Nations Protection Force. Former Yugoslavia-UNPROFOR, United Nations: Department of Public Information.* https://peacekeeping.un.org/en/mission/past/unprof_b.htm

United Nations. (1997). *Angola-UNAVEM III.* https://peacekeeping.un.org/en/mission/past/unavem3.htm

United Nations. (1997). *Strengthening human rights in peace operations.* https://www.ohchr.org/EN/newyork/Stories/Pages/Strengtheninghumanrightsinpeaceoperations.aspx

United Nations. (1997, 4 April). *United Nations human rights field operation in Rwanda.* UN Office of the High Commissioner for Human Rights. https://reliefweb.int/report/rwanda/united-nations-human-rights-field-operation-rwanda

United Nations. (1998, 12 January). *Report of the Secretary-General on the United Nations observer mission in Angola (MONUA).* S/1998/17. https://documents-dds-ny.un.org/doc/UNDOC/GEN/N98/005/13/IMG/N9800513.pdf?OpenElement

United Nations. (1998, 29 June). *Report of the Secretary-General's investigative team charged with investigating serious violations of human rights and international humanitarian law in the Democratic Republic of the Congo.* S/1998/581. https://documents-dds-ny.un.org/doc/UNDOC/GEN/N98/177/22/IMG/N9817722.pdf?OpenElement

United Nations. (1999). *Adopted by the Security Council at its 4046th meeting on 17 September 1999.* http://unscr.com/en/resolutions/doc/1265

United Nations. (1999, 12 July). *Peace agreement between the Government of Sierra Leone and the Revolutionary United Front of Sierra Leone.* S/1999/777. https://peacemaker.un.org/sierraleone-lome-agreement99

United Nations. (1999, 15 November). *Report of the Secretary-General pursuant to general assembly resolution 53/35: The fall of Srebrenica.* A/54/549. https://www.refworld.org/docid/3ae6afb34.html

United Nations. (1999). *Report of the Secretary-General to the Security Council on the protection of civilians in armed conflict.* https://undocs.org/S/1999/957

United Nations. (1999, 25 October). *Security Council establishes United Nations transitional administration in East Timor for initial period until 31 January 2001.* Meeting Coverage and Press Releases.

United Nations. (2000). *Angola-UNAVEM II: Background.* https://peacekeeping.un.org/mission/past/Unavem2/UnavemIIB.htm

United Nations. (2000). *OHCHR in the world: Making human rights a reality on the ground.* https://www.ohchr.org/EN/Countries/Pages/WorkInField.aspx

United Nations. (2000). *Report of the international commission of inquiry on East Timor.* https://reliefweb.int/report/indonesia/report-international-commission-inquiry-east-timor

United Nations. (2000, 21 August). *Report of the panel on United Nations peace operations.* A/55/305-S/2000/809. United Nations. https://undocs.org/A/55/305

United Nations. (2000, 21 August). *Report of the panel on United Nations peace operations (Brahimi Report).* United Nations. https://www.un.org/en/events/pastevents/brahimi_report.shtml

United Nations. (2000, 19 April). *Resolution 1296 (2000): Adopted by the Security Council at its 4130th meeting on 19 April 2000* (para 15). Security Council, S/RES/1296 (2000). http://unscr.com/en/resolutions/doc/1296

United Nations. (2000). *United Nations truce supervision organization.* https://untso.unmissions.org

United Nations. (2001). *Angola-MONUA: Background.* https://peacekeeping.un.org/en/mission/past/monua/monuab.htm

United Nations. (2001). *Report of the Secretary-General to the Security Council on the protection of civilians in armed conflict.* Protection of Civilians in Armed Conflict—SecGen Report, Security Council, S/2001/331. https://www.un.org/unispal/document/auto-insert-177959/

United Nations. (2001). *United Nations operation in the Congo: July 1960–June 1964.* https://peacekeeping.un.org/en/mission/past/onuc.htm

United Nations. (2001). *Republic of the Congo—ONUC background.* https://peacekeeping.un.org/sites/default/files/past/onucB.htm

United Nations. (2003). *Background: United Nations mission in Liberia.* https://unmil.unmissions.org/background

United Nations. (2003). *First United Nations emergency force: November 1956–June 1967.* https://peacekeeping.un.org/en/mission/past/unefi.htm

United Nations. (2003). *Liberia-UNOMIL background.* https://peacekeeping.un.org/sites/default/files/past/unomilS.htm

United Nations. (2003). *Today's peacekeepers: UNAMSIL: The story behind the success in Sierra Leone.* International Day of United Nations Peacekeepers 29 May 2003, Press Kit Fact Sheet 10. https://www.un.org/en/events/peacekeepersday/2003/docs/sierraleone.htm

United Nations. (2003). *United Nations assistance mission for Iraq.* http://www.uniraq.com/index.php?option=com_k2&view=item&layout=item&id=943&lang=en

United Nations. (2003). *United Nations observation group in Lebanon: June–December 1958.* https://peacekeeping.un.org/mission/past/unogil.htm

United Nations. (2004, 2 December). *A more secure world: Our shared responsibility.* Report of the High-Level Panel on Threats, Challenges and Change, A/59/565. https://www.un.org/en/ga/search/view_doc.asp?symbol=A/59/565

United Nations. (2004). *Press briefing on sexual exploitation allegations related to UN mission in Democratic Republic of Congo.* Meeting Coverage and Press Releases. https://www.un.org/press/en/2004/lute041122.doc.htm

United Nations. (2004, 4 October). *Report of the Secretary-General on the Sudan pursuant to paragraph 15 of Security Council resolution 1564 (2004) and paragraph 6, 13 and 16 of Security Council resolution 1556 (2004).* S/2004/787. https://digitallibrary.un.org/record/532668?ln=en#record-files-collapse-header

United Nations. (2005). *A comprehensive strategy to eliminate future sexual exploitation and abuse in United Nations peacekeeping operations.* https://www.un.org/en/ga/search/view_doc.asp?symbol=A/59/710

United Nations. (2005). *Decisions of the Secretary-General policy committee meeting of 26 October 2005.* Decision No. 2005/24—Human Rights in Integrated Missions, United Nations.

United Nations. (2005). *East Timor—UNMISET—Mandate.* United Nations Mission of Support in East Timor. https://peacekeeping.un.org/mission/past/unmiset/mandate.html

United Nations. (2005). *Resolution 1612 (2005). Adopted by the Security Council at its 5235th meeting on 26 July 2005.* S/RES/1612 (2005). https://www.securitycouncilreport.org/atf/cf/%7B65BFCF9B-6D27-4E9C-8CD3-CF6E4FF96FF9%7D/CAC%20SRES%201612.pdf

United Nations. (2005, 28 April). *Security Council establishes one-year political mission in Timor-Leste, Unanimously adopting resolution 1599 (2005).* Meeting Coverage and Press Release, Security Council, SC/8371. https://www.un.org/press/en/2005/sc8371.doc.htm

United Nations. (2005, September). *The 2005 world summit: High-level plenary meeting of the 60th session of the UN General Assembly (14–16 September 2005,*

UN Headquarters, New York). Conferences, Meetings and Events. https://www.un.org/en/events/pastevents/worldsummit_2005.shtml

United Nations. (2005). *Background: Summary.* https://peacekeeping.un.org/en/mission/past/unmihbackgr1.html

United Nations. (2005). *Report of the Independent High-Level Panel on Peace Operations.* https://peacekeeping.un.org/en/report-of-independent-high-level-panel-peace-operations

United Nations. (2006, 13 June). *United Nations determined not to abandon Timor-Leste at critical time of need says Secretary-General, as Security Council meets following recent violence.* Meeting Coverage and Press Releases, Security Council, SC/8745. https://www.un.org/press/en/2006/sc8745.doc.htm

United Nations. (2008). *MONUSCO: United Nations organization stabilization mission in the Democratic Republic of the Congo.* http://www.unmonusco.org/www.un.org/en/peacekeeping/missions/monusco/mandate.html

United Nations. (2008, 7 April). *Report of the Secretary-General on the relationship between the United Nations and regional organizations, in particular the African Union, in the maintenance of international peace and security.* S/2008/186. https://archive.globalpolicy.org/images/pdfs/0407africanunion.pdf

United Nations. (2008, 19 June). *Resolution 1820 (2008). Adopted by the Security Council at its 5916th meeting on 19 June 2008.* S/RES/1820 (2008). https://undocs.org/en/S/RES/1820(2008)

United Nations. (2008). *United Nations peacekeeping operations: Principles and guidelines.* Department of Peacekeeping Operations and Department of Field Support. https://peacekeeping.un.org/sites/default/files/capstone_eng_0.pdf

United Nations. (2009). *A new partnership agenda: Charting a new horizon for UN peacekeeping.* Department of Peacekeeping Operations and Department of Field Support. https://peacekeeping.un.org/sites/default/files/newhorizon_0.pdf

United Nations. (2009, 16 January). *Nepal special representative describes 'Important Achievements' in peace process, hopes world community understanding long-term stability far from being achieved.* Press release: Security Council, S/9575. https://www.un.org/press/en/2009/sc9575.doc.htm

United Nations. (2009). *Office of the special representative of the Secretary-General on sexual violence in conflict (OSRGG-SVC).* https://www.un.org/sexualviolenceinconflict/about-us/about-the-office/

United Nations. (2009, 1 September). *Report of the Secretary-General on the United Nations stabilization mission in Haiti.* United Nations Security Council, S/2009/439. https://www.securitycouncilreport.org/un-documents/document/haiti-s-2009-439.php

United Nations. (2010). *Background: United Nations organization stabilization mission in the DR CONGO.* https://monusco.unmissions.org/en/background

United Nations. (2011). *Background: United Nations mission in Sudan.* https://unmis.unmissions.org/background-0

United Nations. (2011). *Human Rights in United Nations peace operations and political missions.* Office of the High Commissioner for Human Rights, United Nations.

United Nations. (2011, 31 March). *Report of the Secretary-General's panel of experts on accountability in Sri Lanka*. https://www.securitycouncilreport.org/atf/cf/%7B65BFCF9B-6D27-4E9C-8CD3-CF6E4FF96FF9%7D/POC%20Rep%20on%20Account%20in%20Sri%20Lanka.pdf

United Nations. (2011, 12 May). *UNMIS to provide more assistance with Kadugli Agreements*. United Nations Mission in Sudan. https://reliefweb.int/report/sudan/unmis-provide-more-assistance-kadugli-agreements

United Nations. (2012). *Background: United Nations mission in Timor-Leste*. https://unmit.unmissions.org/background

United Nations. (2013, 28 March). *Intervention brigade' authorized as Security Council grants mandate renewal for United Nations mission in Democratic Republic of Congo*. Meetings Coverage and Press Releases.

United Nations. (2013). *Mandate: United Nations assistance mission in SOMALIA*. https://unsom.unmissions.org/mandate

United Nations. (2013). *United Nations multidimensional integrated stabilization mission in Mali*. https://minusma.unmissions.org/en/history

United Nations. (2014). *United Nations multidimensional integrated stabilization mission in the Central African Republic*. https://minusca.unmissions.org/en/about

United Nations. (2015). *Protection of civilians in UN peace keeping*. https://protectionofcivilians.org/wp/wp-content/uploads/2018/03/DPKO-DFS-2015-Policy-on-the-Protection-of-Civilians-in-United-Nations-Peacekeeping.pdf

United Nations. (2015). *Human Rights due diligence policy on United Nations support to Non-United Nations security forces*. Guidance Note and Text of the Policy. https://unsdg.un.org/sites/default/files/Inter-Agency-HRDDP-Guidance-Note-2015.pdf

United Nations. (2015, 17 June). *Report of the high-level independent panel on peace operations on uniting our strengths for peace: Politics, partnership and people*. A/70/95-S/2015/446. https://www.un.org/en/ga/search/view_doc.asp?symbol=S/2015/446

United Nations. (2015, 2 September). *The future of United Nations peace operations: Implementation of the recommendations of the high-level independent panel on peace operations*. General Assembly Security Council, A/70/357-S/2015/682. https://www.securitycouncilreport.org/atf/cf/%7B65BFCF9B-6D27-4E9C-8CD3-CF6E4FF96FF9%7D/s_2015_682.pdf

United Nations. (2015, 16 June). *Uniting our strengths for peace-politics, partnership and people*. Report of the High-Level Independent Panel on United Nations Peace Operations. https://peaceoperationsreview.org/wp-content/uploads/2015/08/HIPPO_Report_1_June_2015.pdf

United Nations. (2015). *Haiti background: Summary*. https://peacekeeping.un.org/en/mission/past/unmihbackgr1.html

United Nations. (2015). *United Nations mission for the referendum in Western Sahara*. https://minurso.unmissions.org/background

United Nations. (2017, 19 December). *Improving security of United Nations peacekeepers: We need to change the way we are doing business*. https://peacekeeping.un.org/sites/default/files/improving_security_of_united_nations_peacekeepers_report.pdf

United Nations. (2017, 20 November). *Letter dated 15 November 2017 from the Secretary-General addressed to the President of the Security Council.* Security Council, S/2017/966. http://www.securitycouncilreport.org/atf/cf/%7B65BFCF9B-6D27-4E9C-8CD3-CF6E4FF96FF9%7D/s_2017_966.pdf

United Nations. (2019). *Declaration of shared commitments on UN peacekeeping operations.* https://peacekeeping.un.org/sites/default/files/dpko-dfs-declaration-shared-commitments-unpeacekeeping-1812605e.pdf

United Nations. (2019, 18 December). *Expert group brief's Security Council's Democratic Republic of Congo sanctions committee on midterm report.* Meetings Coverage and Press Releases, SC/14058. https://www.un.org/press/en/2019/sc14058.doc.htm

United Nations. (2019). *Guidance on casualty recording.* United Nations Human Rights Office of the High Commissioner. https://www.ohchr.org/Documents/Publications/Guidance_on_Casualty_Recording.pdf

United Nations. (2019). *Mandate: Summary of UNISFA mandate.* https://unisfa.unmissions.org/mandate

United Nations. (2019). *The politics of action for peacekeeping.* United Nations University, Centre for Policy Research. https://cpr.unu.edu/the-politics-of-action-for-peacekeeping.html

United Nations. (2020, 19 May). *Acting SRSG Stephanie Williams briefing to the Security Council.* https://unsmil.unmissions.org/sites/default/files/acting_srsg_briefing_to_the_security_council_-_19_may_2020.pdf

United Nations. (2020). *Protection of civilians mandate.* https://peacekeeping.un.org/en/protection-of-civilians-mandate

United Nations. (2020, February). *Secretary-General stresses need for less talk, more action on women, peace, security, in remarks at Book Launch of 'She Stands for Peace'.* UN Secretary-General. https://reliefweb.int/report/world/secretary-general-stresses-need-less-talk-more-action-women-peace-security-remarks-book

United Nations. (2020, 4 June). *Security Council establishes integrated transition assistance mission in Sudan, Unanimously adopting resolution 2525 (2020).* Meeting Coverages and Press Releases, Security Council, SC/14202. https://www.un.org/press/en/2020/sc14202.doc.htm

United Nations. (2020, 13 February). *Situation in Somalia: Report of the Secretary-General.* Security Council. https://undocs.org/S/2020/121

United Nations. (2020). *Human Rights report on civilian casuals, United Nations support mission in Libya.* https://unsmil.unmissions.org/human-rights-report-civilian-casualties-0

United Nations. (2020). *United Nations peacekeeping—Where we operate.* https://peacekeeping.un.org/en/where-we-operate

United Nations Assistance Mission in Afghanistan & United Nations Human Rights Office of the High Commissioner. (2020, February). *Afghanistan: Protection of civilians in armed conflict 2019.* https://unama.unmissions.org/sites/default/files/executive_summary_-_afghanistan_protection_of_civilians_annual_report_2019_english.pdf

United Nations Children's Fund. (2011, 11 January). *Children in Haiti: One year after—The long road from relief to recovery.* http://www.unicefusa.org/assets/pdf/Children-in-Haiti-One-Year-After.pdf

United Nations Economic and Social Council. (1994). *Advisory services in the field of human rights.* Commission of Human Rights. http://hrlibrary.umn.edu/commission/country51/88.htm

United Nations General Assembly Security Council. (2000, 14 July). *Windhoek declaration on the tenth anniversary of the United Nations Transition Assistance Group,* A/55/138=S/2000/693. http://www.equalpowerlastingpeace.org/resource/windhoek-declaration-and-namibia-plan-of-action-2000/#:~:text=A%20follow%20up%20on%20the,peace%20operations%20and%20peace%20processes

United Nations Human Rights Council. (2020). *UN experts say pattern of years of extreme violations in South Sudan must be reserved.* UN Commission on Human Rights in South Sudan. https://www.ohchr.org/EN/HRBodies/HRC/Pages/NewsDetail.aspx?NewsID=25686&LangID=E

United Nations Human Rights Office of the High Commissioner. (2010). *Technical cooperation in the field of human rights.* https://www.ohchr.org/EN/Countries/Pages/TechnicalCooperationIndex.aspx

United Nations Mission in Liberia. (2018). *The story of UNMIL.* https://reliefweb.int/report/liberia/story-unmil

United Nations Office of the High Commissioner for Human Rights. (2010). *Report of the mapping exercise documenting the most serious violations of human and international humanitarian law committee within the territory of the Democratic Republic of the Congo between March 1993 and June 2003, August 2010.* https://www.refworld.org/publisher,OHCHR,,,4ca99bc22,0.html

United Nations Secretary General. (1995, 25 January). *Supplement to an agenda for peace: Position paper of the Secretary-General on the occasion of the 50th anniversary of the United Nations.* United Nations Secretary-General Reports (1994–1995), A/50/60-S/1995/1. United Nations. https://digitallibrary.un.org/record/168325?ln=en

United Nations Secretary General. (2000, 20 October). *Report of the Secretary-General on the implement of the report of the panel on United Nations peace operations.* A/55/502. United Nations. https://digitallibrary.un.org/record/426824?ln=en

United Nations Security Council. (2003, 26 March). *Report of the Secretary-General on Côte d'Ivoire (S/2003/374).* https://reliefweb.int/report/côte-divoire/report-secretary-general-côte-divoire-s2003374

United Nations Security Council. (2007). *Resolution 1740 (2007): Adopted by the Security Council at its 5622nd meeting on 23 January 2007.* https://www.un.org/ga/search/view_doc.asp?symbol=S/RES/1740(2007)

United Nations Security Council. (2009). *Report of the Secretary-General on protection of civilians in armed conflict.* http://www.securitycouncilreport.org/atf/cf/%7B65BFCF9B-6D27-4E9C-8CD3-CF6E4FF96FF9%7D/POC%20S2009277.pdf

United Nations Security Council. (2010). *Regional arrangements (Chapter VIII of UN Charter)*. https://www.un.org/securitycouncil/content/regional-arrangements-chapter-viii-un-charter

United Nations Security Council. (2014). *The international commission of inquiry on the Central African Republic—Final report*. https://reliefweb.int/report/central-african-republic/international-commission-inquiry-central-african-republic-final

United States Holocaust Memorial Museum. (2017). *Background: Political and ethnic violence in Central African Republic*. https://www.ushmm.org/genocide-prevention/countries/central-african-republic/case-study/background/political-and-ethnic-violence

United States Institute of Peace. (1992). *Truth commission: El Salvador*. https://www.usip.org/publications/1992/07/truth-commission-el-salvador

United States Institute of Peace. (1997). *Truth commission: Guatemala*. https://www.usip.org/publications/1997/02/truth-commission-guatemala

United States Institute of Peace. (2000). *What is UNSCR 1325? An explanation of the landmark resolution on women, peace and security*. https://www.usip.org/gender_peacebuilding/about_UNSCR_1325

UNMIS Human Rights Section. (2011, 5 July). *Report on the human rights situation during the SAF military offensive and control of Abyei*.

Vandewalle, D. (2015). Libya's uncertain revolution. In P. Cole & B. McQuinn (Eds.), *The Libyan revolution and its aftermath*. C. Hurst & Co.

Watch List on Children and Armed Conflict. (2009). *UN Security Council resolution 1612 and beyond: Strengthening protection for children in armed conflict*. https://reliefweb.int/sites/reliefweb.int/files/resources/B47350B9C3111673C12575C9006152B8-Watchlist-PolicyPaper-colour-LOWRES.pdf

Watkins, T., Valley, S., & Alley, T. (1995). *Political and economic history of Haiti*. https://www.sjsu.edu/faculty/watkins/haiti.htm

Wheeler, S. (2020, 11 January). UN peacekeeping has a sexual abuse problem. *The Hill*. Human Rights Watch. https://www.hrw.org/news/2020/01/11/un-peacekeeping-has-a-sexual-abuse-problem

Wierda, M. (2015). Confronting Qadhafi's legacy—Transitional justice in Libya. In C. Peter & B. McQuinn (Eds.), *The Libyan revolution and its aftermath*. C. Hurst & Co.

Wikipedia: The Free Encyclopedia. (1997). *United Nations verification mission in Guatemala (MINUGUA)*. https://en.wikipedia.org/wiki/MINUGUA

Williams, P. D. (2010). *Enhancing civilian protection in peace operations: Insights from Africa* (Africa Center for Strategic Studies Research Paper No. 1). National Defense University Press.

Woodward, B. (1984, 23 April). Hangings in Tripoli focus attention on Libyan dissent. *The Washington Post*. https://www.washingtonpost.com/archive/politics/1984/04/23/hangings-in-tripoli-focus-attention-on-libyan-dissent/9c2481e3-1b2d-4b74-8d69-4304afe24ed1/

World Without Genocide. (2017). Darfur Genocide. Mitchell Hamline School of Lawhttp://worldwithoutgenocide.org/genocides-and-conflicts/darfur-genocide

Young, J. (2012). *The fate of Sudan: The origins and consequences of a flawed peace process.* Zed Books.

Zambakari, C., Kang, T. K., & Sanders, R. (2018). The role of the UN Mission in South Sudan (UNMISS) in protecting civilians. In S. C. Roach & Hudson (Eds.), *The challenge of governance in South Sudan: Corruption, peacebuilding, and foreign intervention* (1st ed.). Routledge. https://papers.ssrn.com/sol3/papers.cfm?abstract_id=3128701

Zia-Zarifi, S. (2004). *Losing the peace in Afghanistan.* https://www.hrw.org/legacy/wr2k4/download/5.pdf

ABOUT THE AUTHOR

Ravindran Daniel is an independent expert member of the UN Working Group on the use of mercenaries as a means of violating human rights and impeding the exercise of the right of people to self-determination. He is an expert in international human rights law, with more than 30 years of experience in working on human rights at local, regional and international levels. He specializes in conflict and post-conflict situations. He was the Director of Human Rights Divisions in East Timor, Libya and Sudan of the UN Peacekeeping Operations. He has held senior positions in the Cambodia and Uganda offices of the Office of the High Commissioner for Human Rights (OHCHR). In the 1980s, he worked with the International Commission of Jurists (ICJ), Geneva. He was the secretary of the UN International Enquiry Commission on East Timor. He has conducted numerous academic training and workshops on human rights in various parts of the world. He founded the Asian Forum for Human Rights and Development (Forum-Asia) and was a member of the launching committee that established the International Network for Economic, Social and Cultural Rights (ESCR-Net). He lives in Trivandrum, Kerala, India, and is an avid gardener.

INDEX